IMAGES of America

Taconic Pathways

THROUGH BEEKMAN, UNION VALE, LAGRANGE, WASHINGTON, AND STANFORD

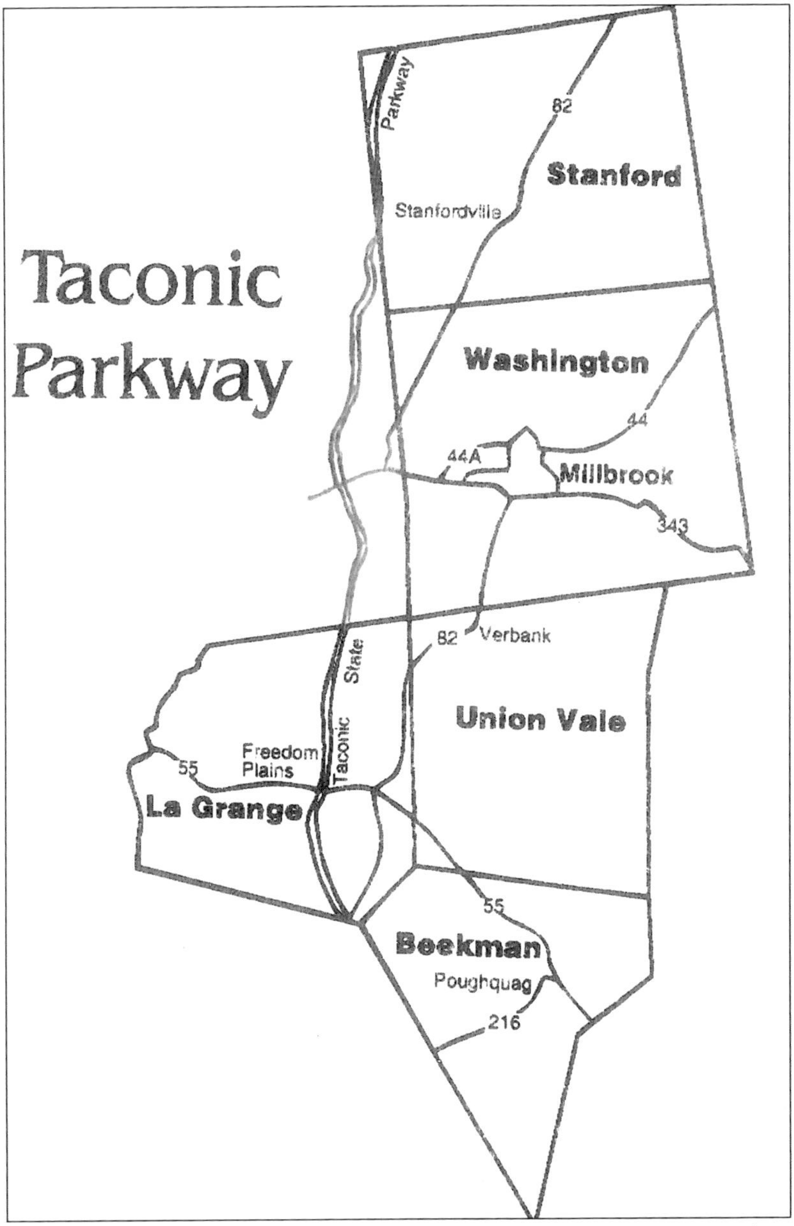

A MAP FROM 2000. While the Taconic State Parkway actually touches only LaGrange and Stanford, it provides access to all five towns, which are—with the exception of LaGrange—mainly to its east. At the end of the 17th century, the English king had given patents (land grants) to various English and Dutch entrepreneurial groups and individuals. The towns shown here were part of the Great Nine Partners, Rombout and Beekman Patents. Through the years, their subdivisions of these patents led to the creation of the towns. The Taconic State Parkway was constructed in Dutchess County mainly between 1936 and 1949. Since that time, the population of Beekman has increased from 1,703 to a projected 12,371 in 2000, and LaGrange has increased from 2,280 to 13,788. The other towns have also experienced growth, although not to the same degree. Proximity to the parkway has been and will continue to be one of the factors influencing the future of these towns. (DCDPEC.)

IMAGES
of America

TACONIC PATHWAYS

THROUGH BEEKMAN, UNION VALE, LAGRANGE, WASHINGTON, AND STANFORD

Joyce C. Ghee and Joan Spence

ARCADIA
PUBLISHING

ISBN 978-0-7385-0475-9

Published by Arcadia Publishing
Charleston, South Carolina

Printed in the United States of America

Library of Congress Catalog Card Number: 00106501

For all general information contact Arcadia Publishing at:
Telephone 843-853-2070
Fax 843-853-0044
E-mail sales@arcadiapublishing.com
For customer service and orders:
Toll-Free 1-888-313-2665

Visit us on the Internet at www.arcadiapublishing.com

CONTENTS

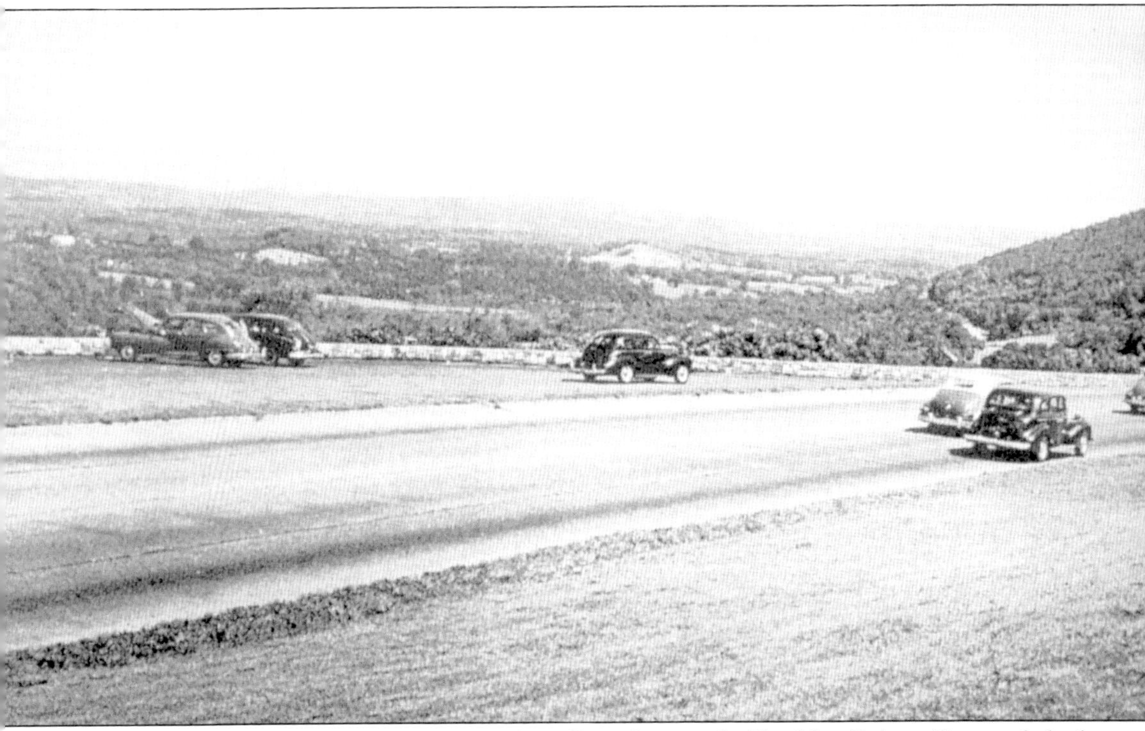

A Taconic Overlook near Miller Hill. From his youth, Franklin Delano Roosevelt had made a hobby of uncovering and exploring the hidden visual and natural beauties of his home county, Dutchess. His run for the state senate in 1910 gave him the opportunity of traveling virtually all of its back roads and, in his own mind, ranking the best views to share with friends or those he wished to impress. When the first leg of the Taconic Parkway in Dutchess County was completed in 1936, opening the southern door to its central corridor, the full impact of FDR's vision of a new experience for recreational automotive travelers was apparent. From an overlook below Miller Hill and Mountain Road, an immense and dramatic panorama was visible. Open farmland and rural communities north and west of the Southern Highlands and Taconics unfolded toward the distant Catskills and Adirondacks. This was a view previously reserved for circling hawks or the fortunate locals who knew the back trails to the heights. (TR.)

INTRODUCTION

While traveling in Dutchess County on the Taconic State Parkway (TSP), the dominant impression is the beauty of a seemingly unchanged natural landscape. Nestled under the shadow of the Taconic (Berkshire) Mountains to the east with views west to the Catskills, the parkway follows a ridge through the center of the county, approximately halfway between the towns and cities on the Hudson River and those in the Harlem Valley bordering New England. In this book, we focus on five central Dutchess towns mainly east of the parkway: Beekman, Union Vale, LaGrange, Washington, and Stanford.

These municipalities are related not only by geography, but also by history and by the families who often settled in several towns. Beekman and Washington were among the original nine towns established in Dutchess County by New York State in 1788. LaGrange, then called Freedom, was formed from Beekman and Fishkill in 1821. In 1827, Union Vale was formed from parts of Beekman and Freedom. Stanford was created from Washington in 1793.

These towns then had existed long before the Taconic State Parkway was even an idea. From the late 18th century into the 20th century, their economies depended mainly upon farming, with some mining and manufacturing enterprises. By the 19th century, one-room schoolhouses and churches dotted the landscape, and farmers came from outlying farms to small hamlets where they could buy the necessities that they did not produce themselves. After the Civil War, the arrival of the railroad led to the development of new hamlets and the village of Millbrook. People from Poughkeepsie and New York City came to relax and enjoy the countryside, with its rolling hills and cool lakes. After World War I, the long decline of agriculture that had begun in the 1880s continued, and the pace of life increased as the horse and wagon gave way to the automobile.

In 1925, Gov. Al Smith appointed the Taconic State Park Commission (TSPC), which was chaired by Dutchess County resident Franklin D. Roosevelt, who later claimed that the parkway was "my invention." Although the design of the parkway mirrored period trends, specific decisions on route and the use of native materials were made by FDR and the TSPC. In 1925, FDR wrote that its "general plan [was] based on the desire first, to open up a very beautiful section at present inaccessible, and, secondly, to provide a new through road from New York City in order to lessen the existing condition on the Post Road and the Harlem Valley Road."

A 1949 editorial in the *Poughkeepsie New Yorker* noted that "only time will answer such questions as to what the extended parkway will mean in terms of [the] development of the central section of the county."

This book shows in part what has happened to the parkway and in each community. The parkway itself, once a way for visitors to drive leisurely through the countryside, has become a route for commuting residents. The communities, too, have undergone many changes caused or accelerated by their proximity to the TSP, by the decline of the family farm, and by the rise of suburban living. The first chapter provides a brief sketch of the planning and construction of the Taconic State Parkway in Dutchess County. The chapters that follow trace some of the significant historical trends in Beekman, Union Vale, LaGrange, Washington, and Stanford, respectively. However, this is not a definitive history of the Taconic State Parkway nor of the five towns. We hope only to pique your interest so that you will seek further information.

Authors' Note: We are fortunate to have been assisted by many individuals and organizations that have provided information and visual materials. Without their help, this book would not have been possible. They are acknowledged at the end of the book. Contributors of visuals are identified by their initials in each caption. Photographs owned or made by the authors are identified as JG or JS.

We recognize that the "truth" of history is always elusive and that it important to use primary sources. We apologize for any errors that have undoubtedly crept in and we welcome corrections. A brief reading list is appended at the end of this book.

One

The Taconic State Parkway

In 1931, at Shrub Oak in Westchester County, Gov. Franklin D. Roosevelt presided at the inauguration of the construction of what became known as the Taconic State Parkway. Thirteen years later, Gov. Thomas E. Dewey, like FDR a Dutchess County resident, opened the 21-mile section from Freedom Plains to Route 199. The parkway was built according to the original vision of the Taconic State Parkway Commission (TSPC) first chaired by FDR: gentle curving grades, forested and turfed medians using native trees and shrubs, bridges and gas stations faced with native stone. Driving on the Taconic State Parkway was itself a recreational experience in which the views of the surrounding landscape played a significant role.

Organized in 1925, the TSPC soon defined the route of the parkway, which, with a few exceptions, remained relatively unchanged during the 40-year construction period. Early on, FDR tried unsuccessfully to acquire Turkey Hollow for a park along the way.

As a commissioner, FDR was also unsuccessful in his efforts to safeguard the budget proposed by the TSPC. He complained vociferously to Gov. Al Smith, who replied temperately; however, the requested budget was not approved. That same year, FDR was elected governor, and the future of the Taconic State Parkway was assured.

For ten years, the name of the parkway was discussed. Among the suggestions were "Eastern Hudson State Park[way]" and "Mohican Trail." By 1949, when the section north to Route 199 was dedicated, it was definitively known as the Taconic State Parkway.

The parkway was conceived in an earlier time when people worked near their homes, and automobiles were used for weekend pleasure drives. Today, the parkway carries its share of harried commuters, as it provides access to towns that were once small and are now growing.

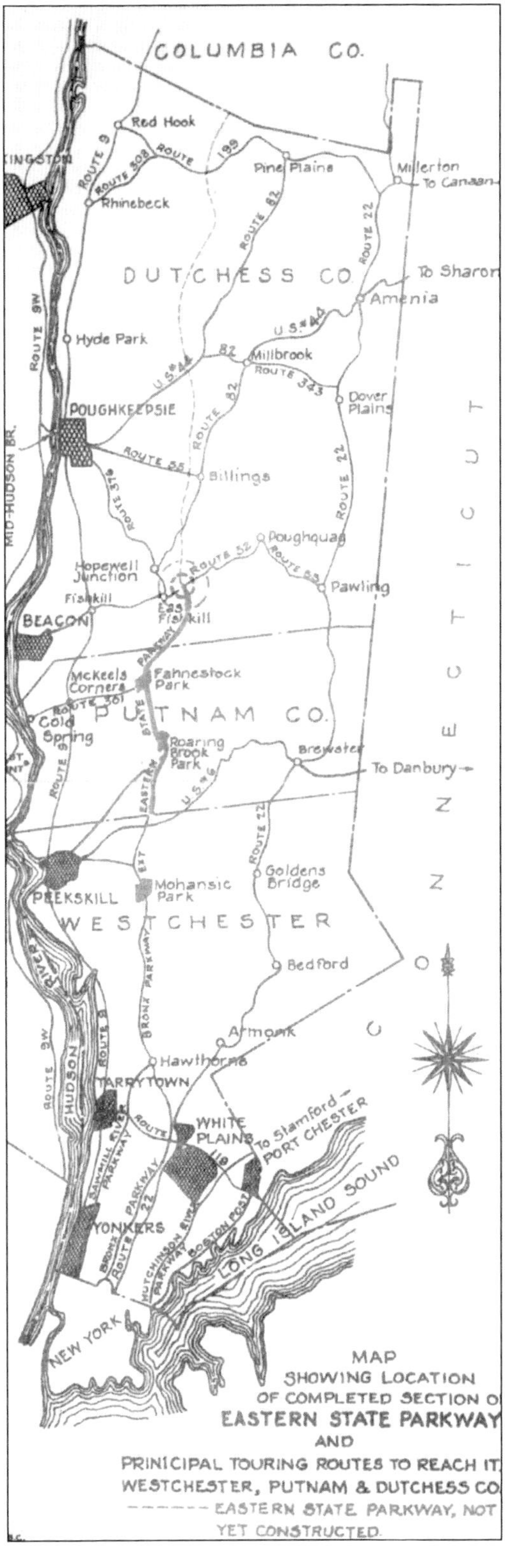

A 1936 Map. The Taconic State Parkway was constructed from the south to the north. This map shows its connection to the Bronx Parkway and its route completed through Putnam County to East Fishkill. The dotted lines indicate its future path through Dutchess County. Located between Route 9 along the Hudson River and Route 22 through the Harlem Valley, the Taconic State Parkway provides access to the central part of the county. Although no town lines appear, the hamlets of Poughquag in Beekman and of Billings in LaGrange as well as the village of Millbrook are clearly indicated. (TR.)

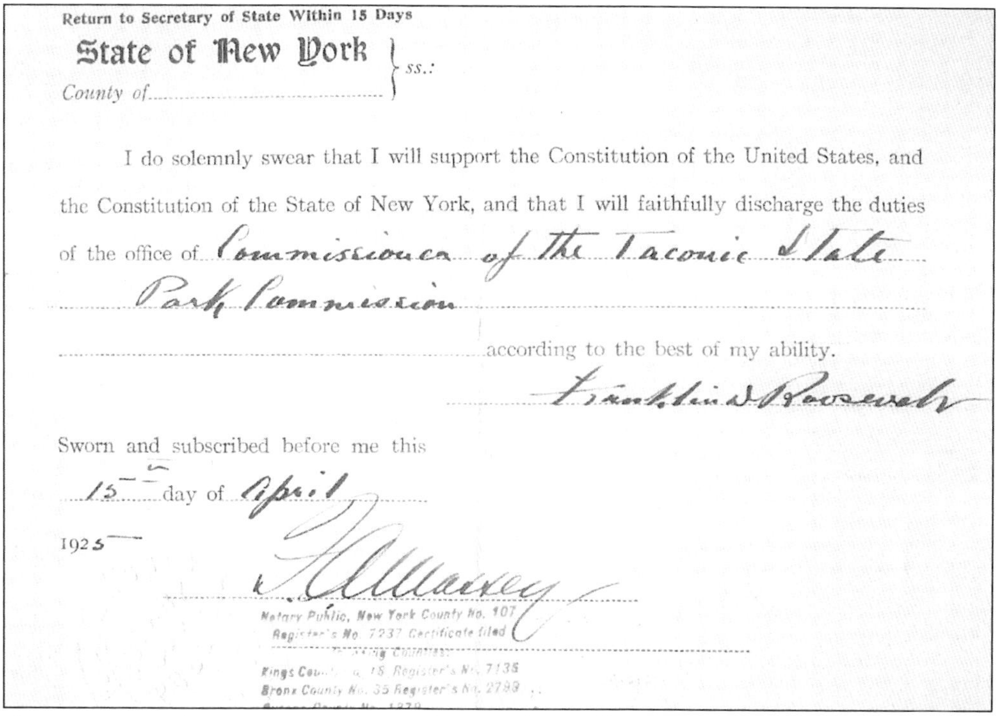

Return to Secretary of State Within 15 Days

State of New York } ss.:
County of.................................

I do solemnly swear that I will support the Constitution of the United States, and the Constitution of the State of New York, and that I will faithfully discharge the duties of the office of Commissioner of the Taconic State Park Commission according to the best of my ability.

Franklin D Roosevelt

Sworn and subscribed before me this 15 day of April 1925

Notary Public, New York County No. 107
Register's No. 7237 Certificate filed
Kings County, No. 15 Register's No. 7135
Bronx County No. 35 Register's No. 2799

CERTIFICATE OF APPOINTMENT TO THE TACONIC STATE PARK COMMISSION (TSPC). Franklin Delano Roosevelt, appointed by Gov. Al Smith to the newly formed TSPC in 1925, became its first chair. From the beginning, Roosevelt envisioned a parkway where the natural beauty of the landscape would be emphasized. He wanted native stone to be used to face its bridges and gas stations. His vision also included service buildings that were constructed in the style of early Dutch vernacular architecture. (FDRL.)

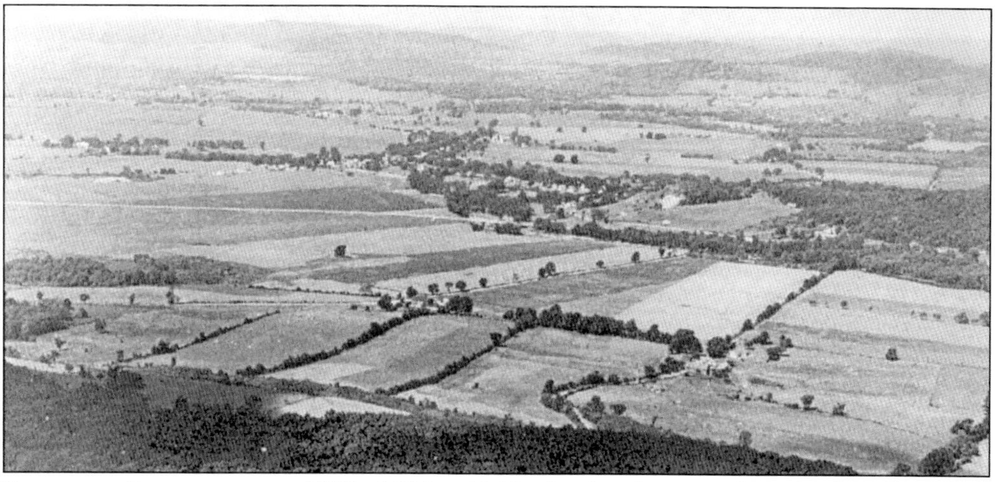

FARMLAND SEEN FROM THE TSP, 1930s, 1940s. In the foreground, trees abound in their natural state, while fields cultivated by generations of farmers extend to the hills on the horizon. FDR's sense of history included a belief in the inspirational and restorative power of the family farm and the traditional rural landscape. Today, agriculture is no longer the dominant use along the route, so trees creep closer to the parkway, providing a buffer between it and recent subdivisions. (TR.)

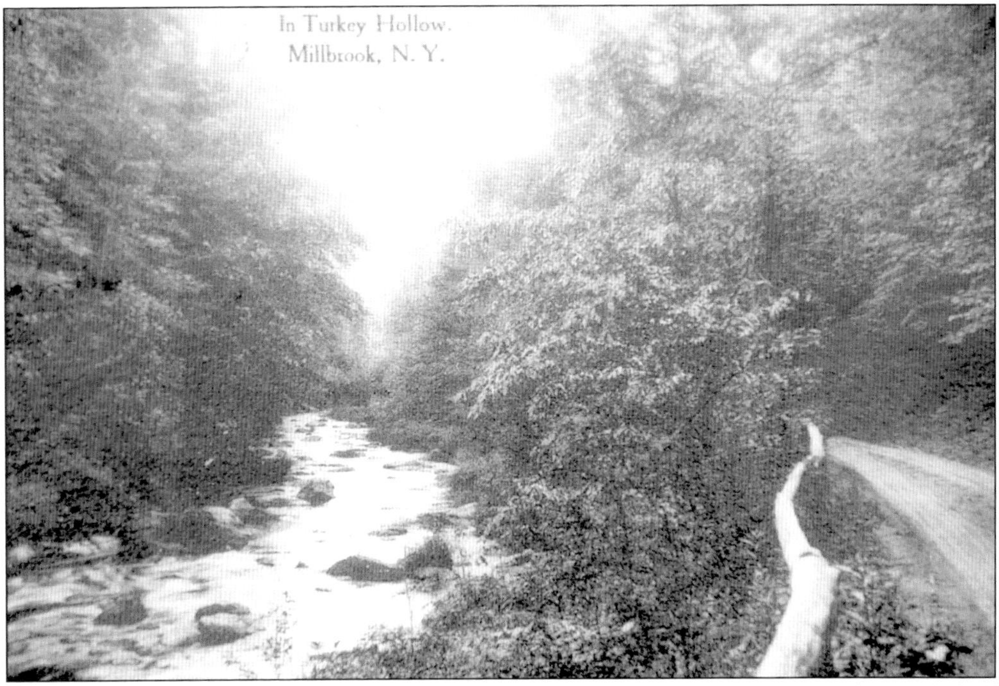

TURKEY HOLLOW, MILLBROOK, EARLY 1900S. In 1926, Franklin Delano Roosevelt—on behalf of the TSP—tried to acquire Turkey Hollow from the Thorne family in Millbrook. Oakleigh Thorne agreed to sell Turkey Hollow for $50,000 while reserving certain farmland for his own use. However, the deal fell through amicably when, as FDR put it, "certain formalities of government [had] to be gone through." (DGTH.)

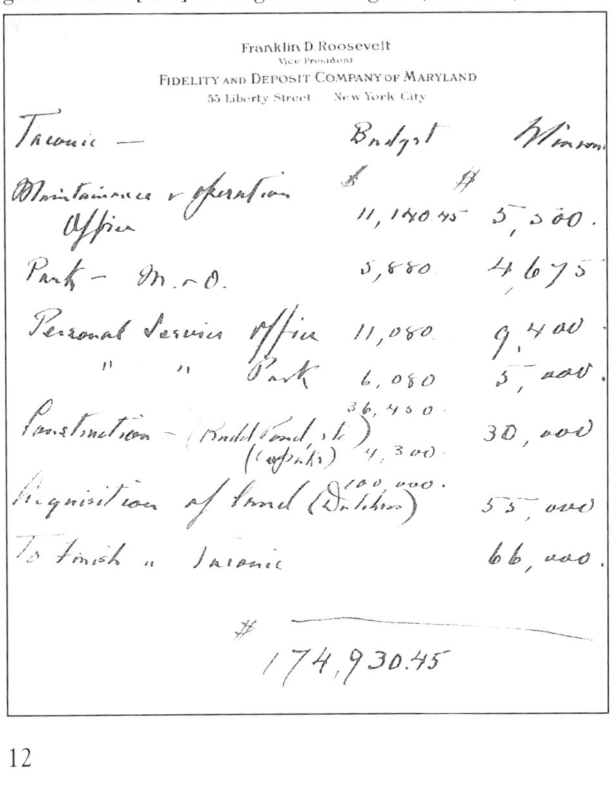
Franklin D. Roosevelt
Vice President
FIDELITY AND DEPOSIT COMPANY OF MARYLAND
55 Liberty Street New York City

Taconic —	Budget	Minimum
	$	$
Maintenance & operation Office	11,140.45	5,500.
Park – M. & O.	5,880	4,675
Personal Service Office	11,080	9,400.
" " Park	6,080	5,000.
Construction – (Roadbed [?], etc.) (asphalt [?])	36,450. 4,300.	30,000
Acquisition of land (Dutchess [?])	100,000.	55,000
To finish " Taconic		66,000.

$ 174,930.45

FDR'S NOTES ON THE TACONIC STATE PARKWAY BUDGET, 1927. Among those "formalities" was budget making. All TSPC budget requests had to be transmitted through the New York State Council of Parks, chaired by Robert Moses, who was as passionate about creating great parks and parkways as Roosevelt, but whose emphasis was on Long Island. The council slashed the proposed TSPC budgets of almost $200,000 to $12,500, causing FDR to appeal directly to Governor Smith. Smith's temperate response soothed FDR, but the TSPC budget was not significantly increased. (FDRL.)

MARY L. HAM ON TYRELL LAKE, 1916. Wearing her "itchy-koo hat," this young woman from Union Vale, who became the mother of Ruth Hogan, seems to be enjoying the lake with its water lilies. The Taconic State Parkway was originally scheduled to be routed near this property owned by the Becks. However, after their appeal to FDR, the route was slightly altered. (RRH.)

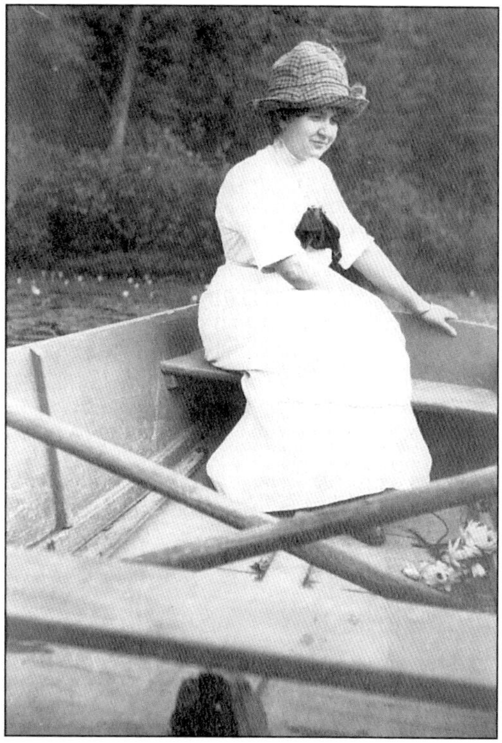

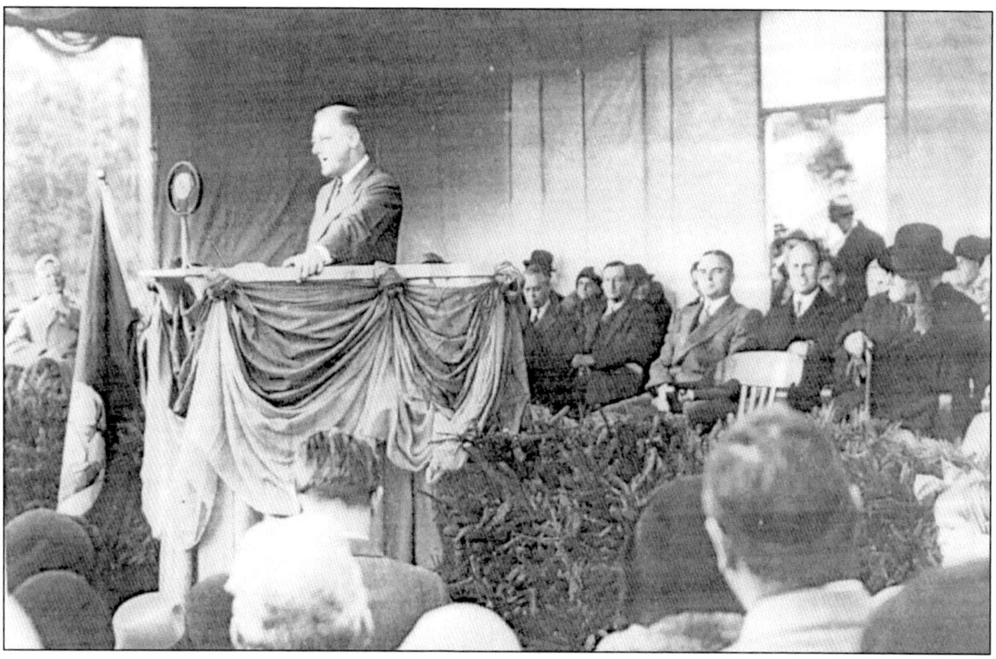

FDR AT THE GROUNDBREAKING FOR THE EASTERN STATE PARKWAY IN 1931. Only a few years had passed since the slashing of the TSPC budgets. However, in the interim, FDR had been elected and reelected governor. In 1931, he presided at the groundbreaking for the new Eastern State Park Highway, which he had always envisioned going as far as Canada. It was hailed at the time as offering a new route from the metropolitan area to the Adironacks. (TR.)

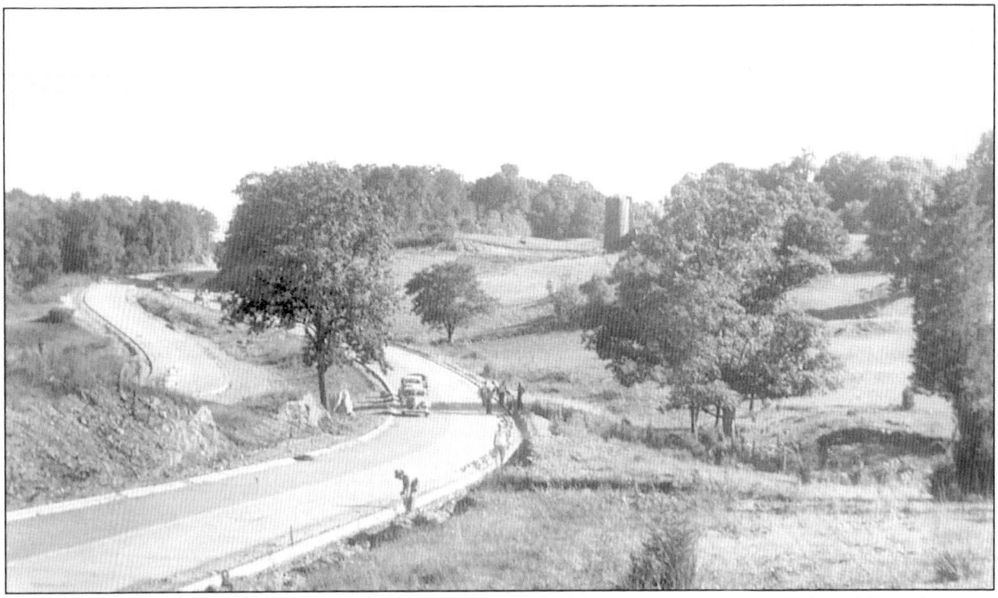

CONSTRUCTION OF THE TACONIC STATE PARKWAY IN DUTCHESS COUNTY, 1940s. The silo is an indication of the farms that bordered the parkway and were sometimes intersected by it, resulting in a number of grade-level crossings. When Governor Lehmann presided at the opening of the parkway in Dutchess County in 1936, it was referred to as the Eastern State Parkway in the *New York Times*, while the *Poughkeepsie New Yorker* called it the Taconic. Because of World War II, 13 years passed before the parkway was completed as far as Route 199. (TR.)

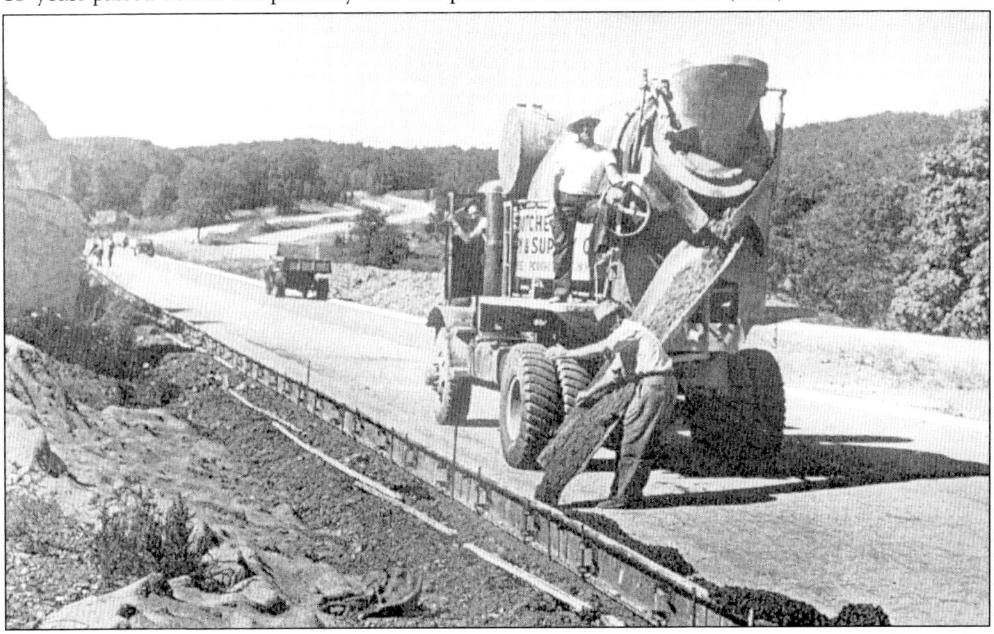

CONSTRUCTION BY THE ARBORIOS, 1949. The Arborio family played a major role in the construction of the parkway from Westchester through Dutchess. The Arborios and Peter Mitchell Inc. were the contractors who constructed the rough grading, drainage, and structures. John Arborio Inc. also did the paving, fine grading, and seeding. The Arborios had also been the contractors for much of the parkway construction south of Route 55 in Dutchess. (TR.)

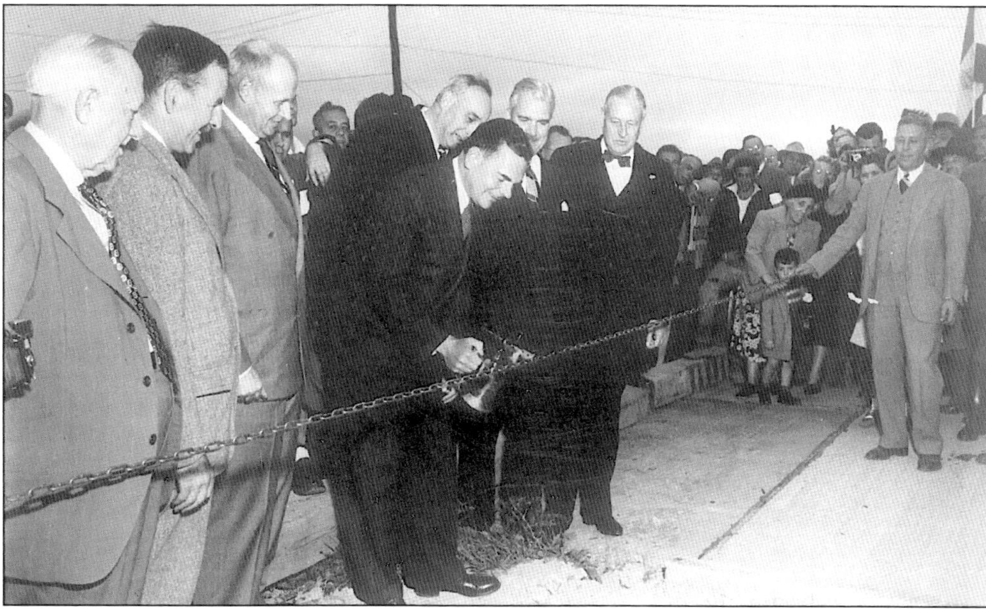

Opening Ceremonies of the TSP, 1949. Gov. Thomas E. Dewey presided at the opening of the 21-mile segment from Freedom Plains to Route 199 in Dutchess County. Just behind him is Robert Moses, who had survived FDR. Paul Winslow, with the bow tie, was the long-term executive secretary of the TSPC. The central section of Dutchess County was now far more easily accessible to those who wanted to enjoy a beautiful and, at that time, a recreational ride to the country. (TR.)

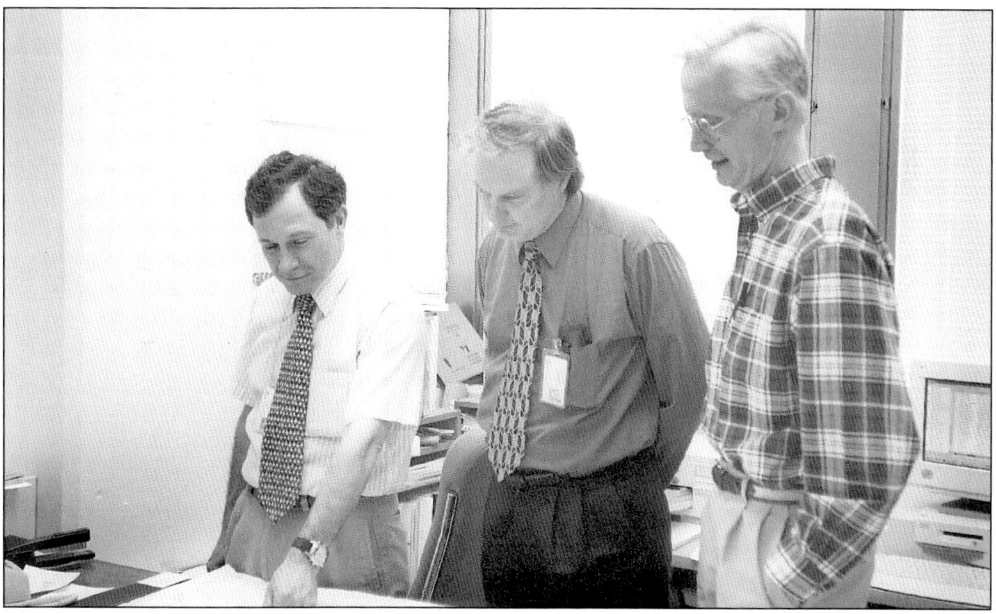

Department of Transportation (DOT) Officials Review Plans of the TSP, 2000. Just over 50 years later, design manager Joe Foglietta, regional design engineer Phil Crocker, and landscape architect Mike George consider the challenge facing DOT and New York State Parks, Recreation, and Historic Preservation: to preserve the parkway in its context as a scenic and historic route while recognizing its modern role as a major high-speed commuter highway. (JS.)

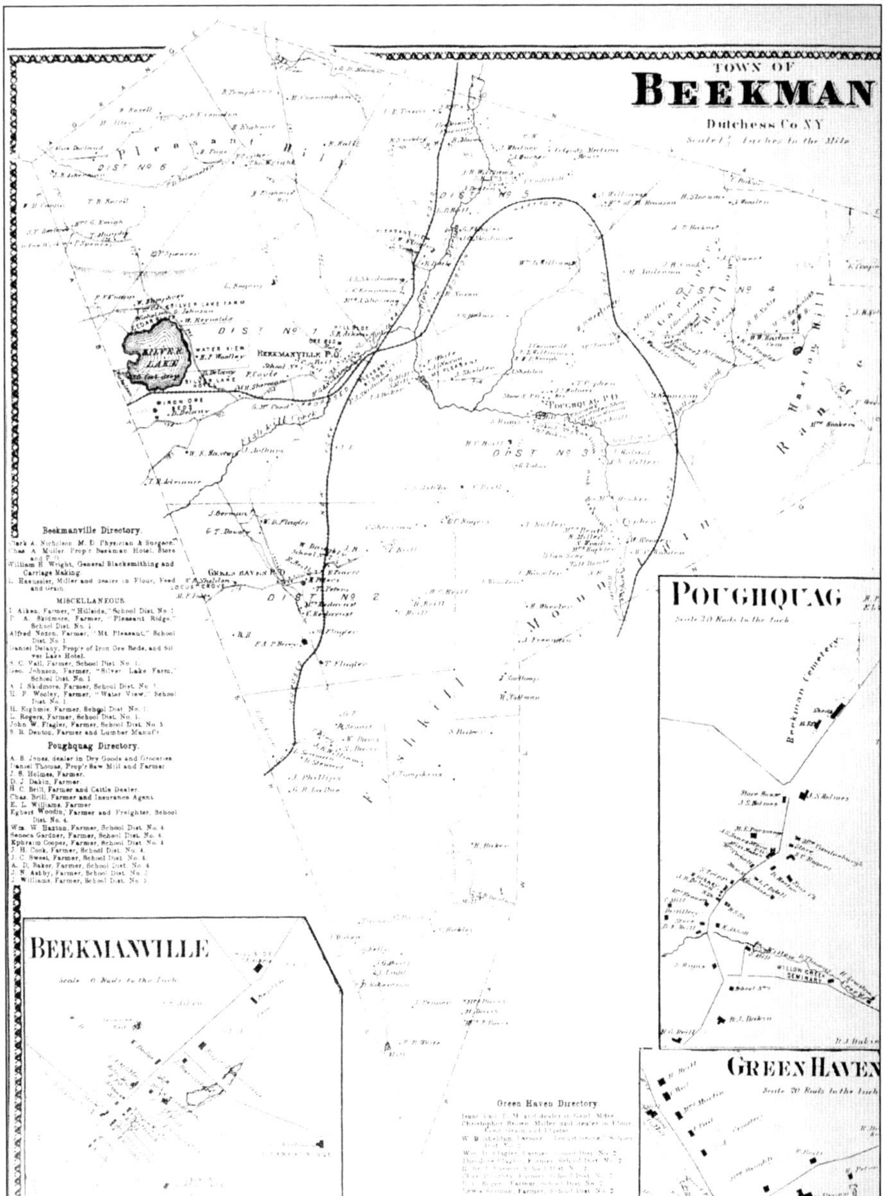

A MAP OF BEEKMAN, 1867. This map, published by F.W. Beers, shows that most of the town was covered with farms. Some familiar names on the map include the Brills, Flaglers, and Van Der Burghs. Also identified are the hamlets Beekmanville, Poughquag, Green Haven, Clove Valley, and Gardner Hollow, where residents and visitors could find the goods and services they needed. The Clove Valley Railroad, a spur of the Newburgh, Dutchess, & Connecticut Railroad, connected iron ore beds to the Beekman Furnace and had a stop at Beekmanville. Green Haven and Poughquag were served by the New York & New England Railroad. The district lines are the geographical boundaries of the areas served by the one-room schoolhouses, which gave way to centralization only in the 1950s. Today, housing developments are replacing farms. (DCHS.)

Two

BEEKMAN

The town of Beekman, created from a portion of the Beekman Patent, was established in 1788. One of the original nine towns of Dutchess County, its current borders date from 1827. During the 20th century, its population has grown from about 1,000 to over 12,000; it is the fastest growing community in the county.

European settlers who began to arrive in the early 18th century included Palatines and Quakers. Later, settlers came from New England, Long Island, and in the mid-19th century from Ireland.

While Beekman has always been a rural area, it was also the site of a thriving mining enterprise. Ruins of the Beekman Furnace remain.

The Methodist Episcopal church and the town hall are in the hamlet of Poughquag. In Beekmanville are the Baptist church, early federal-period homes, and a former hotel. The Mount Zion Baptist church is in Green Haven, today dominated by the state correctional facility.

The only remaining dairy farm in the town is the Green Haven Prison Farm. However, white fences indicate horse farms, and apple trees still blossom in the spring. The Taconic State Parkway continues to open up this area of the county to visitors and weekenders, some of whom become year-round residents. Once, the ride through the beautiful landscape was a prelude to the tranquillity of the destination. Today, new homes are being built almost daily, and many residents now use the parkway to commute to work, often miles away.

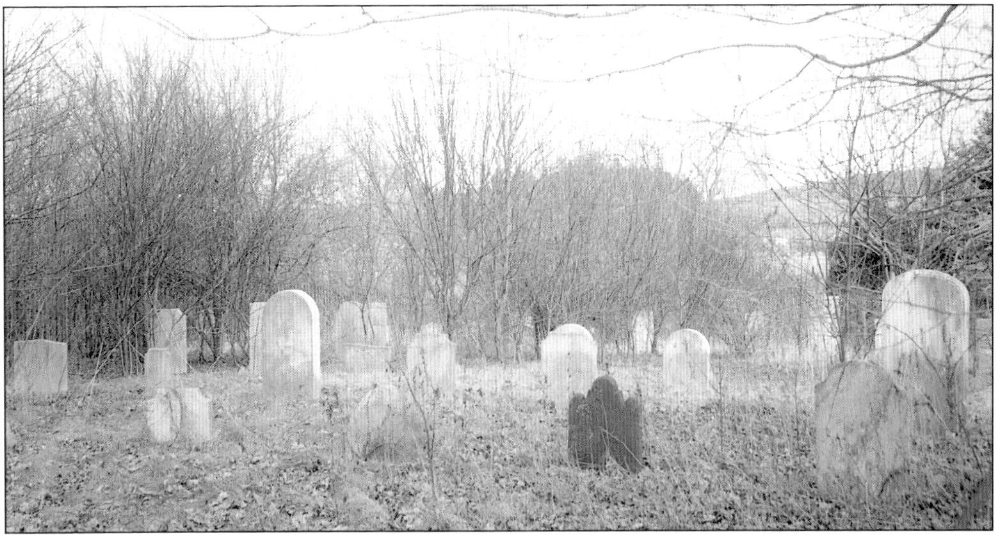

THE FLAGLER CEMETERY, FROG HOLLOW ROAD. This cemetery, where Jean Flagler Matthews gathered the remains of many members of the Flagler family, was dedicated in 1976. Zachariah Flagler came to this country from the Palatine in Germany in 1701, and the 1867 Beekman map lists as farmers several Flaglers. At the beginning of the 20th century, a member of the family became one of the founders of the Standard Oil Company, and the Flaglers are also noted for their role in developing Florida. (JS.)

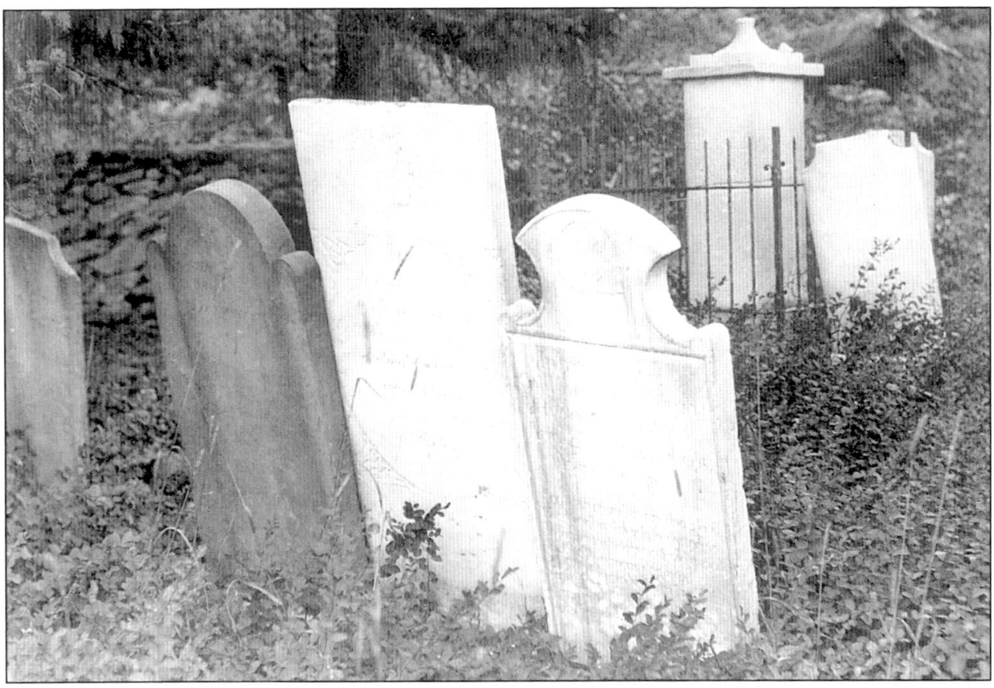

THE GRAVE MARKER OF COL. JAMES VAN DER BURGH, NORTH OF POUGHQUAG, 1794. The colonel commanded a regiment of the Dutchess County Militia in the Revolutionary War, and George Washington dined at his house in 1781. Unfortunately, despite efforts in 1860 of noted historian Benson Lossing to preserve this house, not even Washington's visit could save it. Colonel Van Der Burgh also served as supervisor and assessor. (Margaret DeMott Brown, DCHS.)

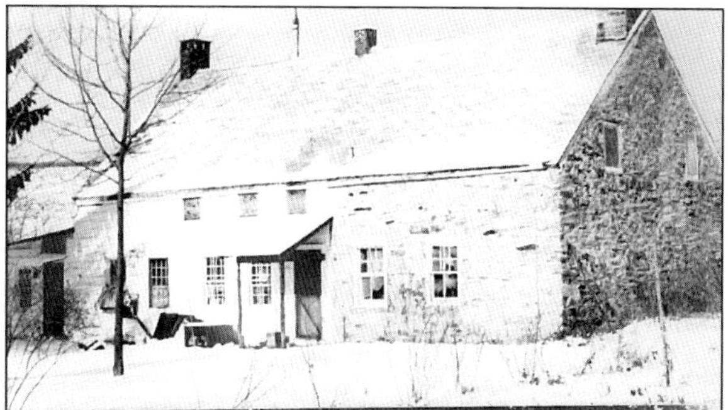

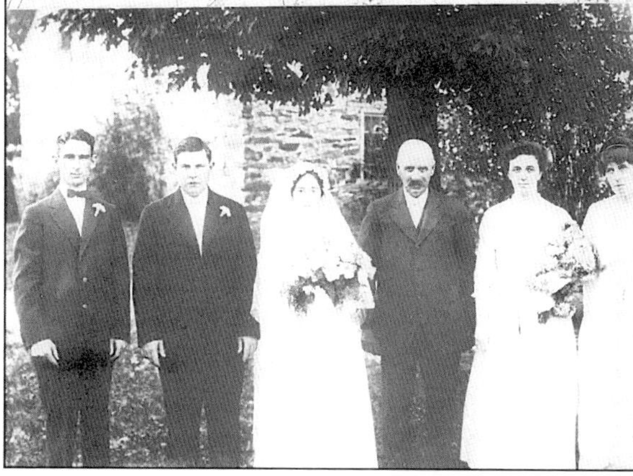

The Stone Abbey, c. 1721, and the Pray Wedding, 1915. This house is reputedly the oldest in Beekman, its stone end dating from 1721 and its wood extension from 1851. The Pray family acquired the house in the 1870s. In addition to the bride, Margaret Pray, and the groom, William Stowe, the wedding party includes her father, Andrew, and her sister, Mary. Mary was born in the house and died there. She married Philip Hoag there a year after Margaret's wedding. Their uncle, Hamilton Pray, invented the ice plow. (AHL.)

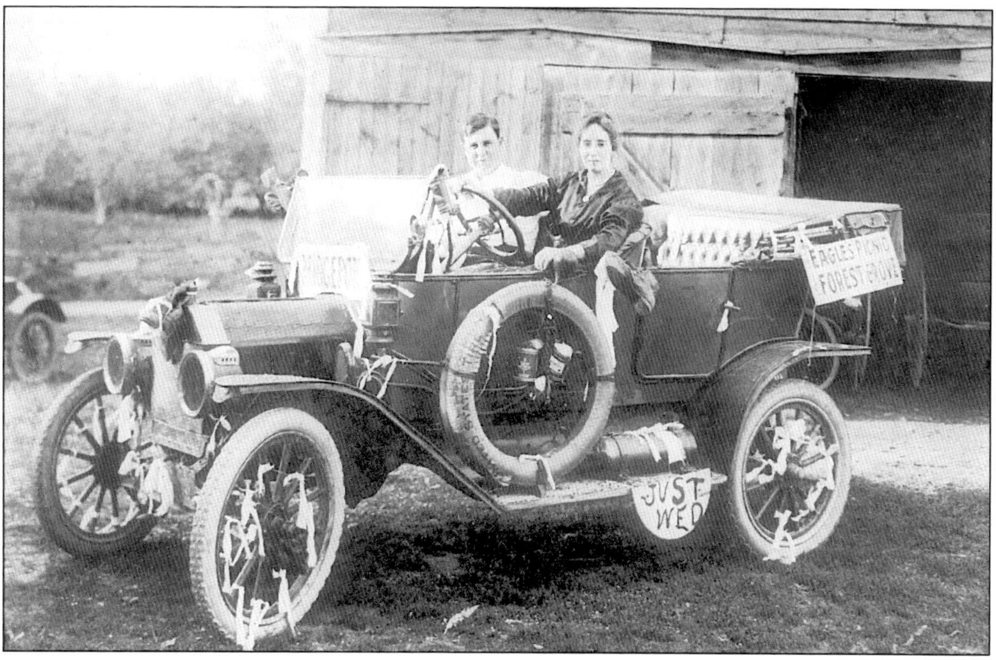

"Just Wed," 1915. With Margaret at the wheel, the bride and groom are about to start off in a car with even its wheels bedecked with streamers. In 1915, when cars were rare and subject to many breakdowns, it would not have seemed likely that they would become so much a part of American life, enabling people to have weekend homes and to live far from work. Today, orchards, such as the one in the background, continue to give way to subdivisions. (AHL.)

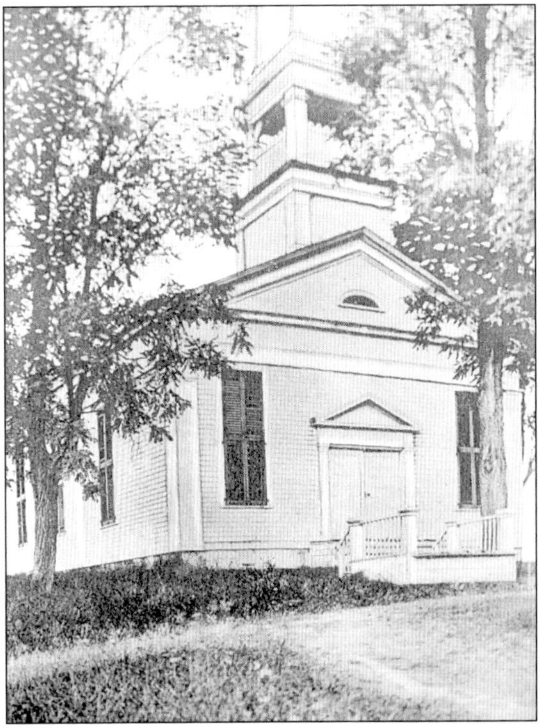

The Methodist Episcopal Church, Poughquag. This early-20th-century postcard shows the Methodist Episcopal church, which was built within the boundaries of the Beekman Cemetery and dedicated in 1840. Among its founders were the Brills, who were early settlers in the area and became large landowners. (BL.)

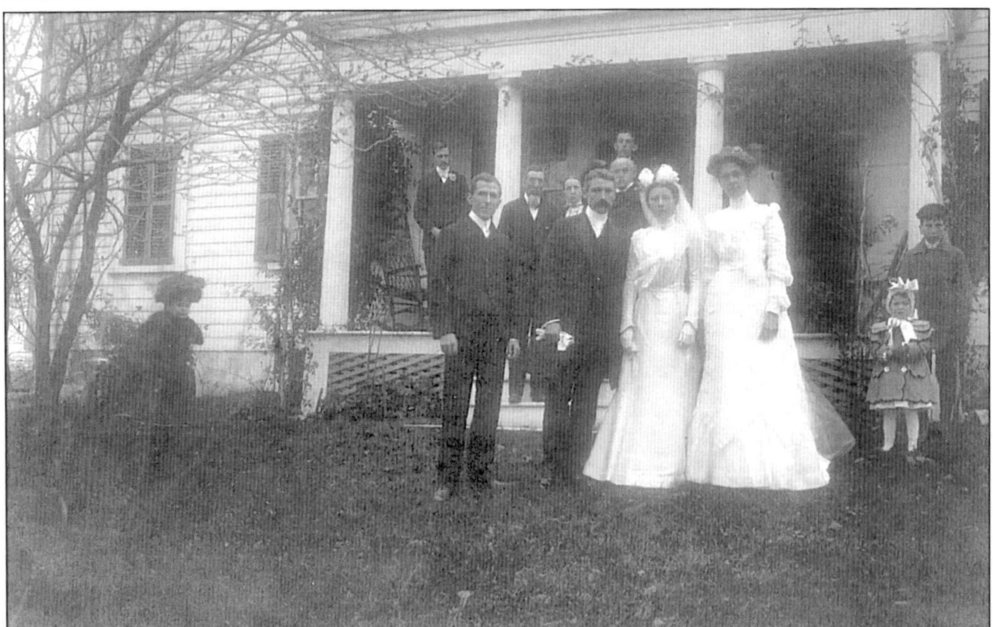

The Wedding of Mary Williams and Gerow W. Brill, 1901. As many 19th-century weddings were celebrated at home, it should not be so surprising that this wedding was the first celebrated in the Methodist Episcopal church. Statia Brill Ramage, the couple's daughter, and her husband, Robert, moved back to Poughquag in 1948 and became active in every facet of church activities. Their children—Peggy, Gay, Gerry, and Bill—were also part of the church community. (GM.)

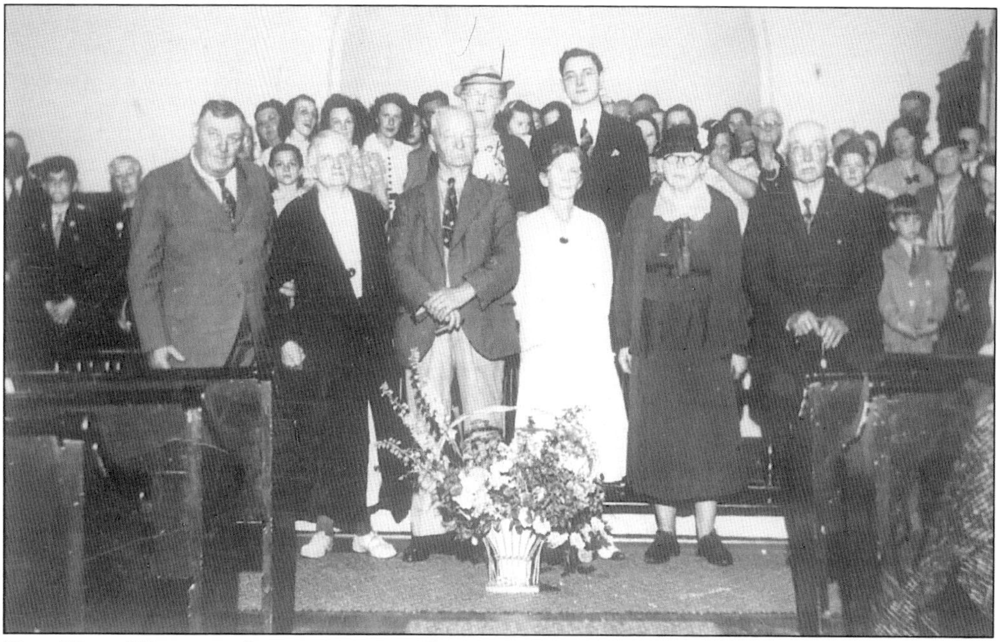

The 50th Wedding Anniversary of Roland and Anne Brill, c. 1930. The Methodist Episcopal church has continued to be a center for family occasions and celebrations. In the front row are Mr. and Mrs. James Stowe, Mr. and Mrs. Brill, and Mr. and Mrs. Reuben Place. The hamlets were small, and the population of the entire town of Beekman in 1930 was only 764, so that everyone seemed to know everyone else, promoting a real feeling of community. (RRH.)

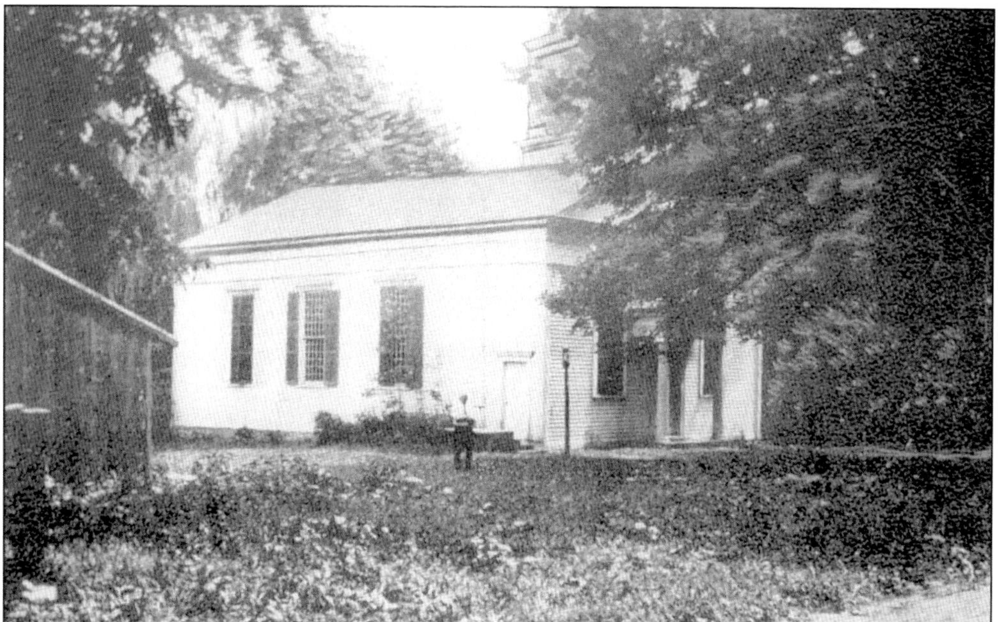

The Baptist Church, Beekmanville, c. 1900. In addition to Poughquag, Beekmanville was also a thriving hamlet. The Baptist church was built c. 1840 on land given by Egbert Delong, whose family included other early settlers of the area. In 2000, the church proudly celebrated its 160th anniversary. (VV.)

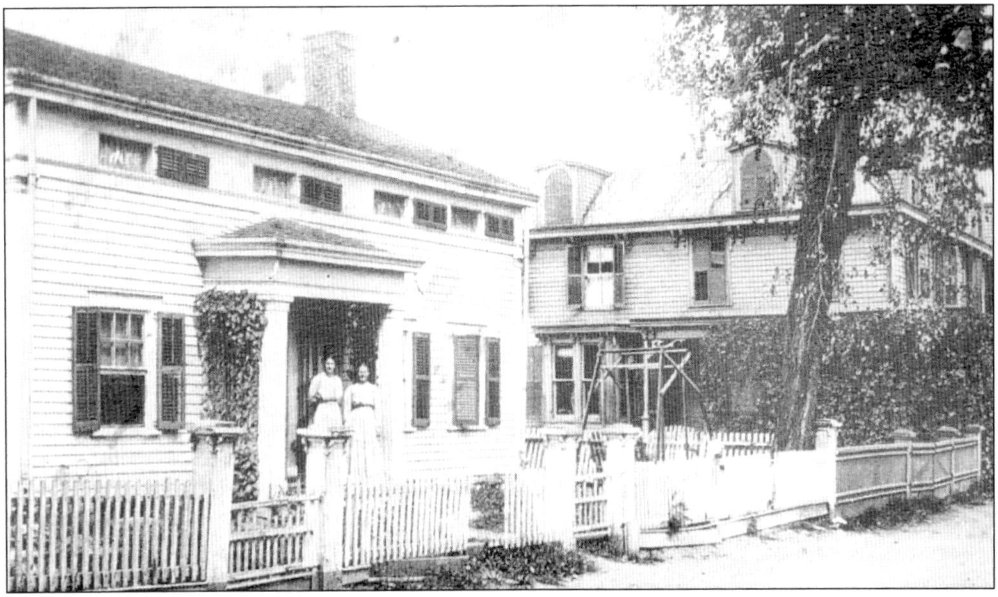

Beekmanville Hamlet, early 1900s. Shown is a typical Federal-style house surrounded by a picket fence. The ladies on the porch may be about to settle themselves on the swing in the front garden. The 1867 Beers atlas lists a doctor, a blacksmith, a dealer in flour, feed, and grain, as well as a number of farmers living in the hamlet. (BL.)

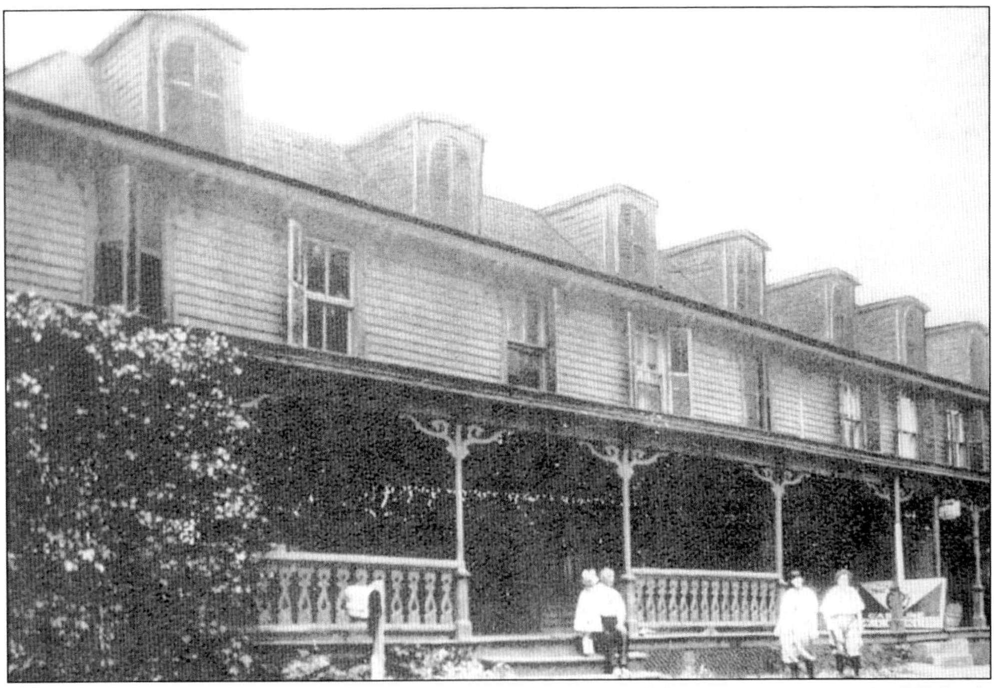

Beekmanville Hamlet Hotel, early 1900s. This turn-of-the-century postcard of Baker's Hotel is a reminder that the beauty and tranquillity of the Dutchess County landscape have long been a draw for city dwellers. There have always been connections between the country and cities, sometimes city dwellers seeking rest and recreation, sometimes country farmers looking for markets for their products. (VV.)

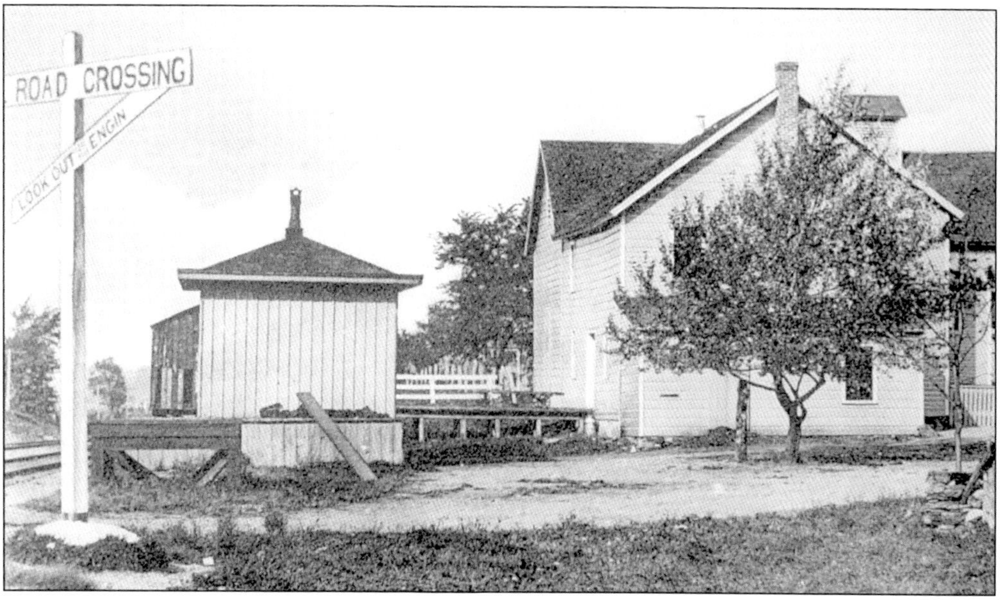

A Green Haven Creamery, early 1900s. This postcard from Vincent Vail's collection makes clear the link between this small hamlet and sometimes faraway markets. The Mutual Milk and Cream Company creamery was right next to the railroad, which provided the necessary means of transporting milk to customers in New York City. (VV.)

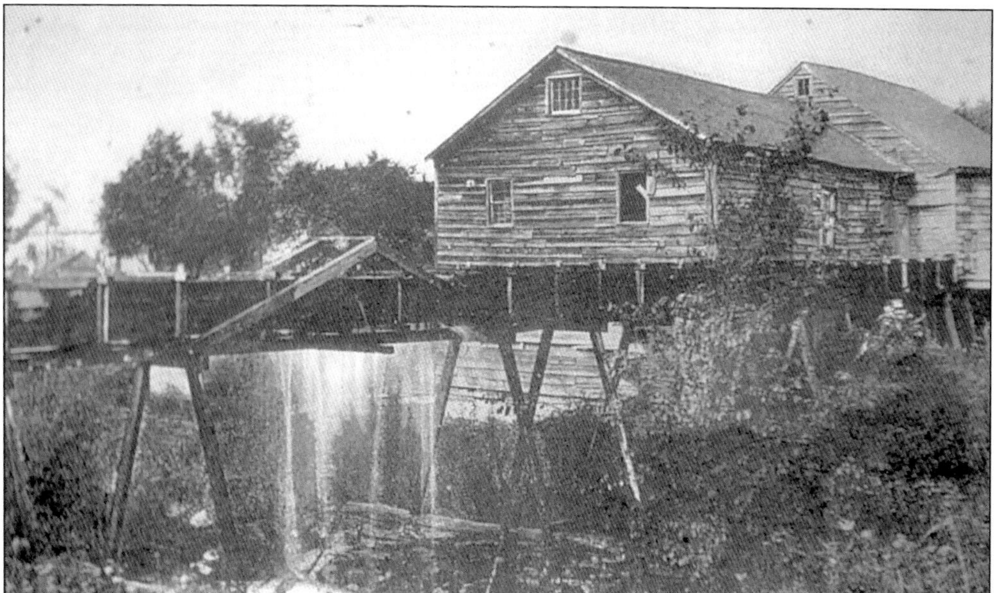

The Old Mill, Green Haven, early 1900s. Electricity did not come to many rural areas until the 1930s. Until then, water supplied the power necessary to run the mills situated along the streams. Most hamlets had at least one mill where farmers brought their grain to be ground or their felled trees to be sawn. (HC.)

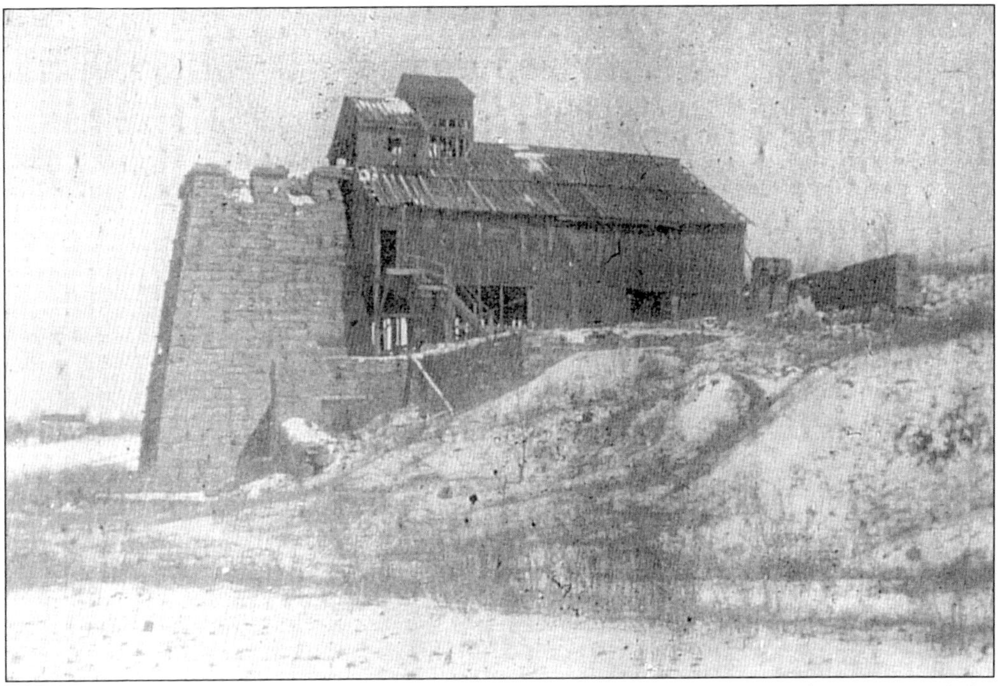

The Beekman Furnace, Furnace Road. All that remains today is the lower part of the structure. Iron was discovered in Beekman by W.E. Haxtun about 1846, and a mine on Baker Road was opened by Albert Tower in 1869. In 1873, the Clove Spring Iron Works built an anthracite furnace on what is now Furnace Road. This furnace had a 48-foot stack and produced 25 tons of pig iron per day. It ceased functioning in 1896. (VVTH.)

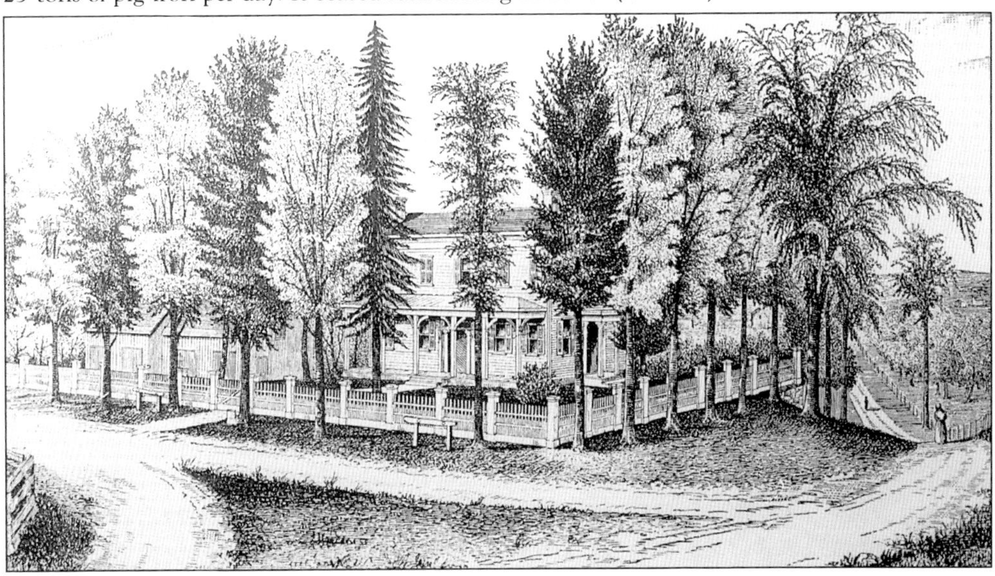

The Summer Residence of A. Tower, Esq., c. 1870s. This sketch is from James Smith's *History of Duchess County*, published in 1882. It is obvious that iron mining was profitable, at least for a while. W.E. Haxtun purchased the property in the late 1860s and lived there for a number of years. However, the discovery of purer ore in the Mesabi resulted in the closing of mines in Dutchess County.

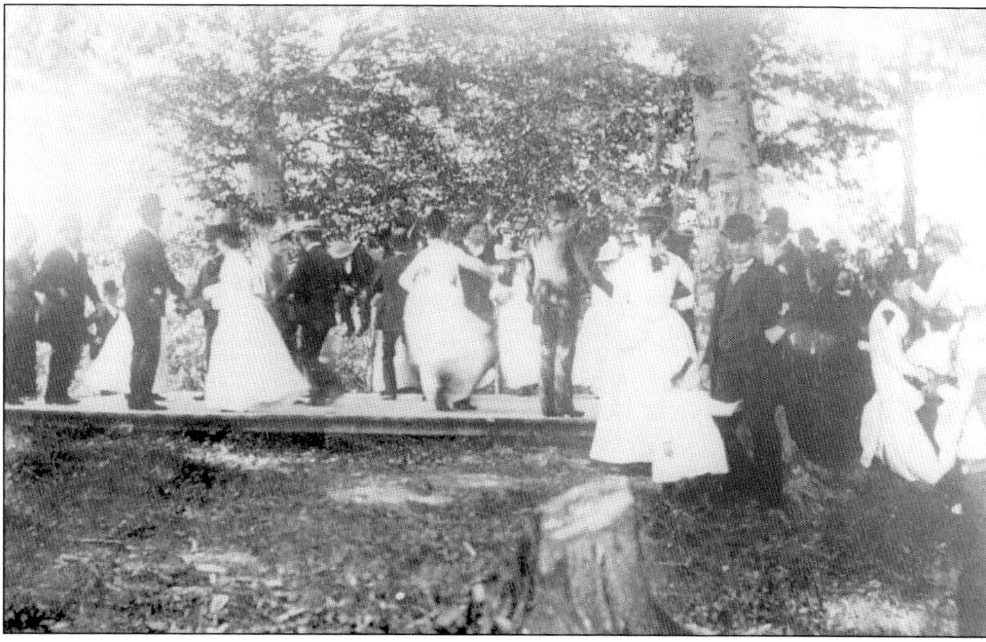

Irish Dancers at a Miners' Picnic, c. 1888. The Irish were spirited dancers, as shown in this photograph that captures their quick movements. They were also hard workers in the iron mines. According to an article by Lee Eaton, Daniel David Delaney had acquired land that had iron ore beds south of Sylvan Lake. By 1850, he had a functioning iron mine where he employed Irish immigrants. By the 1860s, Delaney had become a millionaire; in 1867, he built the Sylvan Lake Hotel. (UVHS.)

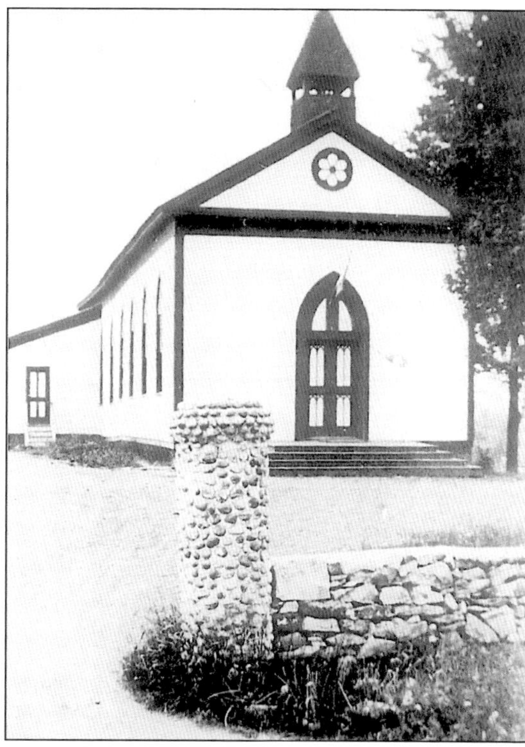

The St. Denis Church, Beekman Road. In 1858 or shortly thereafter, Daniel David Delaney donated land, and with the assistance of the Irish miners, the first St. Denis church was built just over the line in East Fishkill. There was also a chapel named Our Lady of Mercy, built by the miners in the Clove in the mid-1880s. It closed after WWII. St. Denis burned in 1935, but a new church building was constructed, dedicated the following year. (VVTH.)

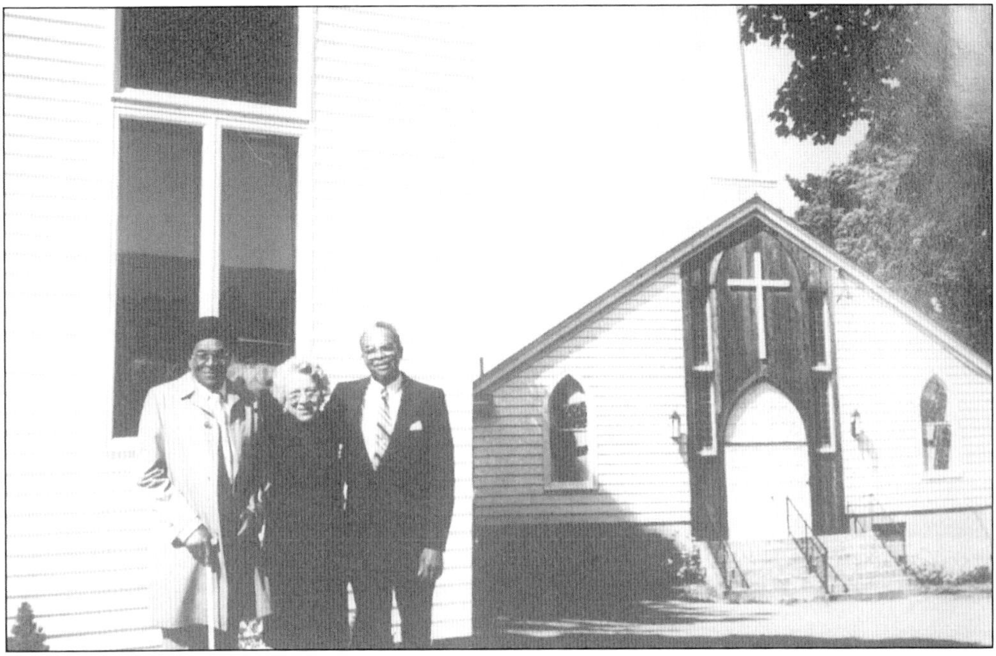

THE MOUNT ZION BAPTIST CHURCH AND CHURCH LEADERS, GREEN HAVEN. This montage shows the Mount Zion Baptist Church, which was founded in 1902 by Sr. Mary Johnson. The first chairman of the deacons was Deacon Byrd, whose son the Reverend Charles E. Byrd served as pastor from 1936 to 1952. The original building has been significantly renovated and expanded. Deacon James Wright, Church Mother Beatrice Johnson, and Chair of the Deacons Thomas Coleman continue the tradition of service. (BL/JS/JG.)

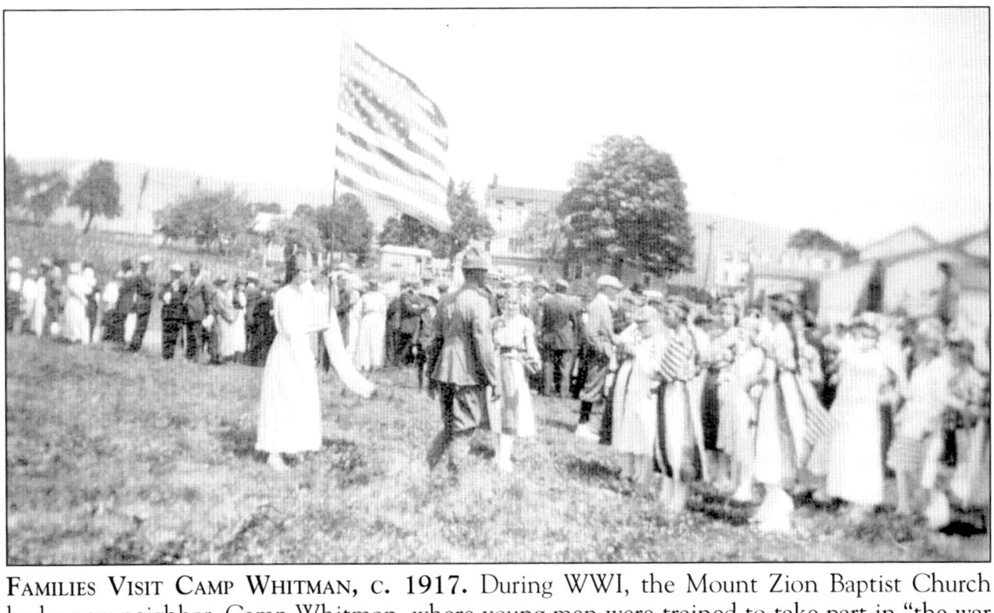

FAMILIES VISIT CAMP WHITMAN, C. 1917. During WWI, the Mount Zion Baptist Church had a new neighbor, Camp Whitman, where young men were trained to take part in "the war to end all war." Just before WWII, a state prison was built here but not occupied. Today, the correctional facility is a vast presence. However, it is seldom recorded as part of local history because of laws that limit photographing the building and its occupants. (RRH.)

HENRY SLOCUM WITH HIS SON, FRANK, C. 1912. The Slocums are in front of the house on Pleasant Ridge, where Frank was born. Henry and his wife, Lillian, whose father had worked in an ore mine, ran the general store in Poughquag for many years. It was a meeting place for everyone and a place where you could get practically anything. (TC.)

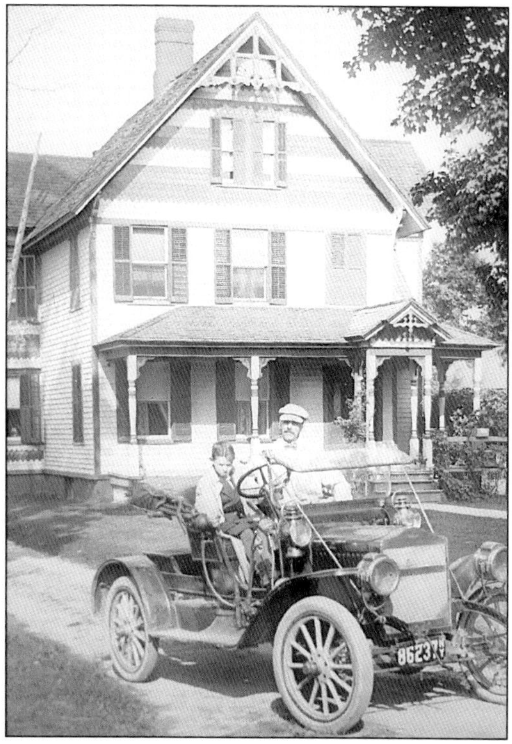

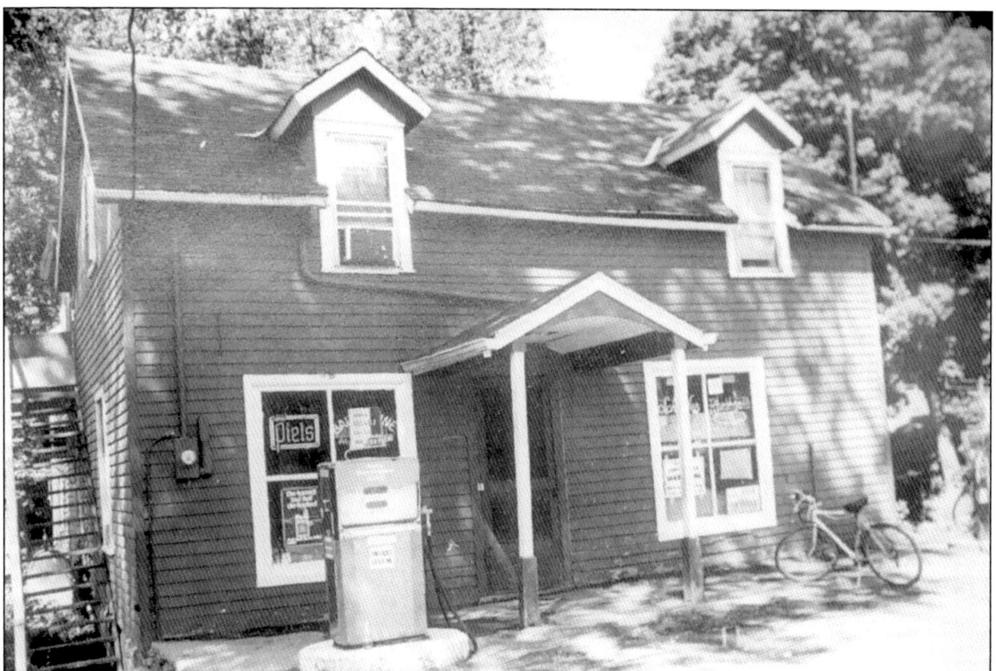

THE SLOCUM-KNAPP STORE, 1977. The Knapps took over the store from the Slocums. Blanche Hait, the Knapp's daughter, recalls that during the 1920s and 1930s, when people were short of money, Mr. Knapp was known to say "just hang up the groceries," which meant putting the bill on a wooden peg. The store burned in the 1990s. (BL.)

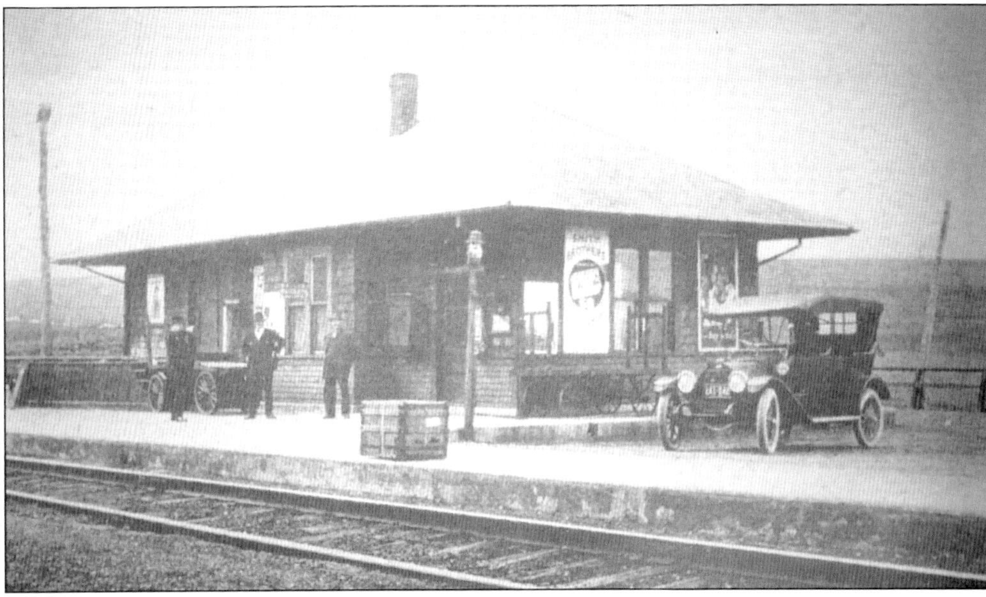

POUGHQUAG DEPOT, EARLY 1900S. Poughquag was on the New York & New England Railroad, previously chartered as the Boston, Hartford, & Erie Railroad. It was later acquired by the Central New England Railway in the 1900s and finally by the New York, New Haven, & Hartford Railroad in the 1920s. Statia Ramage remembers arriving by train at the depot on Depot Hill Road. (RRH.)

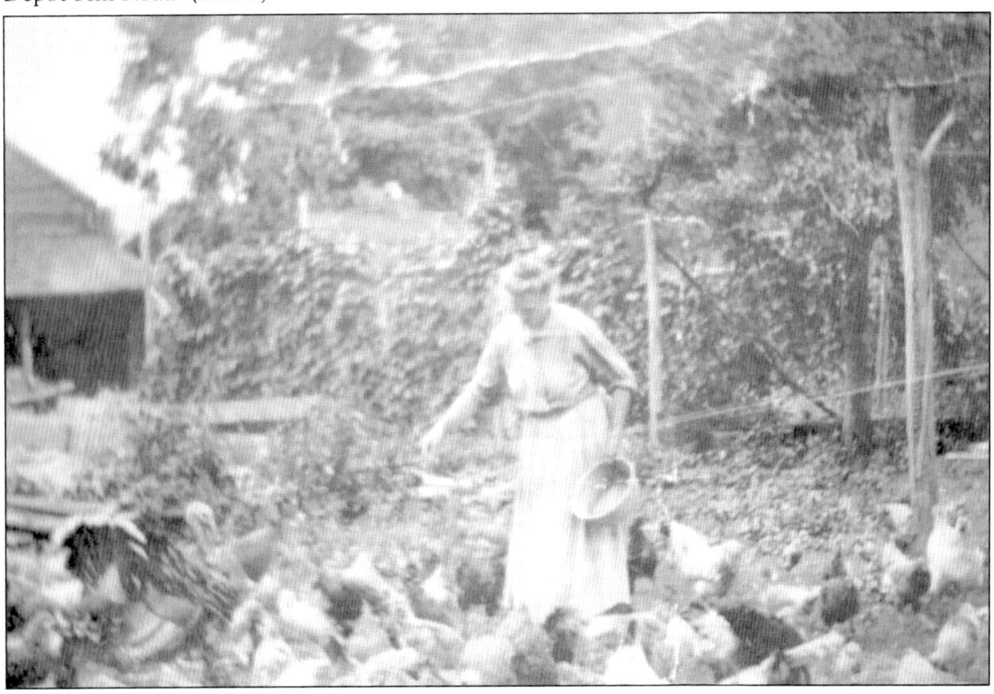

ELIZABETH LYNCH HOGAN, 1936. Mrs. Hogan, Bob Hogan's grandmother, is shown feeding the chickens on the Hogan farm in Poughquag. The life of a farmer's wife was not easy, with no running hot water and no electricity. While she lived to see electricity come into her house, the oil burner came after her death. (RRH.)

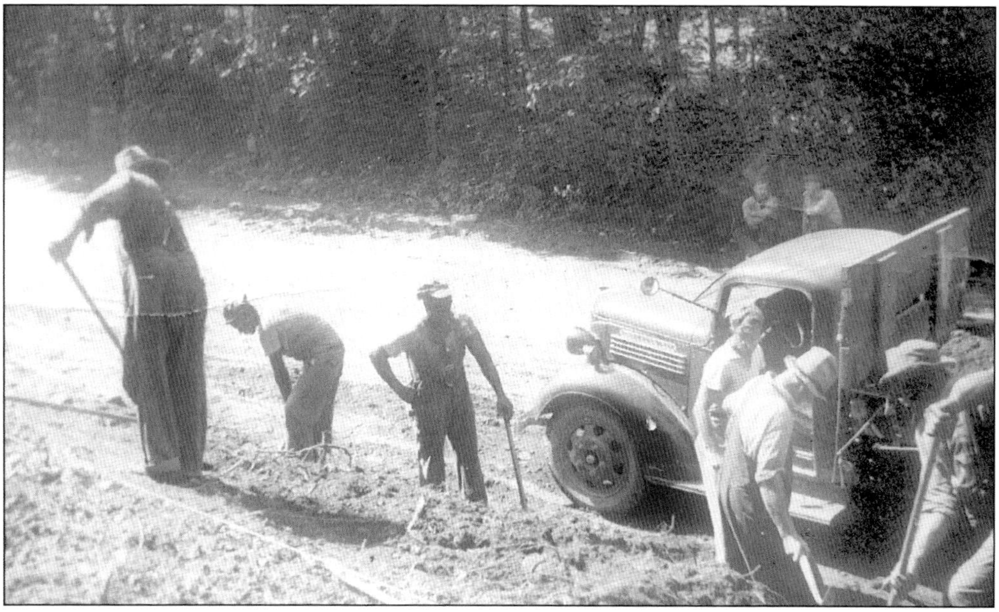

Road Building, 1936. This road building in 1936 was a harbinger of the changes that have come and continue to come to Beekman. In the same year, the segment of the Taconic State Parkway to East Fishkill was dedicated. Route 55 from Billings to Poughquag was not paved until 1946. Nevertheless, automobiles were making the town more and more accessible to city dwellers who began to spend weekends and summers in its quiet beauty. (RRH.)

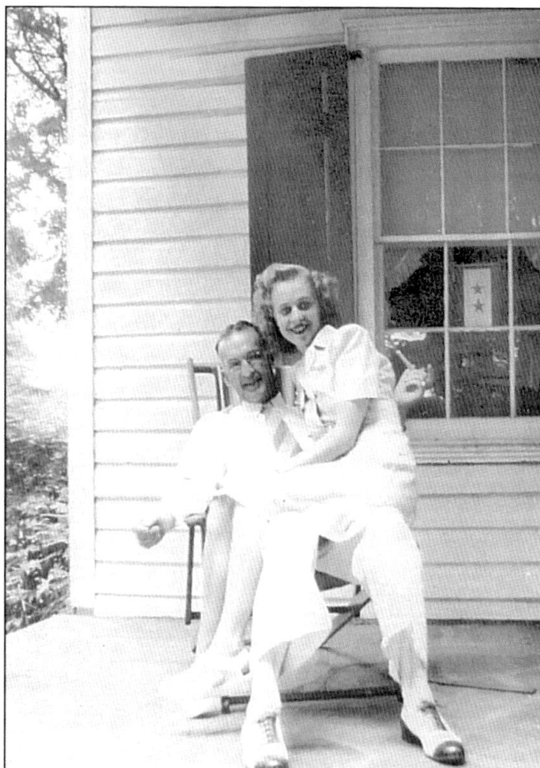

Bill Gardner and Loretta Flanigan, 1940s. Two members of town supervisor Bill Gardner's family, Bob and Eugene Hogan, were in service during WWII, as indicated by the two stars in the window. Despite this, Gardner is enjoying life while his nephew's fiancee, Loretta, sits on his lap. In 1940, the town needed a firehouse and hoped to obtain help from the WPA. One morning, Gardner was summoned by John Mack to his pond, where he found President Roosevelt. It seems that there were no funds available for firehouses, but town halls were a different story! (RRH.)

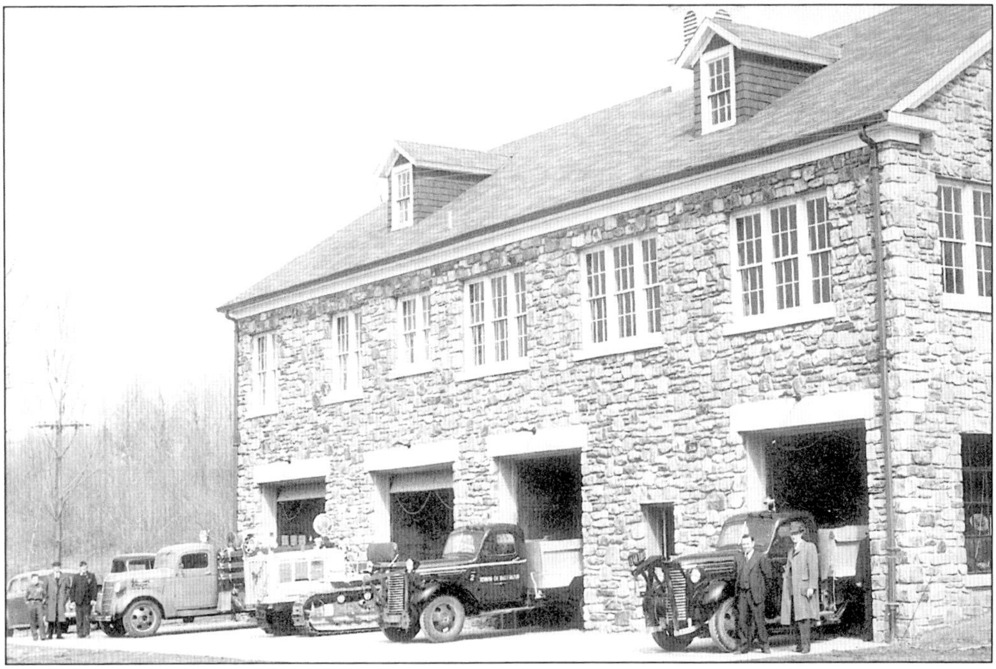

THE BEEKMAN TOWN HALL AND FIREHOUSE, 1940S. The fire engines were housed in the lower story of this building until the 1970s, when members of the fire company purchased land on which a new firehouse was constructed, financed by a bond issue approved by the voters. The Ladies Auxiliary was established in 1945 and the Beekman Rescue Squad in 1967. Discussions are now underway on the impact of town growth on the future needs of the fire department. (RRH.)

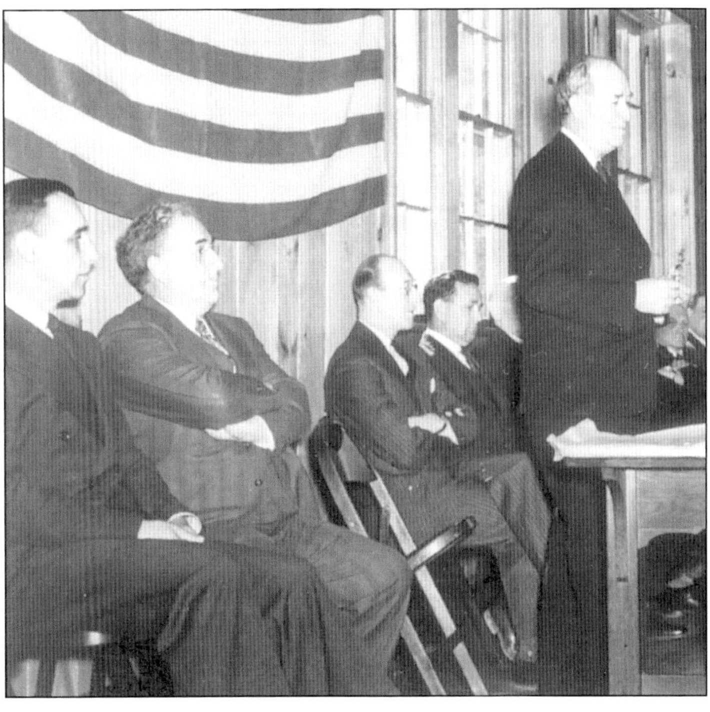

DEDICATION OF THE TOWN HALL, 1942. Judge John Mack—who had a longstanding political friendship with FDR, having nominated him for the presidency—speaks at the dedication. His 1,000-acre place in the Clove was known for its beautiful gardens. Seen second from the right is Spencer Shepherd, the first fire chief, and next to him at the extreme right is supervisor Bill Gardner, who was also the first president of the Beekman Fire Protectives. (RRH/JG.)

THREE YOUNG LADIES IN THE 1940S. Ella Odell, Theda Slocum, and Helen "Ruby" Woodin seem to be without a care in the world. Theda's father-in-law, Henry, had been postmaster. After his death, his wife, Lillian, took over; the post office was moved from the store to the extension of the house where Theda Slocum still lives. After WWII, "Ruby" Woodin, who had been a mail carrier, became the postmaster. She was also one of founders of the rescue squad and its first president. (TC.)

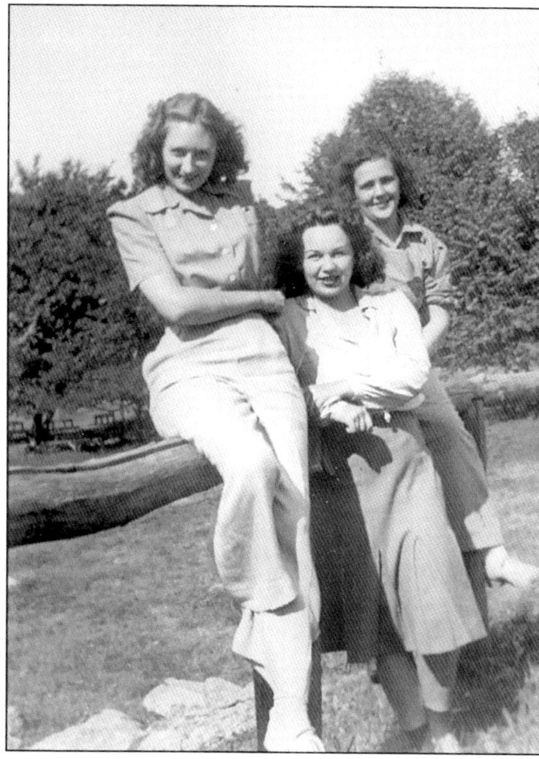

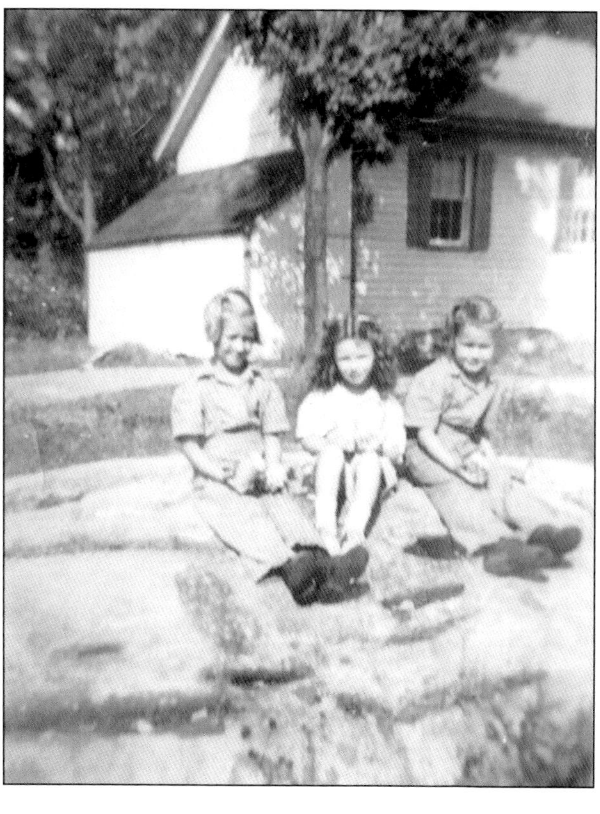

PLAYING HOOKEY IN THE 1940S. The daughter of Theda Slocum, Tony Slocum Capalbo, the child in the middle, is not sure today whether she and her two friends—Shirley Woodin Phillips and Mary Woodin Capalbo—were "playing hookey" on that beautiful day or simply had a holiday from school. Whichever it was, they seem to have been unable to stay away from school, at least the Gardner Hollow School where "Ruby" Woodin, Shirley and Mary's mother, did substitute teaching when not delivering mail. (TC.)

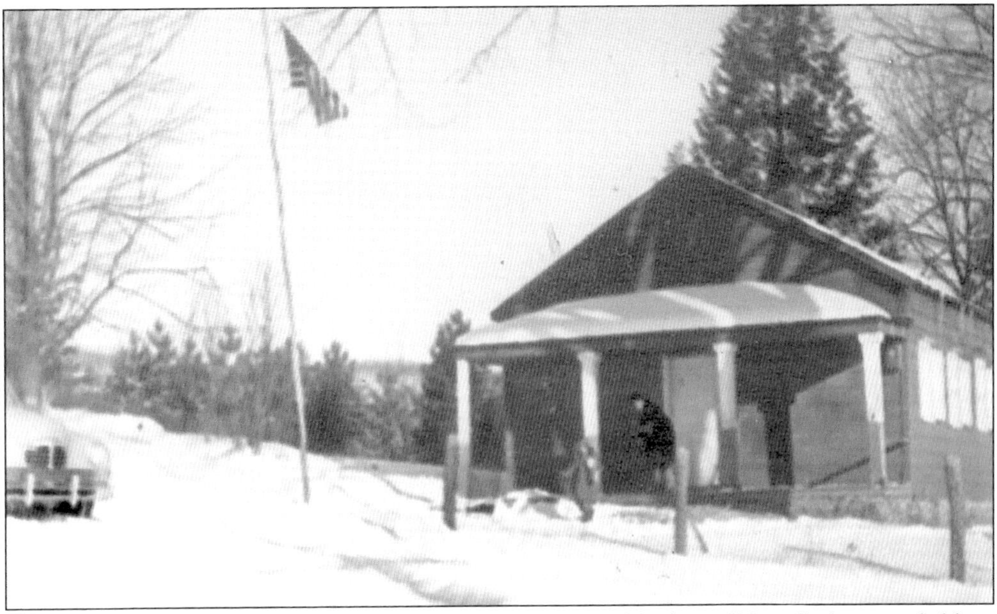

GARDNER HOLLOW SCHOOL NO. 4, C. 1950S. The little girl looks well bundled up, as children had to be when they had to walk to school in all weather. Amy Hoag Lynch recalls that her grandfather, her mother, she, and her daughter all attended this school. It was only about the time of the consolidation of the Beekman one-room schoolhouses with the Arlington Central School District that a bus fleet was acquired. (AHL.)

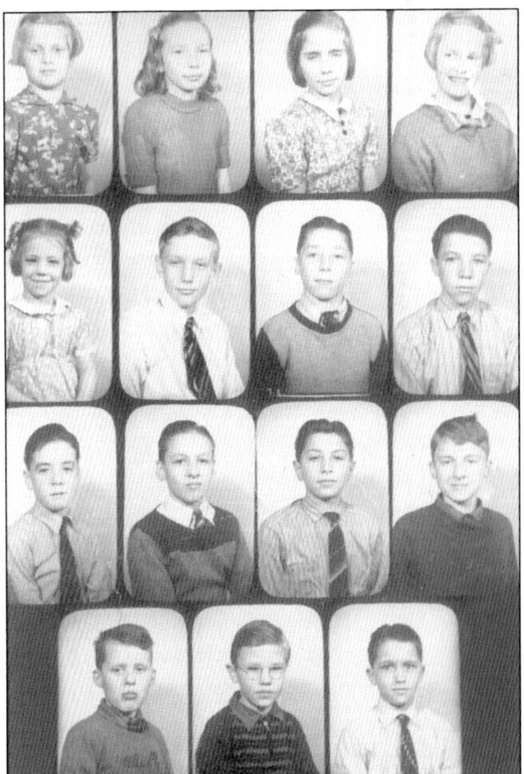

CHILDREN AT THE BEEKMAN SCHOOL DISTRICT NO. 5, ON CLOVE VALLEY ROAD, C. EARLY 1940S. On the extreme left in the bottom row is Vince Vail, who is now the Beekman town historian. The Gregory and Baker children were also in this class. When the school was no longer used, it became a residence, which burned in 1987. (VV.)

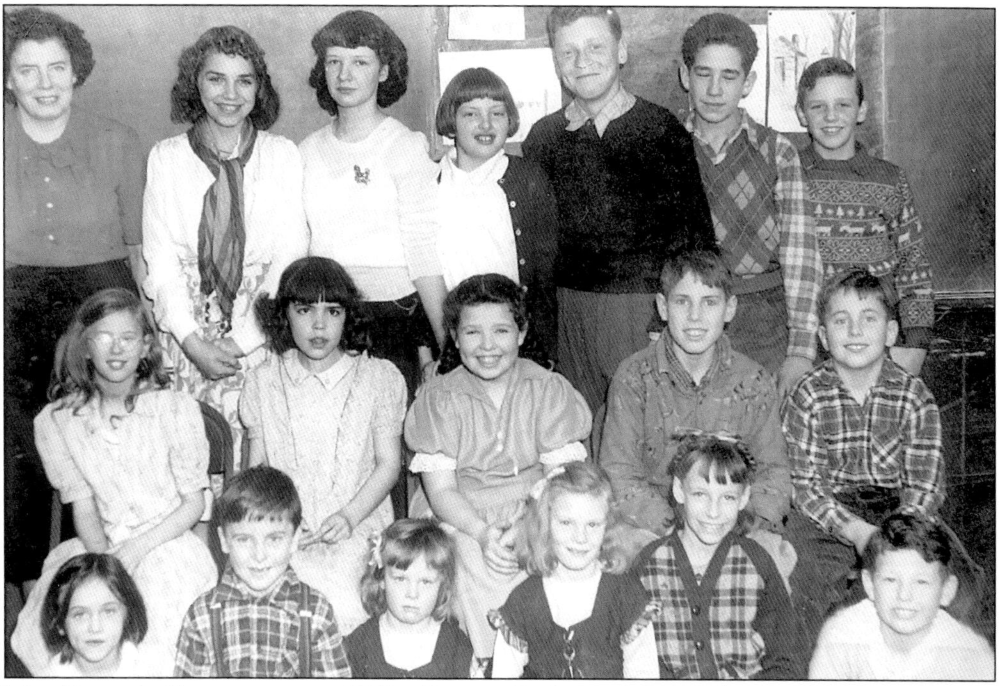

MISS DODGE'S CLASS, C. EARLY 1950S. Bernice Dodge is shown with one of the last groups of children to be taught in this one-room schoolhouse on Clove Valley Road. As the town grew, a consolidated school district was formed. The one-room school teachers—Mrs. Hoag, Mrs. DeForest, Mrs. DeRosa, Mrs. Robinson, and Miss Dodge—became part of the Arlington School District in the early 1950s. Beekman children first attended the Todd Hill School and later the Beekman Elementary School. (VVTH.)

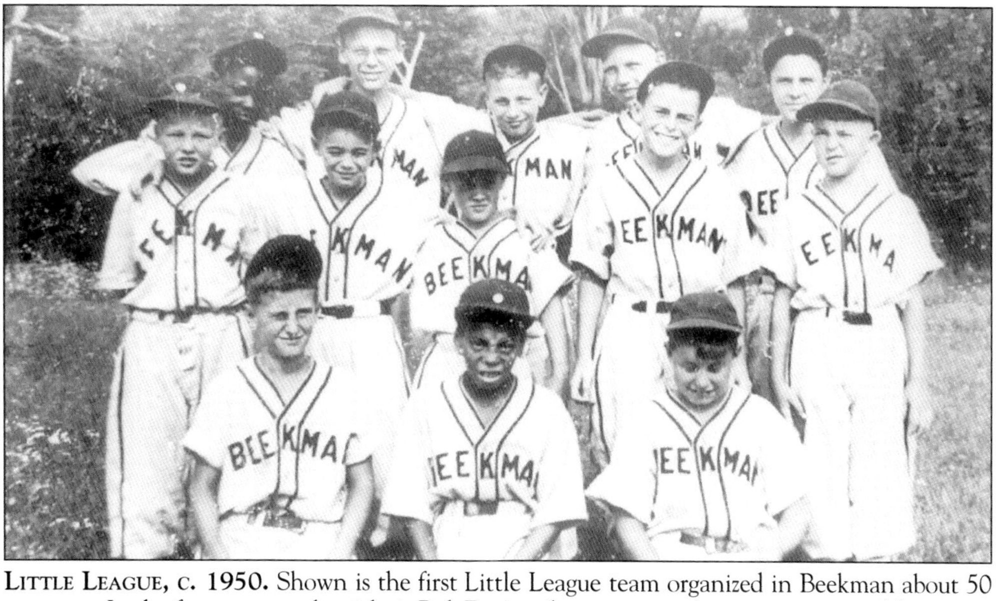

LITTLE LEAGUE, C. 1950. Shown is the first Little League team organized in Beekman about 50 years ago. In the front row on the right is Bob Ferris, who grew up to become a justice of the peace. Today, Beekman youngsters play soccer and football as well as Little League. Parents spend many hours transporting their children to practice and games, but to them it is well worth it. (RF.)

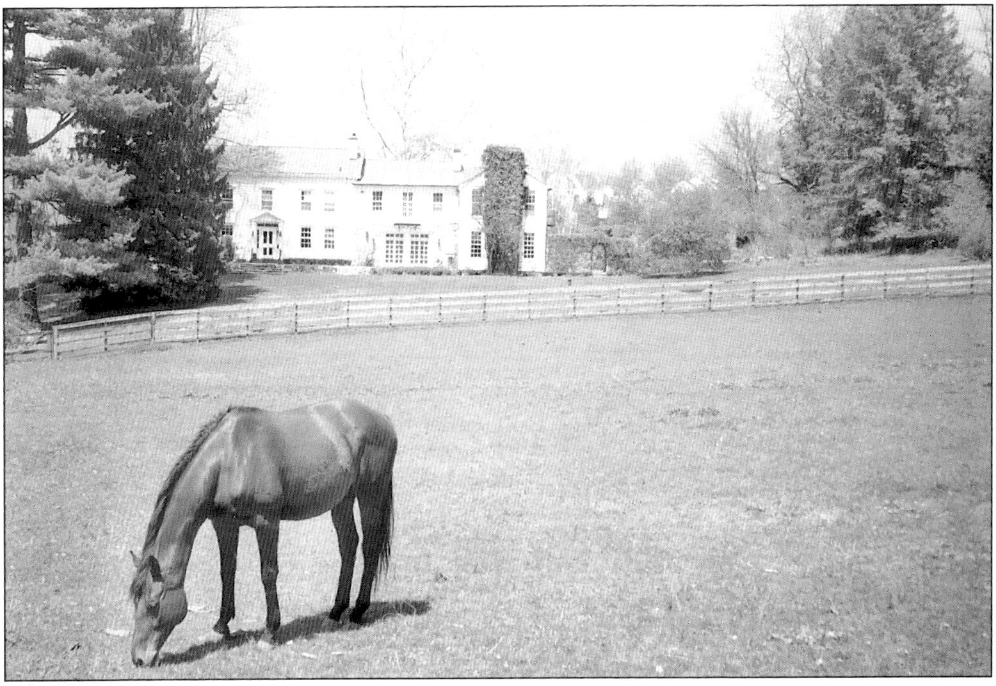

The FDR Jr. House, 2000. In the late 1940s, Franklin D. Roosevelt Jr., the son of the president, acquired this property made up of a number of small farms that had been put together by the Fortington family. FDR Jr. raised polled Herefords, but he later became interested in horse breeding. In the 1980s, the Roosevelt property was sold to Dalton Farm. (JS.)

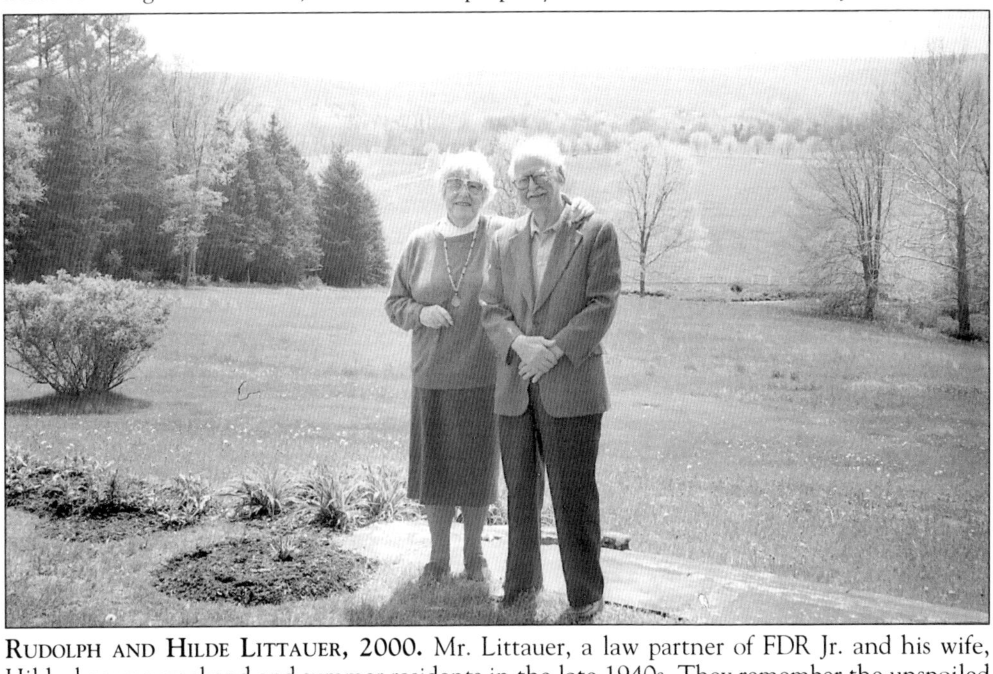

Rudolph and Hilde Littauer, 2000. Mr. Littauer, a law partner of FDR Jr. and his wife, Hilde, became weekend and summer residents in the late 1940s. They remember the unspoiled beauty and friendliness of the area. Today, they watch with concern as house after house is built upon what was formerly farmland. The rate of change has become very fast. (JS.)

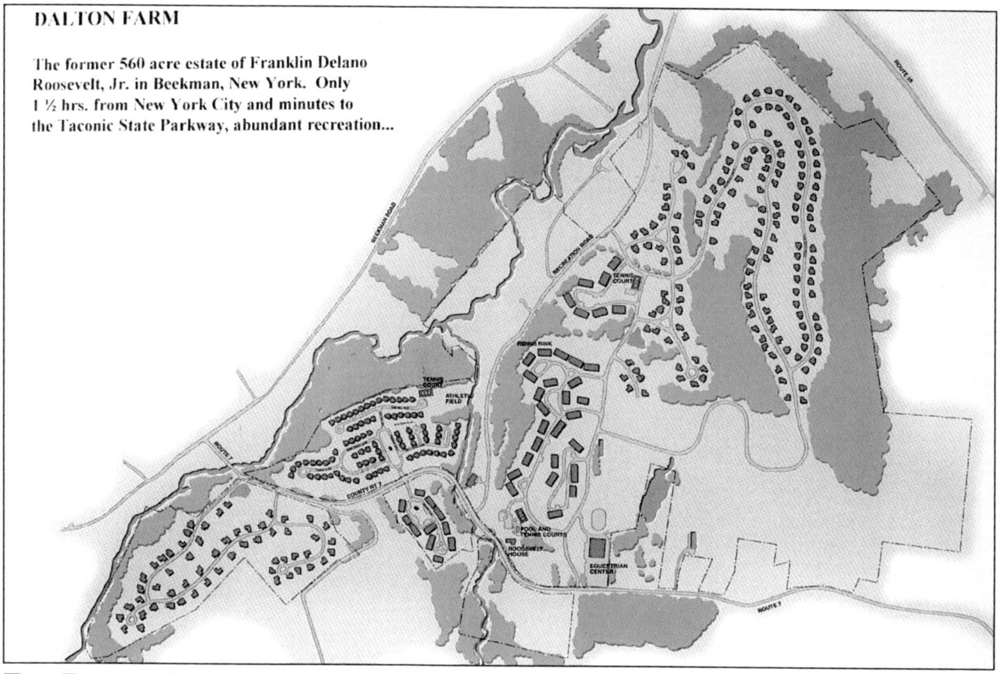

The Dalton Farm, 2000. This brochure for the development of the former Roosevelt property emphasizes its proximity to New York City and the Taconic State Parkway. A planned community, of which 60 percent of the acreage will remain forever green, Dalton Farm also stresses a "village" theme, in some ways an effort to recreate an earlier time. FDR Jr.'s house has become the clubhouse, and the property contains a working horse farm, equestrian center, lake, pool, and tennis courts. (DF.)

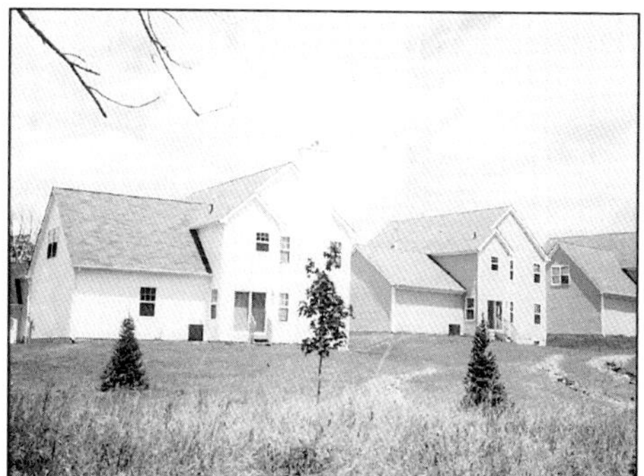

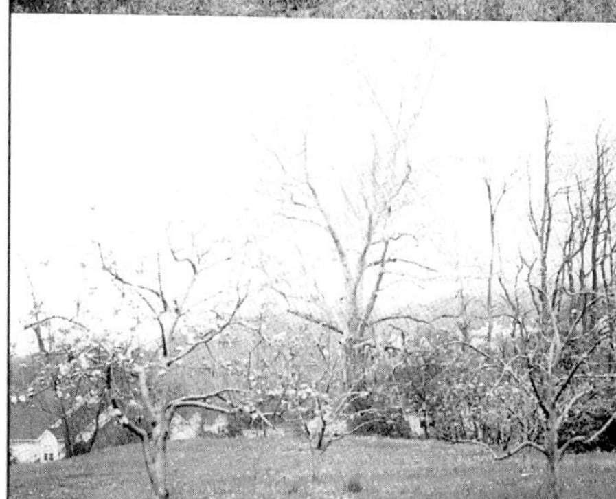

Apple Orchards–Housing Development, 2000. This montage of apple orchards and newly built homes shows the "old" and the "new." The Barton Orchards, which border these houses, are on land once owned by the Fortingtons. Now featuring a "pick your own" system, the orchards were also "new" at one time. Change, always inevitable, is often unsettling, bringing with it new problems as well as new opportunities. (JS.)

BEEKMAN READING CENTER VOLUNTEERS C. 1970S. For a number of years, the Beekman Reading Center, the precursor to the library that was formally established c. 1987, was housed in a former school in Green Haven. Under the direction of Lee Eaton, the former chairman of volunteers, it now functions in a storefront in a small shopping area on Route 55. With all the new residents, the town has outgrown this space, and plans are underway to build a new library. (BL.)

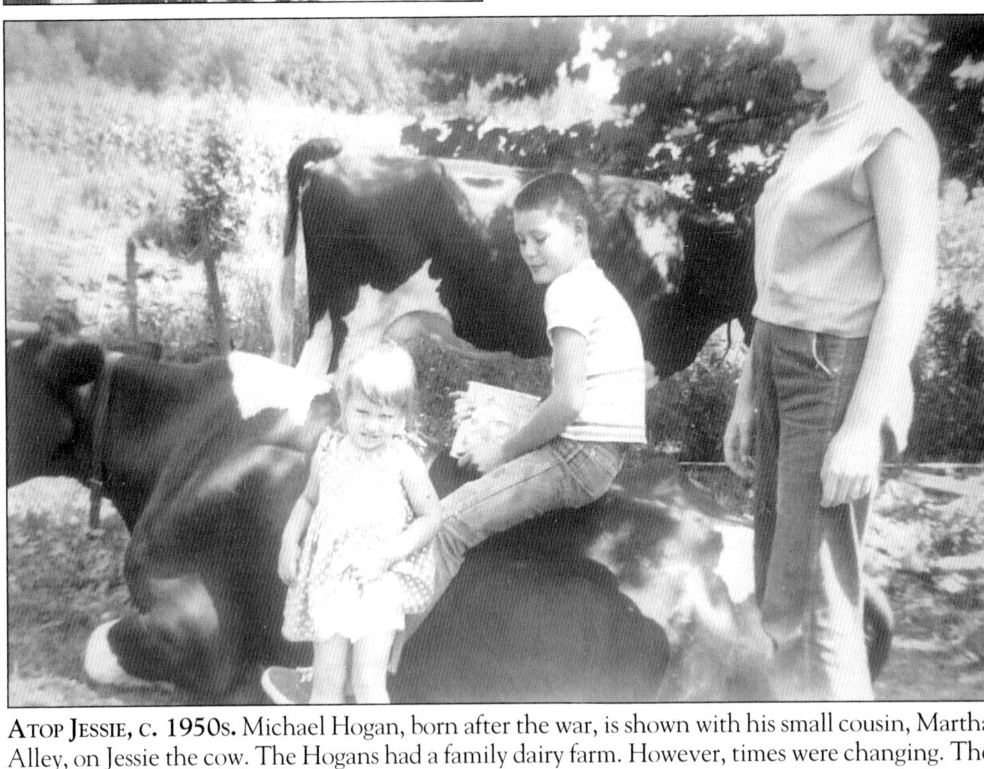

ATOP JESSIE, C. 1950S. Michael Hogan, born after the war, is shown with his small cousin, Martha Alley, on Jessie the cow. The Hogans had a family dairy farm. However, times were changing. The price that farmers were able to get for their milk was not keeping pace with the prices of the goods and services the farmers had to buy, and land taxes continued to rise. (RRH.)

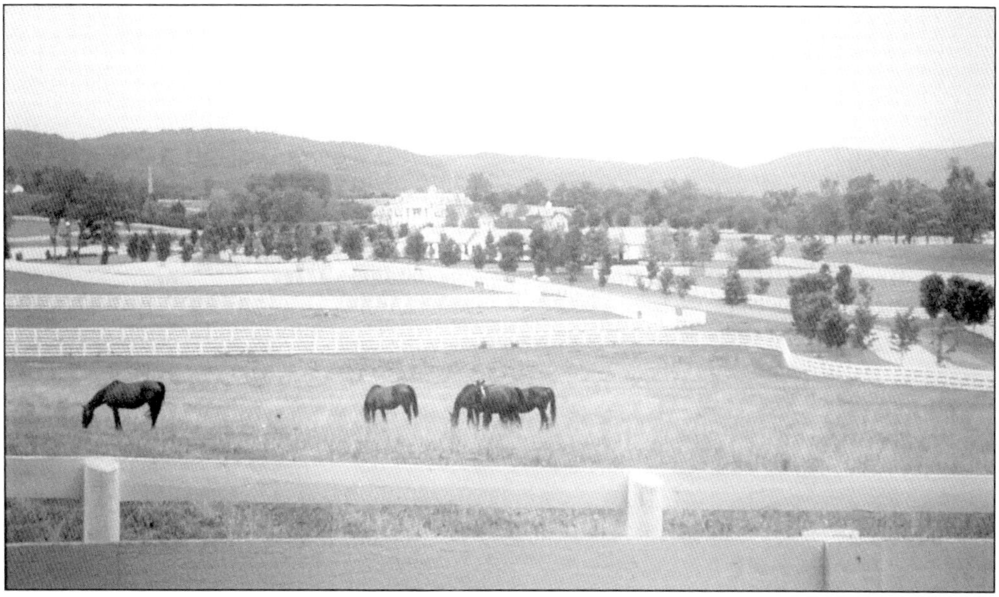

SUGAR MAPLE FARM, 1996. Sugar Maple, an internationally renowned horse breeding farm, is a very different kind of farm. Miles of white fences mark its borders. Among the horses bred here was Champagneforashley, a three-year-old who was a favorite to win the Kentucky Derby in 1990 until a last-minute injury scratched him from the running, disappointing Dutchess County fans. (JG.)

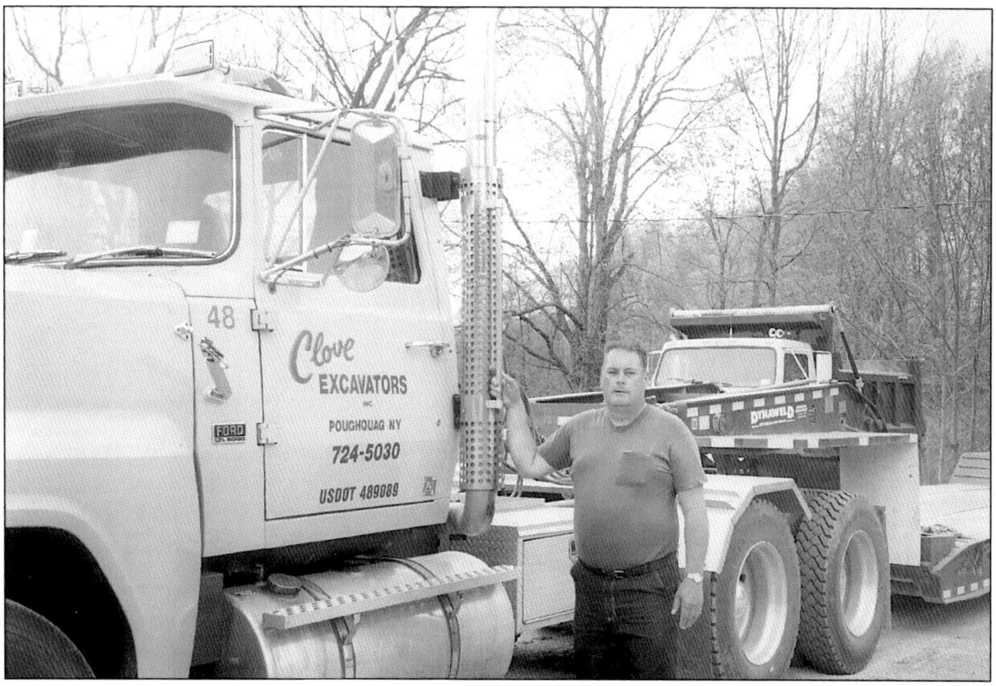

MICHAEL HOGAN AND CLOVE EXCAVATORS, 2000. The Hogans gave up their dairy farm and, in 1966, started Clove Excavators, of which Mike is now president. Dairy farming was no longer economically feasible, and the demand for rebuilding old roads and constructing new ones is ever increasing. Mike Hogan now has a "herd" of trucks. (JS.)

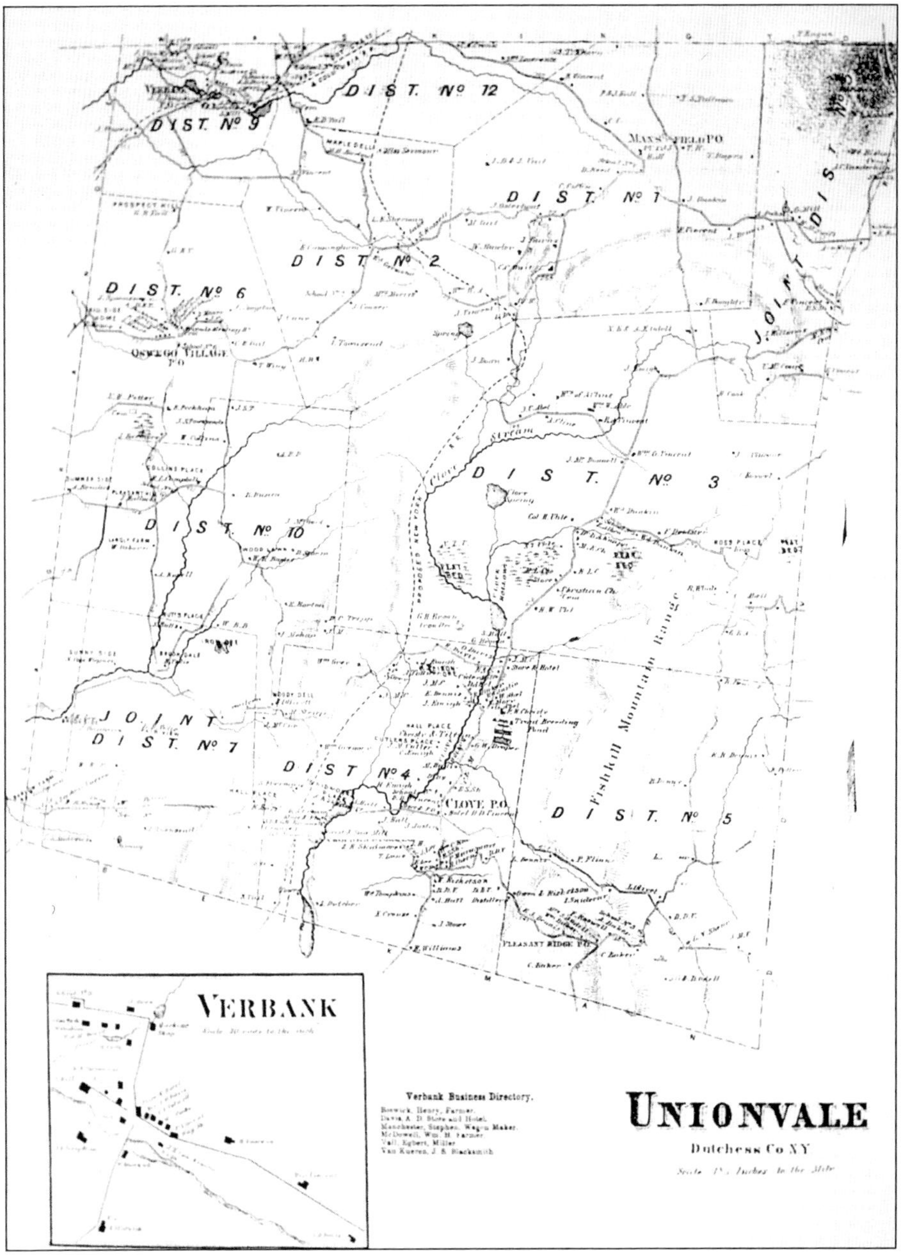

A Map of Union Vale, c. 1867. In 1867, before the coming of the railroad, Verbank, located in the northwest corner of the town, was a thriving hamlet. When the Dutchess & Columbia Railroad arrived just a few years later, a depot was established there. Another was also established about a mile to the northwest at Verbank on the Green, which then became the major hamlet. South of Verbank was Oswego Village, where a hamlet including a Friends school grew up around the Friends meetinghouse. Extensive ore beds were to be found in the broad valley between East and West Mountains extending north to south through the center of the town known as "the Clove". The Clove Valley Railroad branch from Sylvan Lake to Clove Valley was opened in 1877. The map also shows settlement in the Clove and at Crouse's Store (now the Tymor area) to the west. (DCHS.)

Three

Union Vale

Union Vale, formed in 1827 from parts of Beekman and Freedom (later LaGrange), is one of the most rural of Dutchess County towns. In its center, Clove Valley—named for the cleft or clove in the mountains at its northern end—runs 6 miles from north to south and is about a mile wide. Union Vale was first settled at the beginning of the 18th century by Palatines, New Englanders, and people from Long Island.

Farming was the basis of the economy, although mining played a major role, given the discovery of iron ore in the early 1800s. Large areas of forest were cleared to make the charcoal needed to run nearby furnaces. Verbank Village, settled in the last part of the 18th century, was for years the center of tanning and charcoal industries. However, with the demise of the furnaces and the coming of the railroad, Verbank on the Green, settled mostly after the Civil War, became the dominant hamlet with a milk factory, post office, stores, and houses. The mills were fueled by water power, supplied by creeks and ponds.

The town was divided into school districts, each with a one- or two-room schoolhouse, the last of which closed in 1961. Fishing and hunting continue to be favorite pastimes of local residents and those who belong to one of the several rod and gun clubs.

The active fire department and ambulance service formed in the 1950s serves the community and provides a focus for many activities. Tymor Park, presented to the town by Ralph and Jean Connor and dedicated in 1975, has become the center for town government and recreation. Today, the town is in transition, as large housing developments sprout up where once were farms.

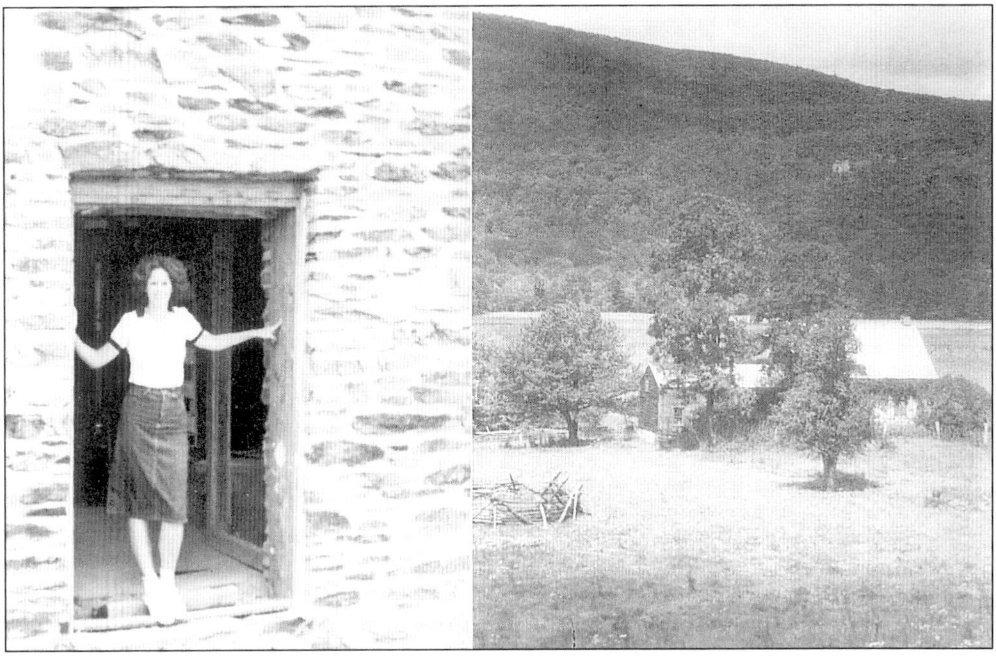

THE OLDEST HOUSE IN TOWN. A one-and-a-half-story structure of stone, the house built in the Clove in 1740 by Nicholas Emigh, a Palatine, had fallen into disrepair when Peter and Deborah Krulewitch bought it. They had the house recreated using its 2-foot-thick stone walls, its original rafters, some of the interior partitions, and some of the original staircases. Nearby is the large Clove Spring. (DPK/Margaret De Mott Brown, DCHS.)

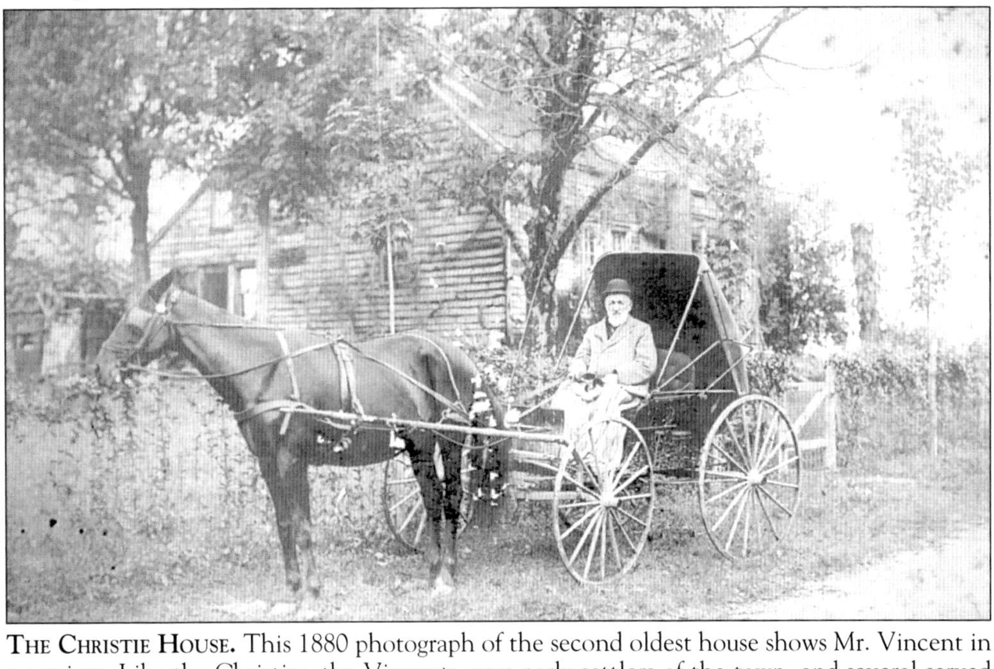

THE CHRISTIE HOUSE. This 1880 photograph of the second oldest house shows Mr. Vincent in a carriage. Like the Christies, the Vincents were early settlers of the town, and several served as town supervisors. Built by John Peter Hall in 1747, the house was dismantled and moved to the town of Pawling in the 1980s. (UVHS.)

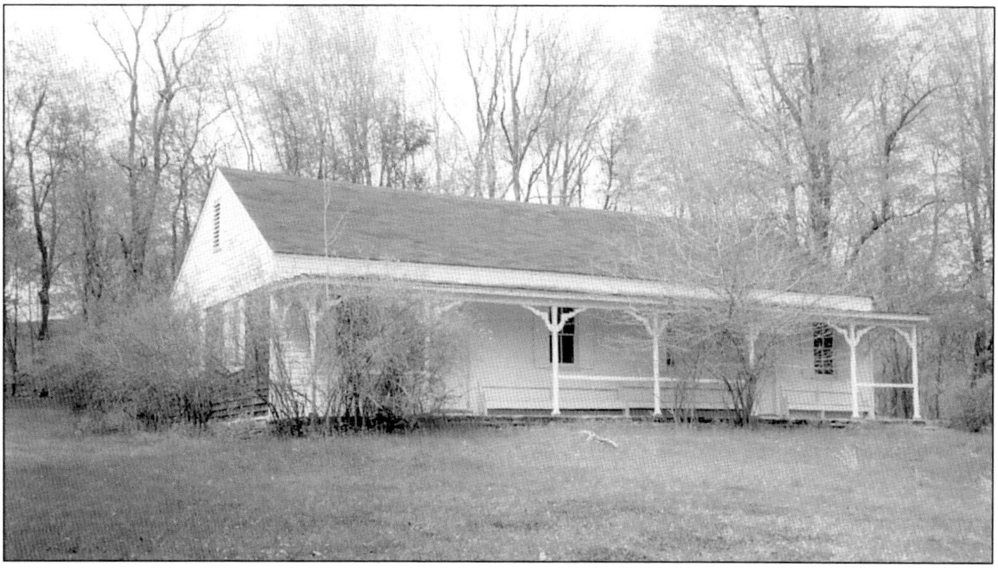

THE OSWEGO MEETINGHOUSE. This meetinghouse, which was once within the boundaries of Freedom (now LaGrange), was built in 1828, replacing the first log meetinghouse built in 1761. The Friends, originally from New England, came to the area before 1750. In 1751, the group purchased 2 acres for its meetinghouse and cemetery. They were once surrounded by a school and hamlet, which have since disappeared. Their neighbor is now the Sky Acres airport, established in 1965. (JS.)

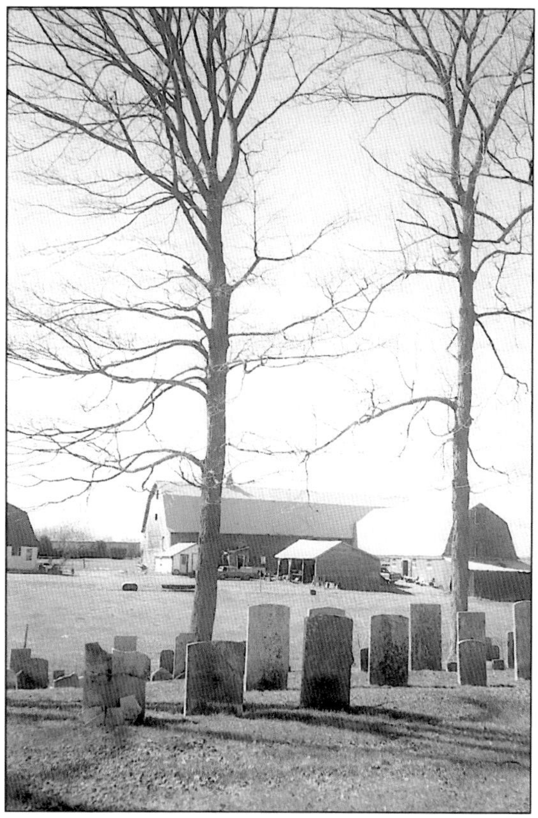

POTTERS' CEMETERY. Like the Oswego Meetinghouse, the cemetery at the corner of NY Route 55 and County Route 21 is near the town's boundary with the town of LaGrange, of which it was once part. A Methodist church building was erected here early in the 19th century, but in the1860s it was removed to a site in LaGrange. In the distance are the barns of Ray Vail's farm. (JS.)

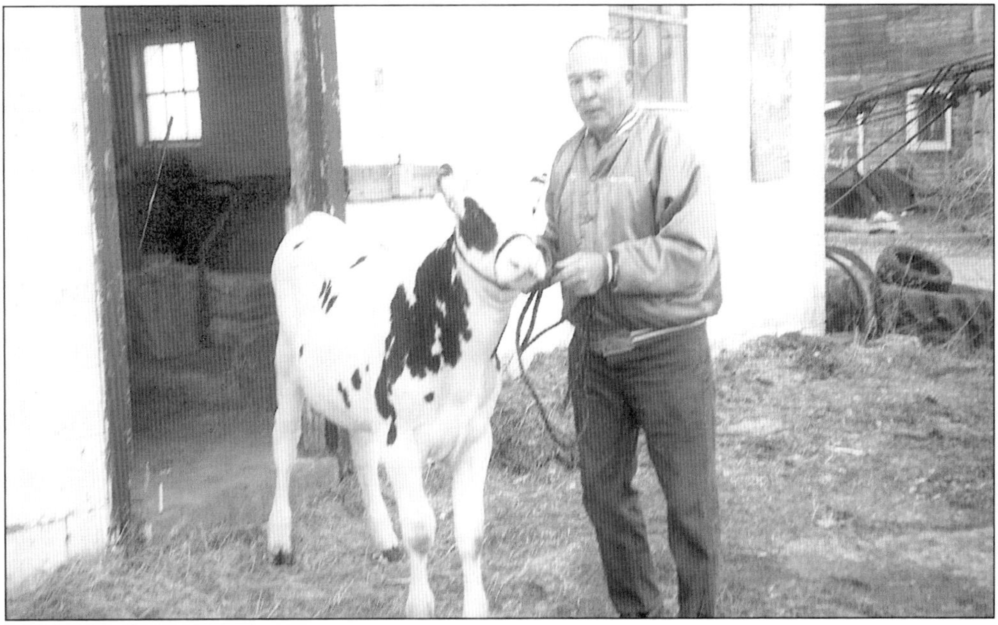

RAY VAIL AND JOYCE, 2000. Ray Vail still owns this farm, Kenray, which has been in his family since 1794. A 4-H leader for over 50 years, Vail was named an "outstanding young farmer" by the Junior Chamber of Commerce; he has raised many champion cows. However, he is no longer in the dairy farm business, having sold the farm on the other side of Route 55 and auctioned off most of his cows. Today, Union Vale has no dairy farms. (JS.)

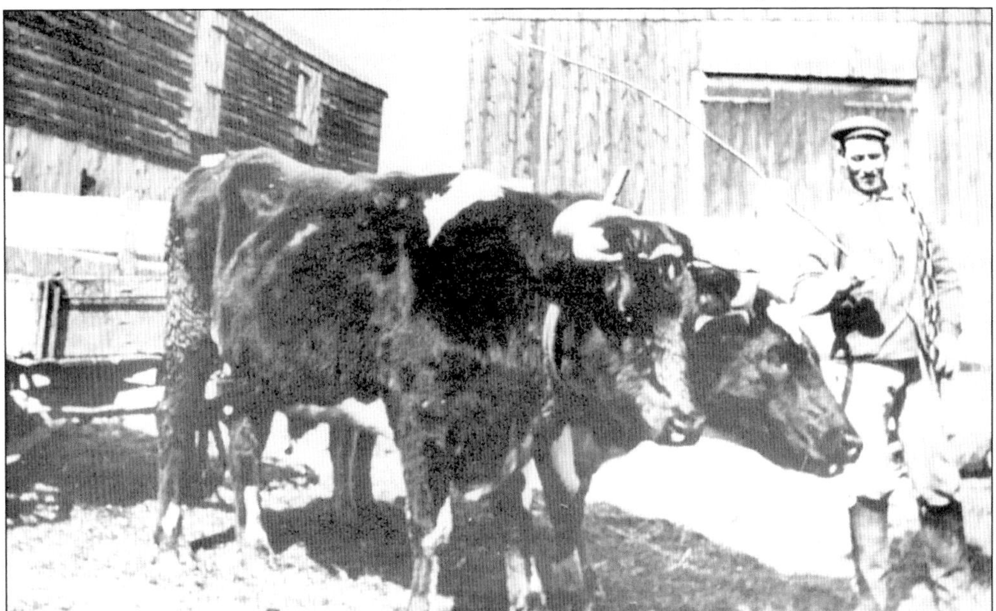

OXEN WITH FLOYD COE, C. 1900S. In the background are the barns of Gordon Andrews at a time when oxen were almost as common on farms as tractors are today. They were used to plow, harrow, and haul logs. Farmers in the Clove—such as the Coes, Andrews, and Uhles—took turns hauling their milk to the Sheffield Farm Creamery and Milk factory in Verbank, where it was bottled and sent to New York City. (UVHS.)

MRS. MARGARET ABEL, 1880S. Mrs. Abel, with her violin, appears in this lovely photograph by a Poughkeepsie photographer. She looks calmly forward through her spectacles as she sits in a very ornate chair. She belonged to another prominent family in Union Vale, the Abels, who today carry on a tree farm business. (UVHS.)

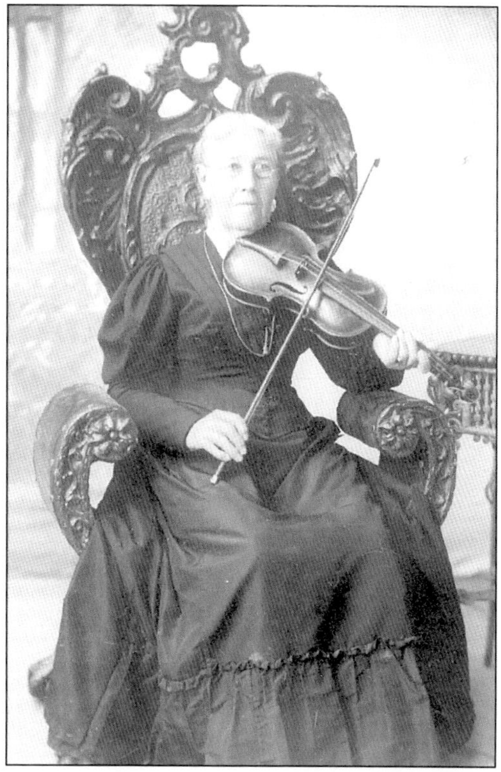

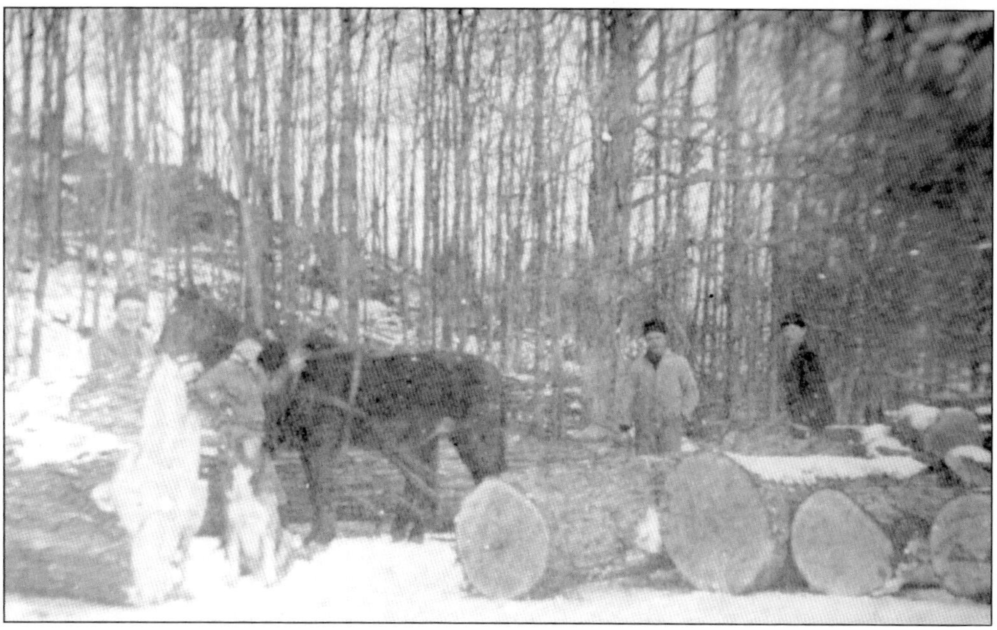

LOGGING IN THE CLOVE, LATE 1800S. While Union Vale is one of the most rural communities in the county, ore beds were discovered and mined during most of the 19th century. Much of the charcoal was produced in Verbank. Huge trees were felled during the winter and burned in charcoal pits from April to October. The discovery of pure ore in the Mesabi Range led to the closing of mines here, too. (UVHS.)

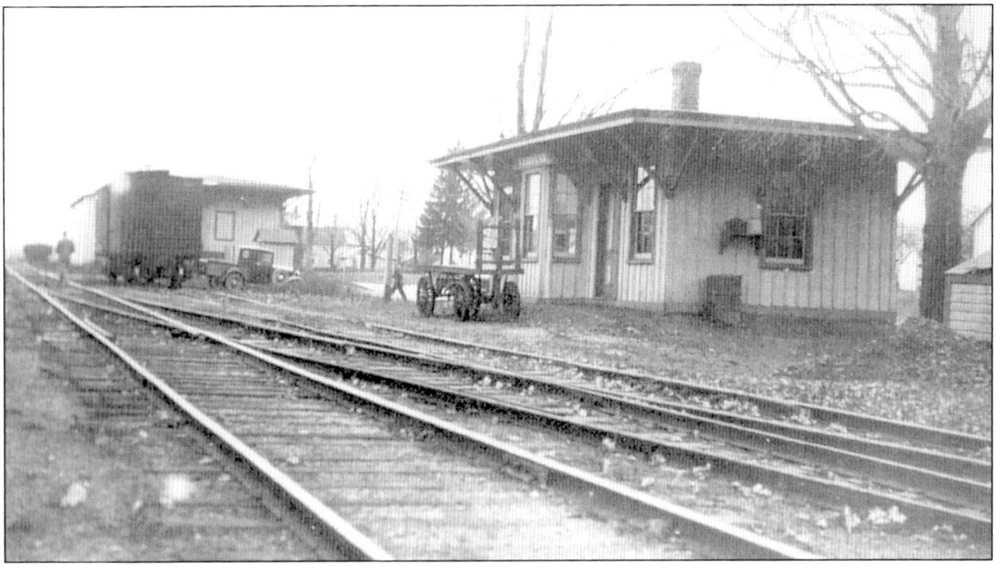

The Railroad Station at Verbank on the Green. While there was a combination freight and passenger station on the Newburgh, Dutchess & Connecticut Railroad just a mile southeast at Verbank Village, the coming of the railroad after the Civil War spurred the development of this hamlet. Before automobiles, trucks and paved roads railroad service was very local. In addition to the freight and railroad station there was a post office, feed store, and Methodist church. (HC.)

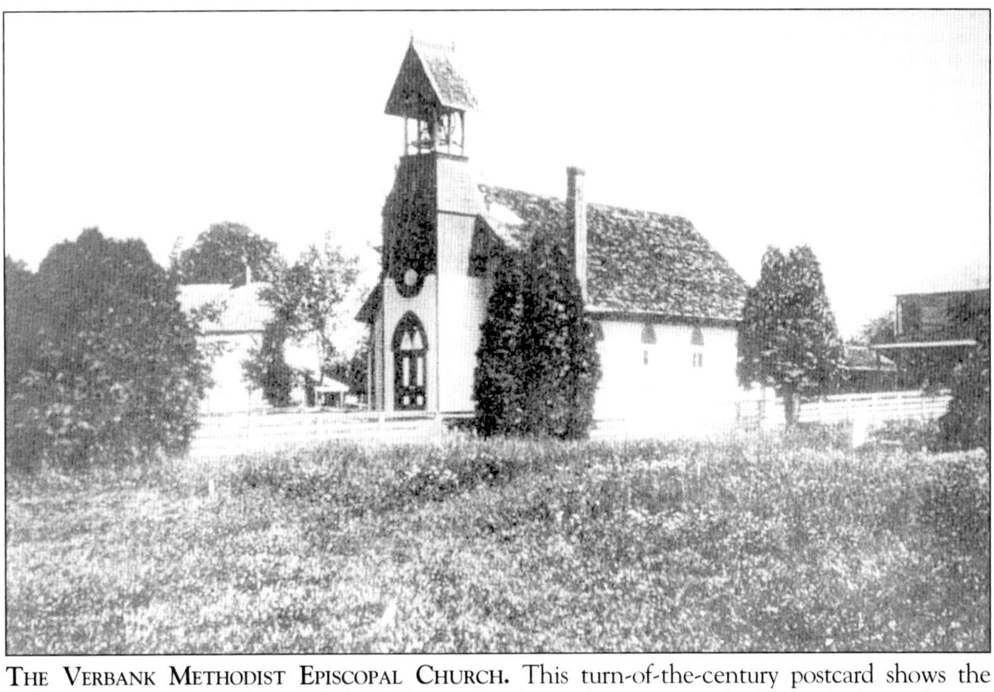

The Verbank Methodist Episcopal Church. This turn-of-the-century postcard shows the Methodist church, which was dedicated in 1878. An earlier structure had been built on the site of the Verbank School. Union Vale had no church structures until 1825, when a group called Christian Liberty Departure built in North Clove. Methodists also built there in 1834. (UVHS.)

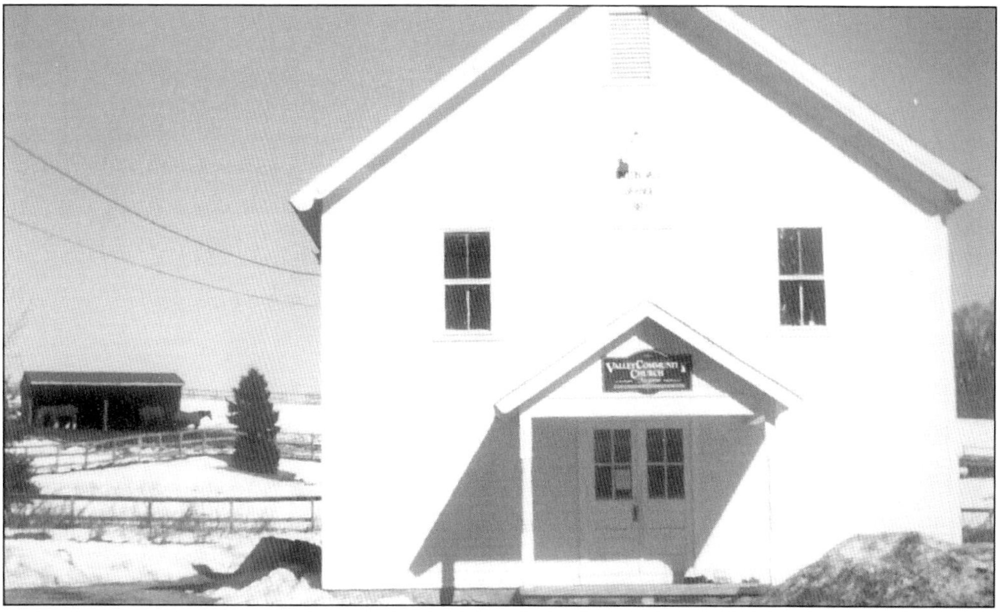

The Grange. Since its organization in the North Clove Schoolhouse in 1900, the Grange has been a center of activity, also sponsoring 4-H Clubs, Boys and Girls Scouts, and a Junior Grange for young people. It was at the Grange that discussions led to the establishment of a fire district. Jim Andrews, who has been an active Grange member for over 65 years, says, "For years the church and the grange were all we had." In 2000, the Grange celebrated its 100th birthday. (JG.)

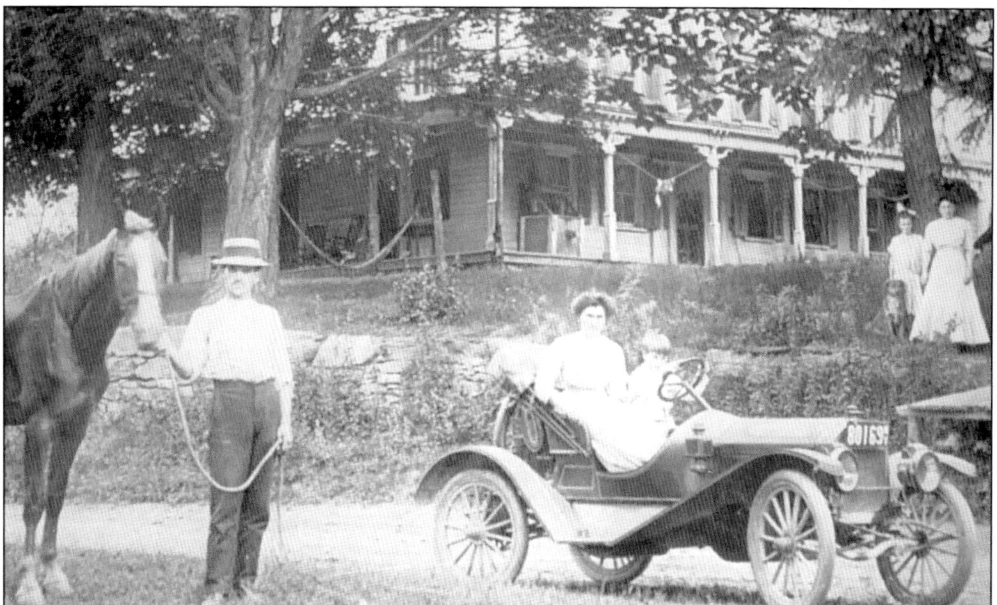

Sutton Place Farm, Formerly at the County Routes 9 and 21 Traffic Circle, c. 1900. Here the horse and car are beginning a coexistence that would last until after WWII. Since the advent of the car, little boys like this one have enjoyed pretending to drive while others, including the family dog, look on. Later, the farmhouse became a saloon and finally was torn down. (UVHS.)

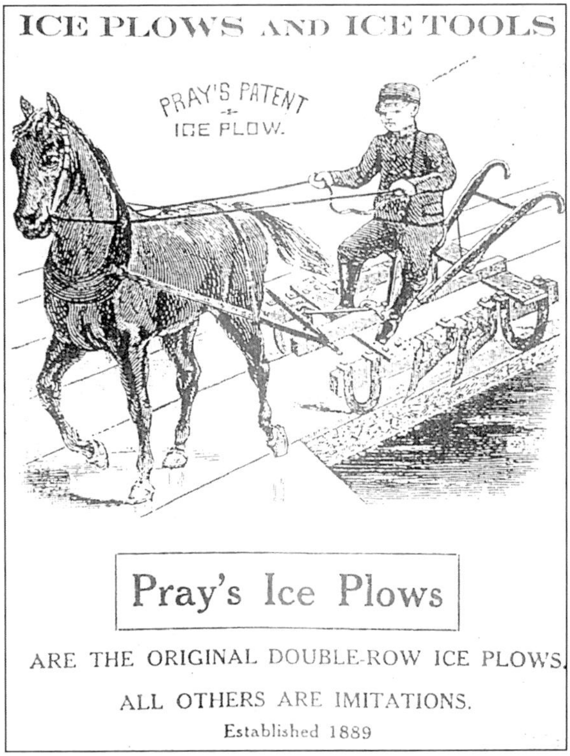

PRAY'S ICE PLOWS, C. 1890S. This is an advertisement for Hamilton Pray's ice plows, which were patented by the inventor in 1889. In the days of no electricity and no refrigerators, ice was a very precious commodity. Before ice plows, gathering ice to be stored for the summer had to be done by hand, a laborious and cold undertaking. Jim Andrews recalls that 1930, the year they got electricity, was the last year they filled the icehouse. (JA.)

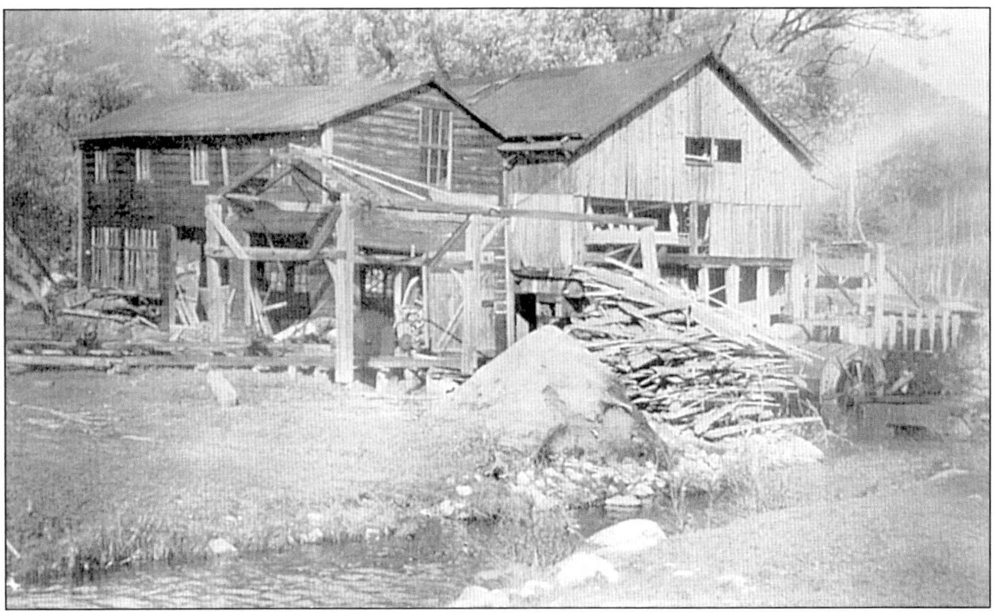

PRAY'S MILL, NORTH CLOVE, C. 1900. Before electricity, water supplied the power to run the machinery to make the ice plows as well as to repair tools. Hamilton Pray's son, William, had a workshop here for many years. While he owned the dam creating the millpond, the pond itself belonged to the Clove Valley Rod and Gun Club . When the club made an island in the pond, the source of power for the mill was decreased, allowing it to operate only a few hours in dry seasons. (JA.)

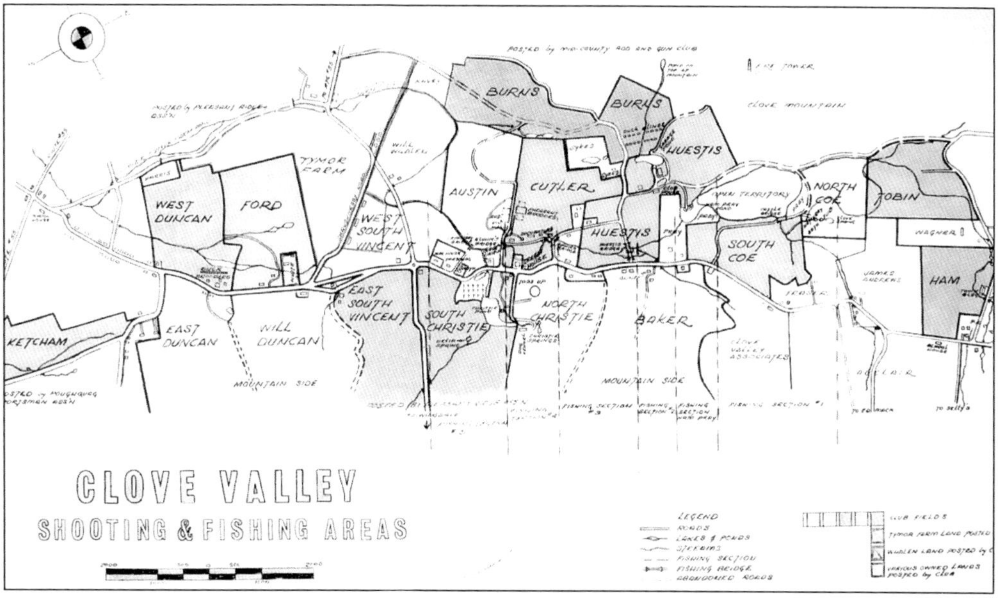

CLOVE VALLEY SHOOTING AND FISHING AREAS, C. 1945, ADAPTED 1971. There are several clubs devoted to these sports, including the Clove Valley Rod and Gun Club, founded in the early 1900s, the Verbank Hunting and Fishing Club, and the Mid County Rod and Gun Club, founded in 1948. The latter purchased 220 acres of land on Waterbury Hill Road. Volunteers built the present clubhouse and other buildings; they continue to maintain them. (UVHS.)

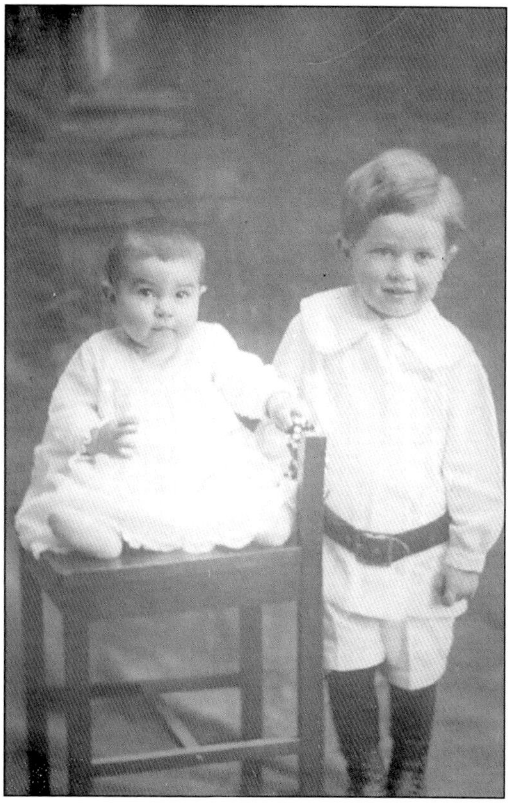

VINCENT AND HELEN COFFIN, C. WWI. The Coffin homestead was on Old Camby Road, once called Coffin Road. In 1906, Episcopal Bishop Greer acquired land near where he established Hope Farm, a home for disadvantaged children from New York City. Later, Hope Farm was renamed the Greer School; today, it has become the Fountains, a retirement community. (JC.)

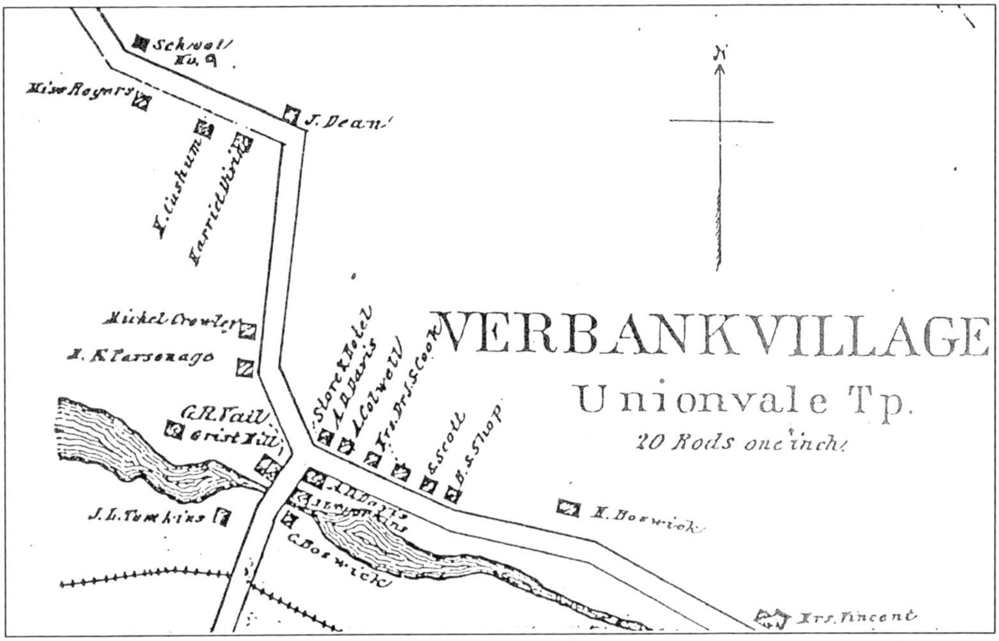

VERBANK VILLAGE, 1867. School No. 9 is shown in the northwest corner of Verbank Village on this Beers map of Union Vale. While the Methodist church does not appear, its parsonage is there. Water from the creek supplies the power to run the gristmill. A.H. Davis runs both a store and hotel, and his houses appear to be across the street. (DCHS.)

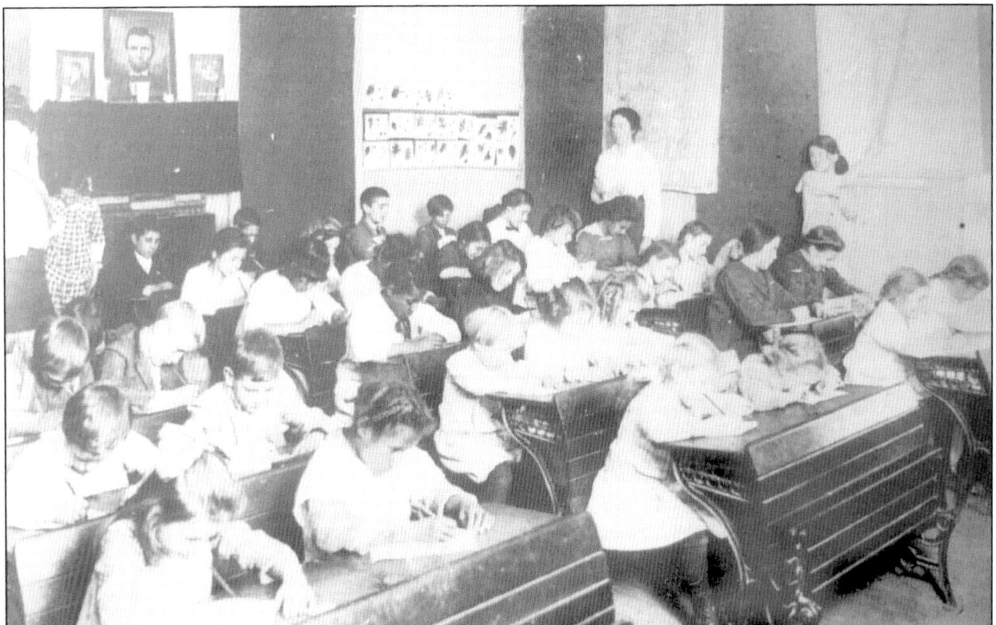

VERBANK SCHOOL NO. 9, C. 1914. The children all seem intent on doing their lessons. Mostly sitting two to a desk, they range in age from a tot of about five to young ladies. The older children helped to instruct the younger ones. This school remained in use until 1961. Children are now part of centralized school districts and are transported daily by bus. (UVHS.)

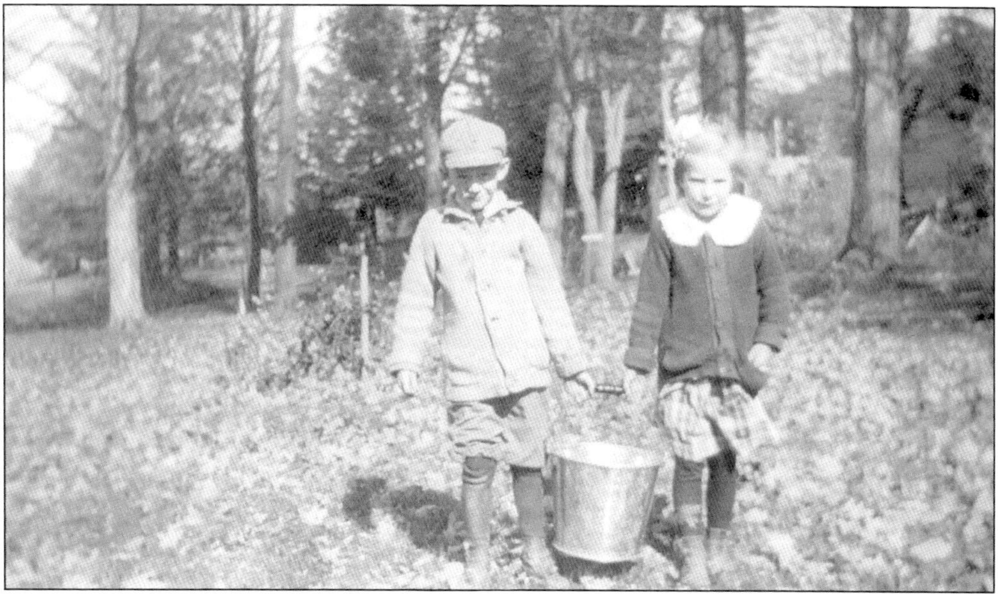

ANNIE AND WILLIE PIERSON, C. 1910. These children are shown bringing water to the North Clove Schoolhouse (No. 3), where there was no running water, no electricity, and no indoor plumbing. A stove heated the room in winter, but it must have become dark in the cold winter afternoons. Mary Lucy Ham, pictured on page 13, taught at the school, where she had once been a pupil. (RRH.)

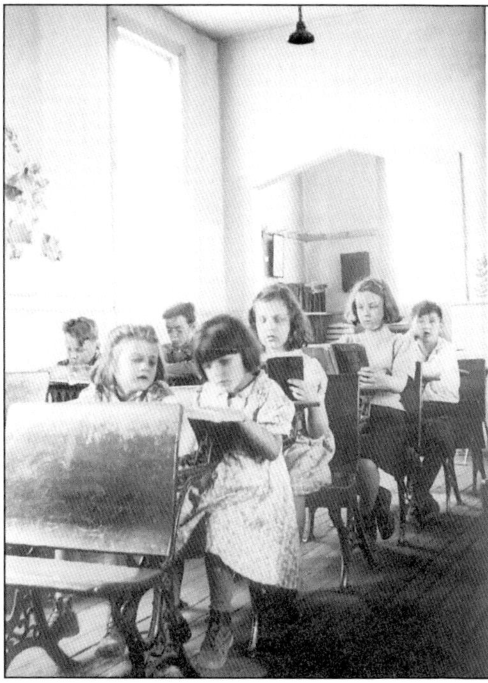

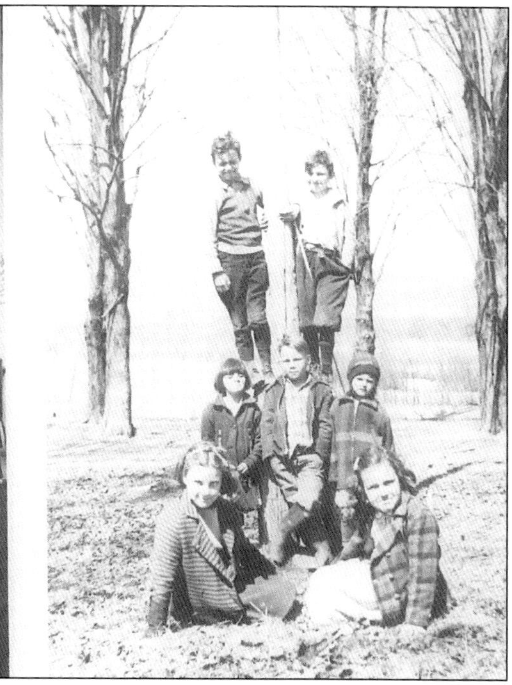

NORTH CLOVE SCHOOL NO. 3, 1941. The girl in the left front row looks intrigued by the book that her seat mate is reading. Behind her, Jean Hitsman is concentrating on reading while the boy in the back seems to be daydreaming. To the right, a group poses for a photograph. The boy to the left of the pole is Franklyn Hitsman. The schoolhouse still stands on County Route 9. (AF/MLdeF).

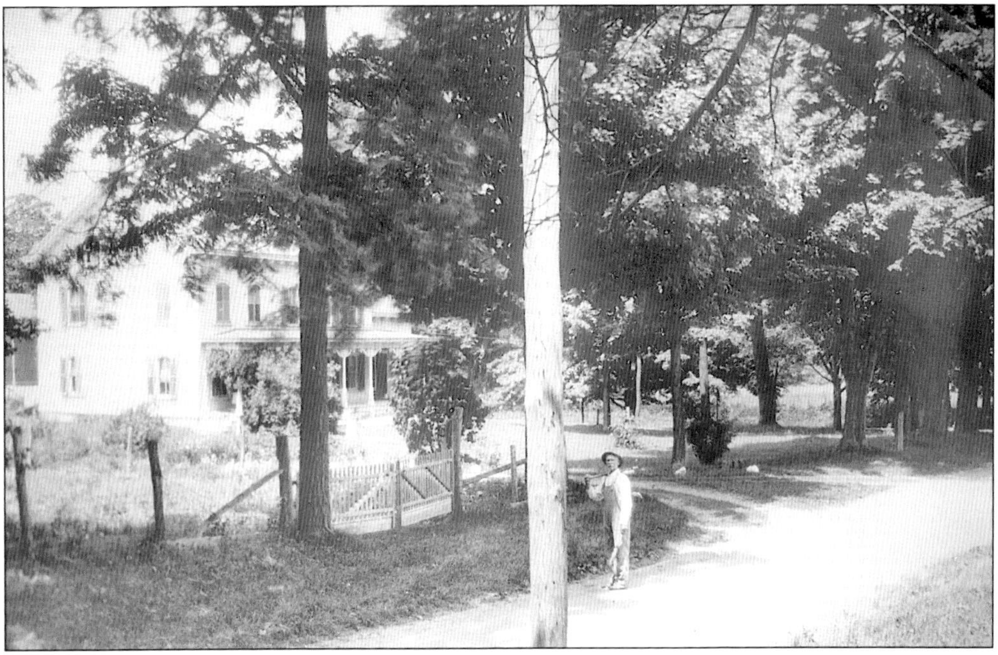

The Ham Homestead, c. 1925. This homestead in North Clove was built in the mid-19th century and belonged to John Ham, Mary Ham's father. Although he was educated to become a teacher and taught in the schoolhouse next-door to the present Union Vale Firehouse, he spent most of life as a farmer. His brothers, who were twins, had left the farm to go to the Dakotas, where they hitched teams of elks rather than oxen. (RRH.)

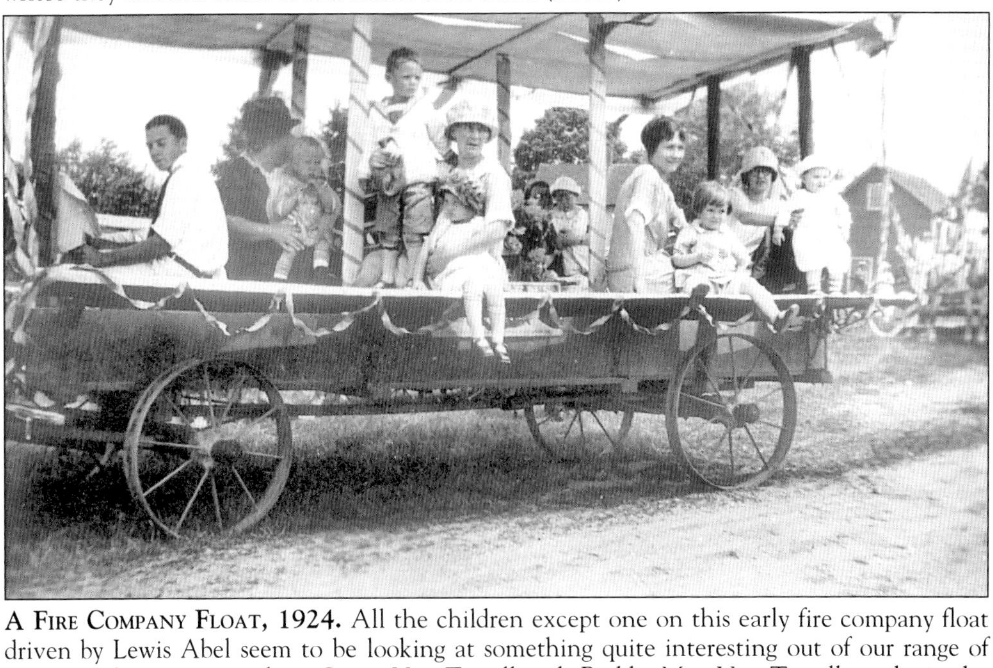

A Fire Company Float, 1924. All the children except one on this early fire company float driven by Lewis Abel seem to be looking at something quite interesting out of our range of sight. At the extreme right is Susan Van Tassell with Buddy. Mrs. Van Tassell taught in the Verbank two-room schoolhouse on the corner of Verbank Village Road and Route 82. She also taught in Millbrook and later at the Greer School. (MF/MB.)

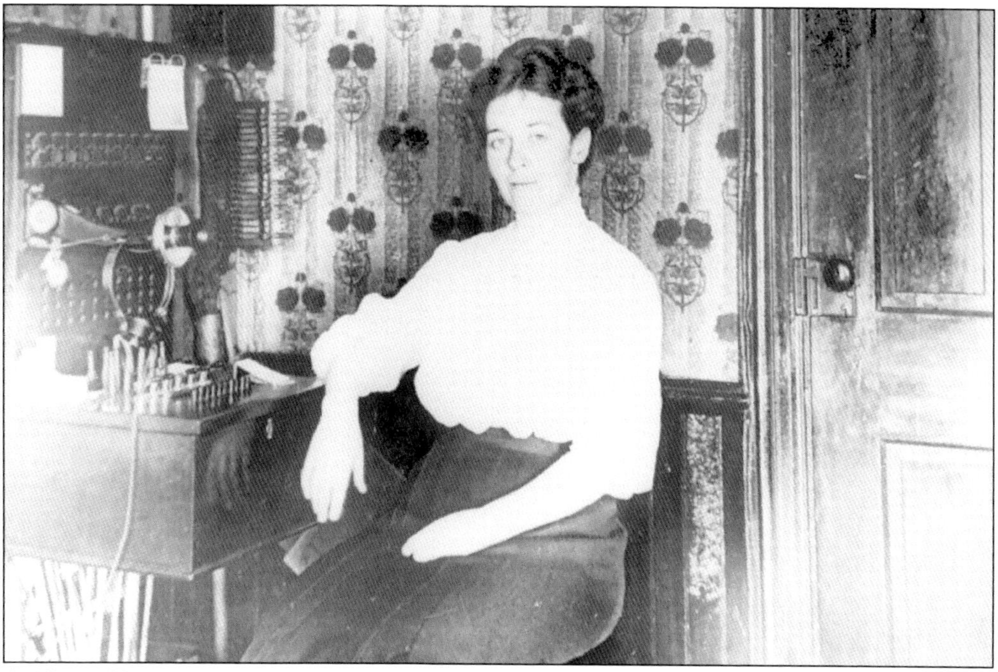

A Home Telephone Operator at the Switchboard. The North Central Clove office of the telephone company was located at Mrs. Huestis's boardinghouse, which was across from the Clove Valley Rod and Gun Club annex. Florence Coe White was the "hello girl" before Mrs. Huestis. At one time, the post office was also in the basement. Mrs. Huestis was certainly preferable to today's recorded voice saying, "Press one for . . . . Press two for . . . ." (UVHS.)

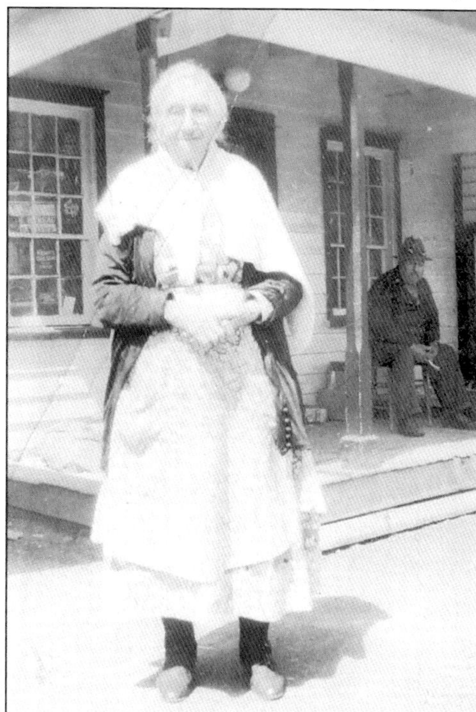

Helen Penny Lasher, 1934. People received personal service not only from the telephone operator, but also at Mrs. Lasher's store in Clove Valley. An example of the small general store, it stocked everything from food staples to sewing materials. Even after WWII, farm families were quite self-sufficient, canning and later freezing their own produce. They would only go into town perhaps once a month to buy 100-pound sacks of oatmeal and sugar. (UVHS.)

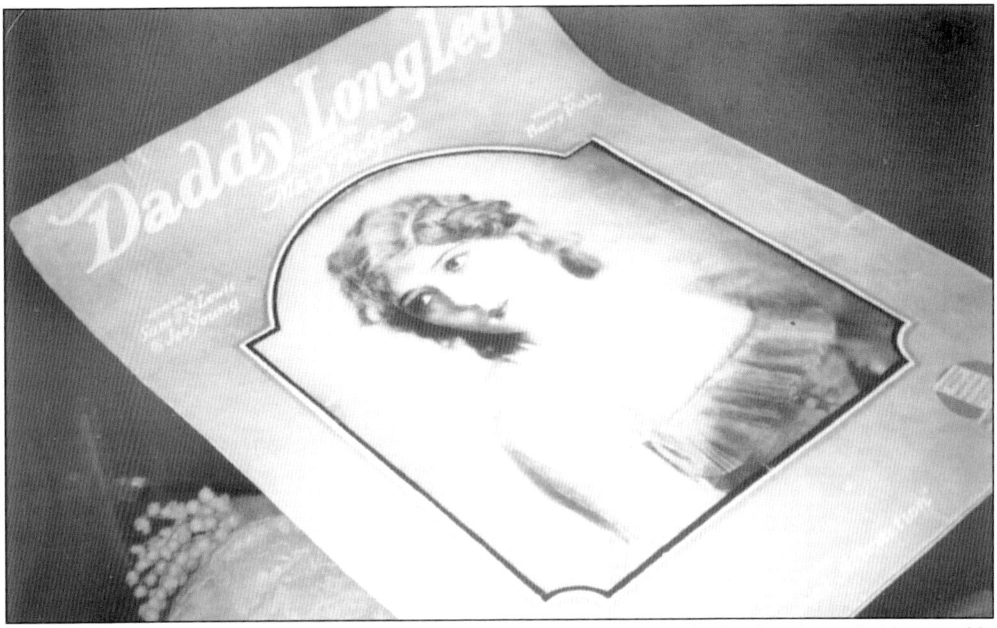

DADDY LONGLEGS. Jean Webster, Mark Twain's niece, created the book and film *Daddy Longlegs*, as well as *Dear Enemy*, and the "Patty" books. A 1901 graduate of Vassar College, she and her husband, Glen Ford McKinney, lived opposite Tymor Park in a Georgian house built in the early 19th century by Andrew Skidmore. Skidmore, it is said, used the profits he gained from the early iron industry. *Daddy Longlegs* was turned into a movie starring Mary Pickford. (UVHS.)

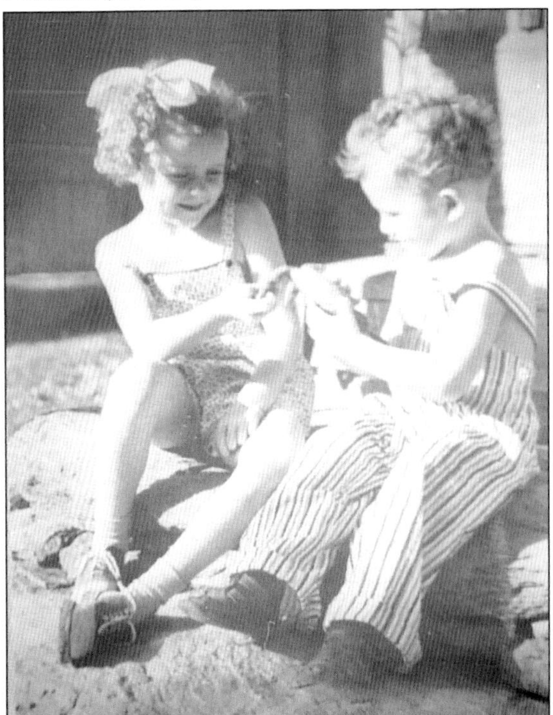

JIM AND GAIL COFFIN, C. 1940. The son and daughter of Vincent Coffin, these children are not playing with a daddy longlegs, but rather with what appears to be a lizard. They lived near Hope Farm and also enjoyed playing with live animals. Jim, who has moved to the hamlet of Verbank on the Green, says he still does—that is when he's not working on his shovelback band. (JC.)

THE FIRE TOWER. The fire tower, built in 1928, is 73 feet high and is located about 5 miles southeast of Verbank. The tower existed for just one purpose, which according to Oscar Ferris—who was a forest observer for the Conservation Department for over 20 years—was simply "spotting fires." While it has not been in use since the 1970s, the fire tower is a reminder of the time when it played an important role in safeguarding the community. The view of the countryside from the tower was spectacular. (LH.)

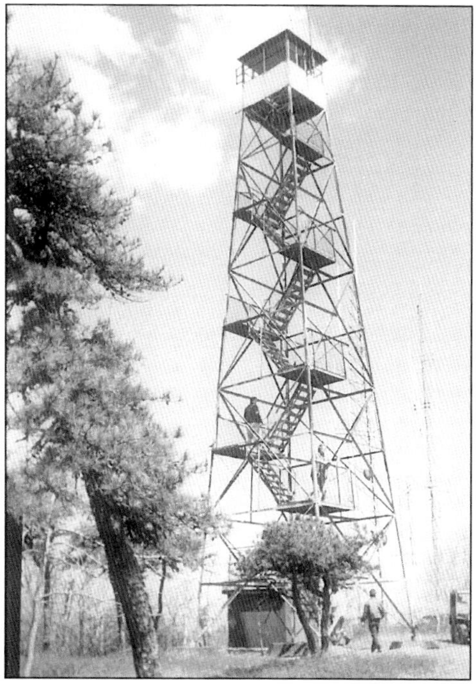

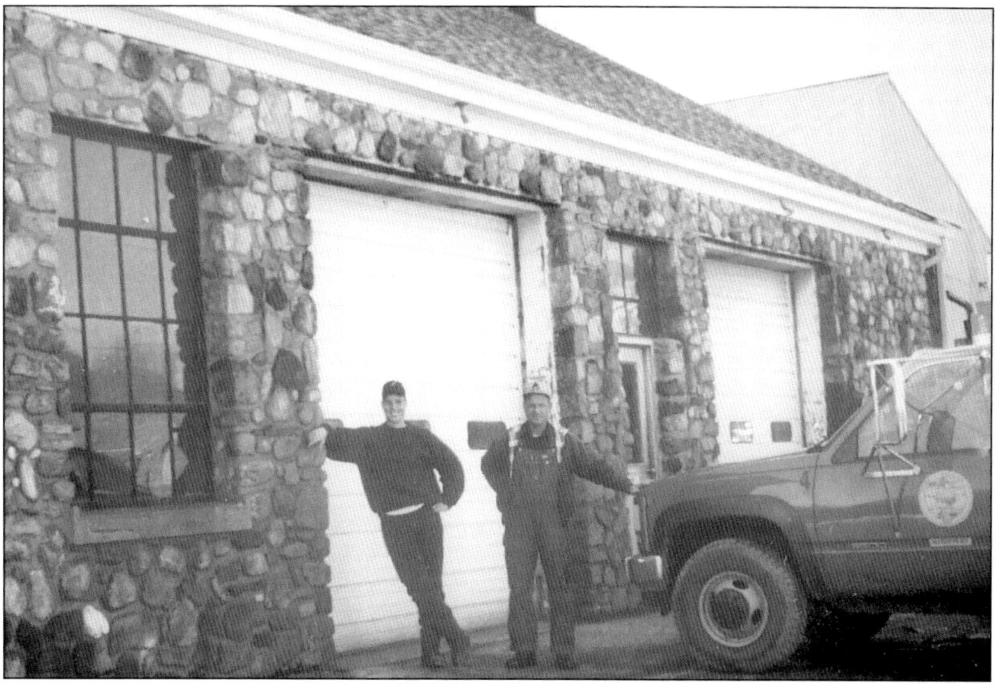

THE TOWN GARAGE, NORTH CLOVE ROAD. Town employees Mike Matteo and Russell Sokol stand in front of the garage, which was constructed by the WPA in 1941. FDR's affection for native stone is reflected in this building, as in many others in Dutchess County. The town board met in a small room there, while public meetings and elections were held in the nearby Grange building. In the 1960s, buildings were acquired on Route 55 for town offices. In 1995, a new town hall was dedicated in Tymor Park. (JG.)

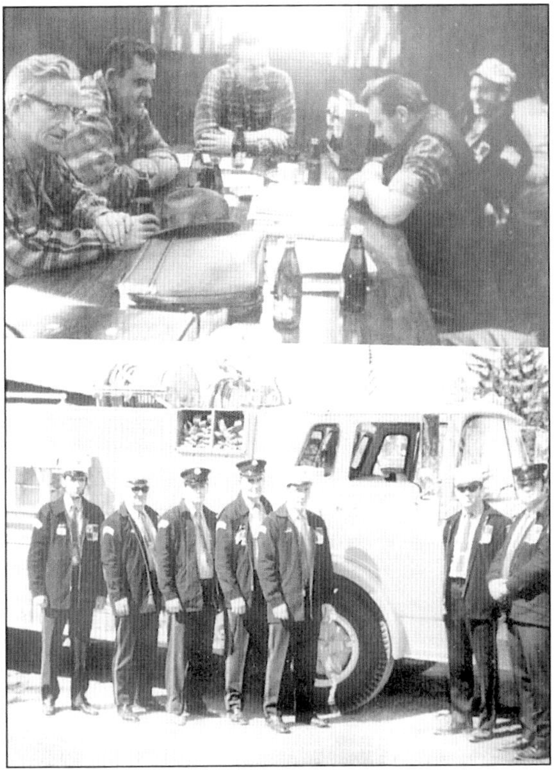

THE UNION VALE FIRE DEPARTMENT, C. 1972. Due to the efforts of many, a fire district was created in 1952. Twenty years later, some of its members are seen as they await the delayed arrival of their new fire engine, "Yellow Bird." After being misdirected en route several times, it finally arrived and became the pride of the department. It was the first yellow fire engine in the county. (UVFD.)

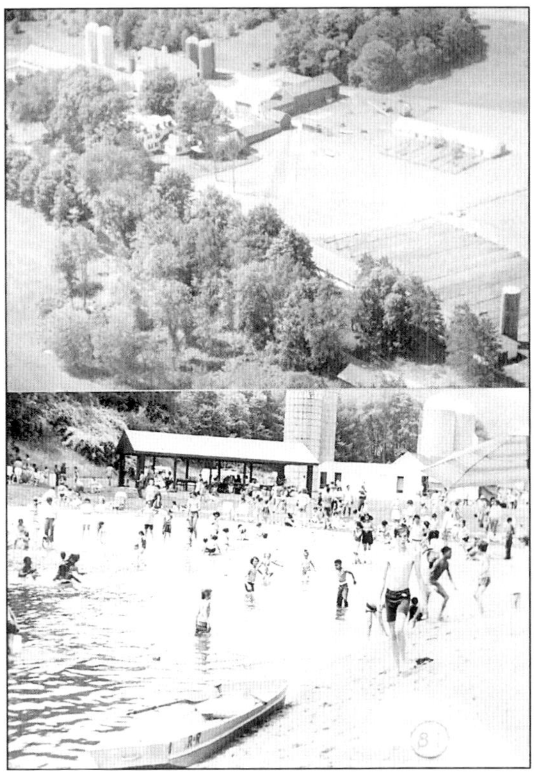

THE DEDICATION OF TYMOR PARK, 1975. In 1971, Ralph and Jean McKinney Connor (Jean Webster's daughter) donated 500 acres to the town for use as a park. In 1993, a pool replaced the pond where the water, which was fed by springs in the Fishkill Creek, had been *very* cold. Tymor Park is in daily use as the town's governmental, cultural, and recreational center. Family dinners, Community Day, Oktoberfest, and the Festival of Lights are also held held in the park. (UVHS.)

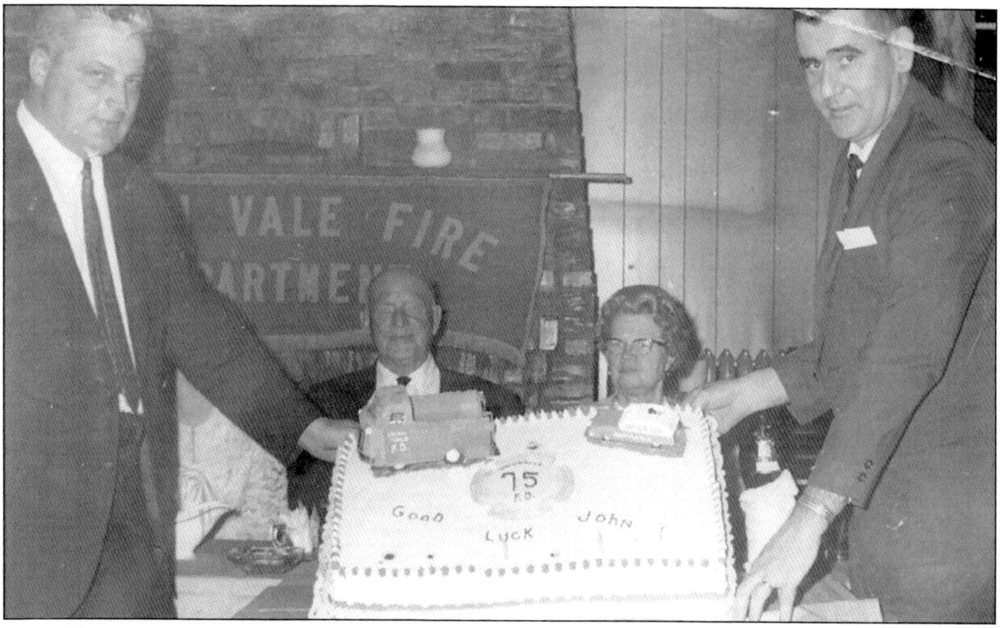

John Tietjen's 75th Birthday, 1969. Pictured at the Verbank Village Inn are Robert Fettes, Mr. Tietjen, and Jack Farmer. Bob Fettes—who served as president of the fire department, ambulance corps, and rescue squad—devoted his life to his community and even designed and managed the building of the first addition to the firehouse, which was later named in his honor. Jack Farmer, longtime member of the department, has served as chairman of the board of fire commissioners. (UVFD.)

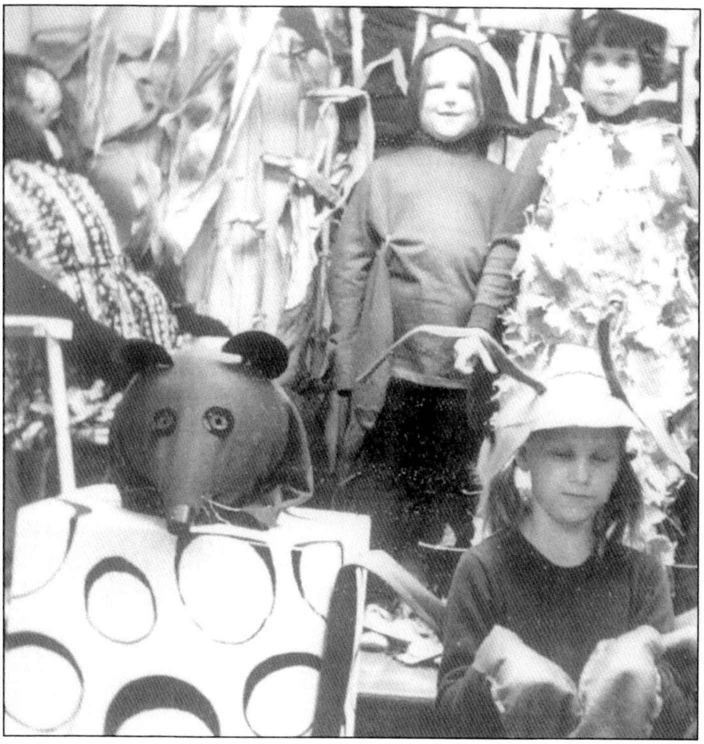

A Halloween Party, 1971. The fire department, which has firehouses on Route 82 in Verbank and in the Clove, is also a center of social activity. The ladies auxiliary holds this annual Halloween party as well as a ham supper in the spring. The ambulance corps sponsors a ham dinner in the fall. Carnivals also take place every year. Most importantly, the fire department and ambulance corps are always there when needed. (UVFD.)

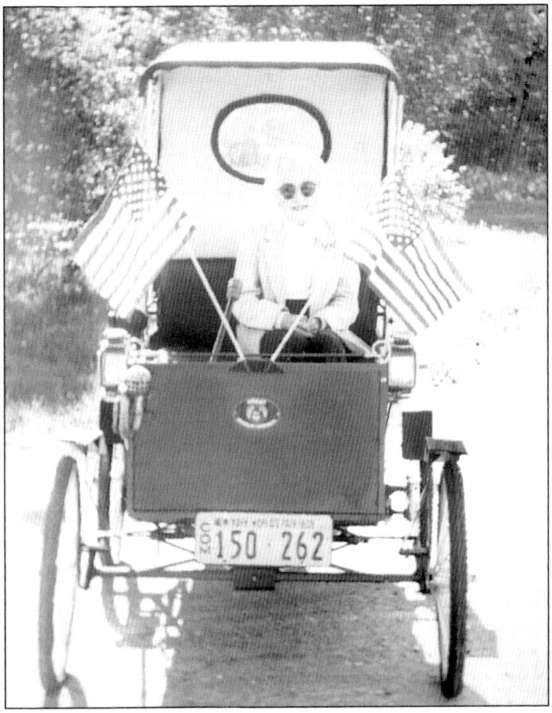

Lydia Brown, 1990s. A Grange member for 75 years and still going strong at the age of 96, Lydia Brown is shown riding in a car created by Jim Coffin. The daughter of Edward J. Quinlan, a carpenter and rural mail carrier, Lydia became the wife and assistant of Melville J. Brown. He was the postmaster of Verbank for 35 years as well as a store owner. Their son, Melville, is on the postcard sold by the historical society. The postcard shows him with the fire alarm made from a railroad engine wheel ring. (JC.)

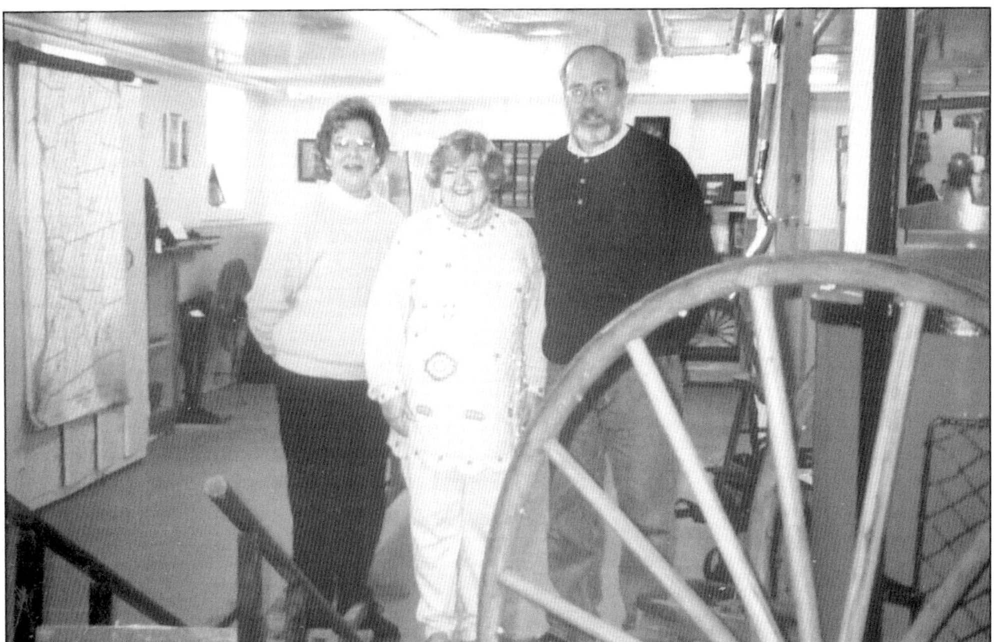

The Union Vale Historical Museum, 2000. Judith Coombs is the former town supervisor; Joann Miracco is the town historian and president of the historical society; and Rev. Jim Wickstead is the volunteer museum curator and pastor of the Valley Bible Fellowship Church. This church is located in what was known as the Clove Christian Church where Abigail Hoag Roberts, ancestor of Amy Hoag Lynch, played a leading role. The museum, which was started by Irena Stolarik, former town historian, has information and artifacts pertaining to town life. (JG.)

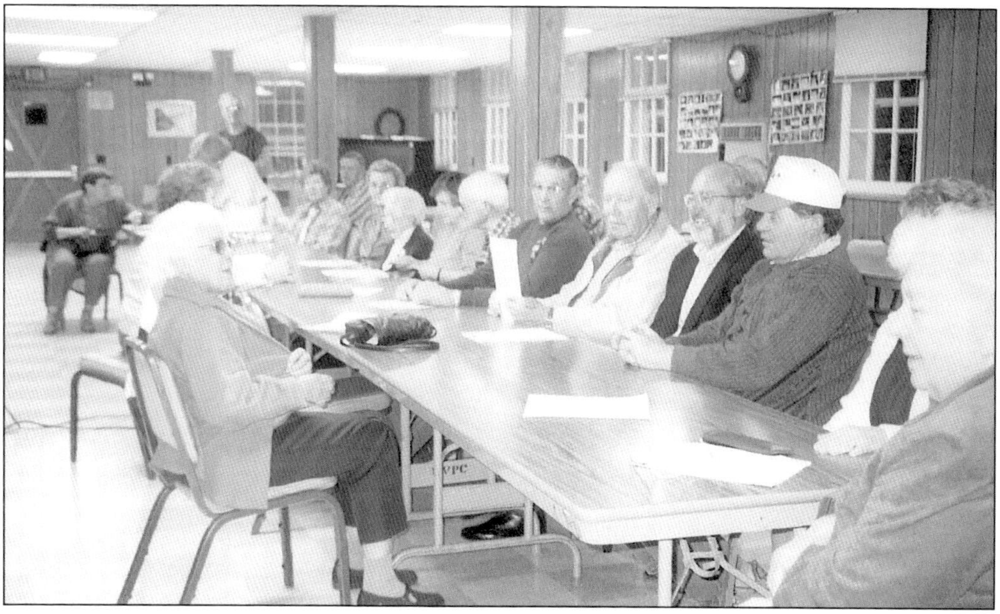

UNION VALE HISTORICAL SOCIETY, 2000. A recent meeting of the society chartered in 1969 was held at Tymor Park. The society brings together natives and newcomers who care about the history of their town. As development pressure continues to increase, it becomes even more important to preserve a sense of place and to instill a sense of a community. (JG.)

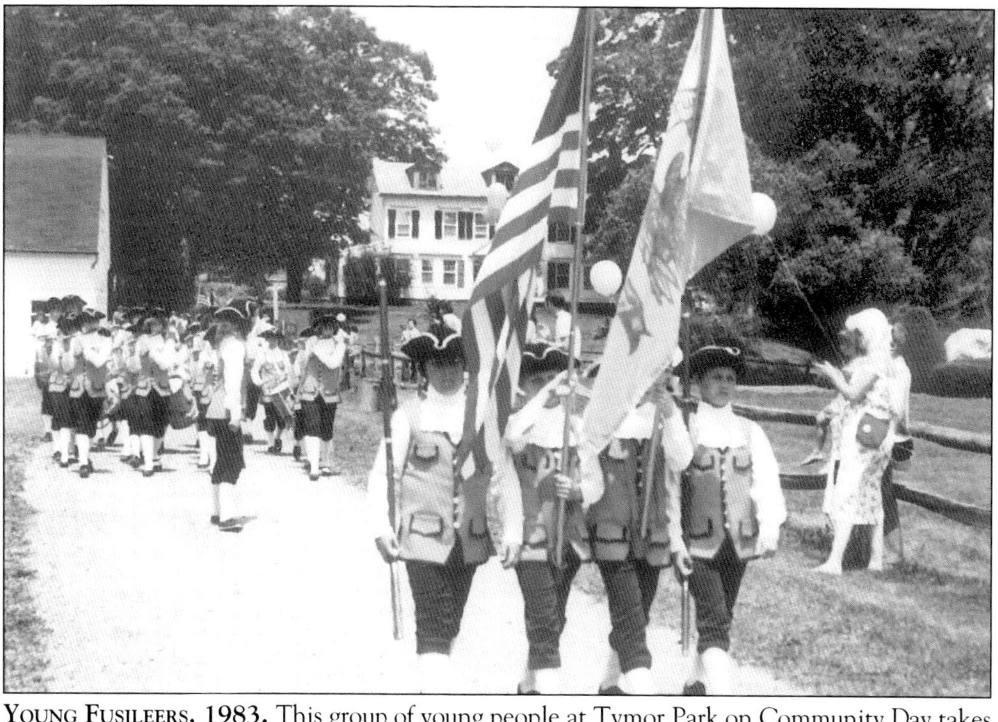

YOUNG FUSILEERS, 1983. This group of young people at Tymor Park on Community Day takes part in various parades and festivals throughout the county. Lots of practice is required to produce the precision with which they play and march. They are a reminder of the importance of involving young people in preserving their heritage. (UVHS.)

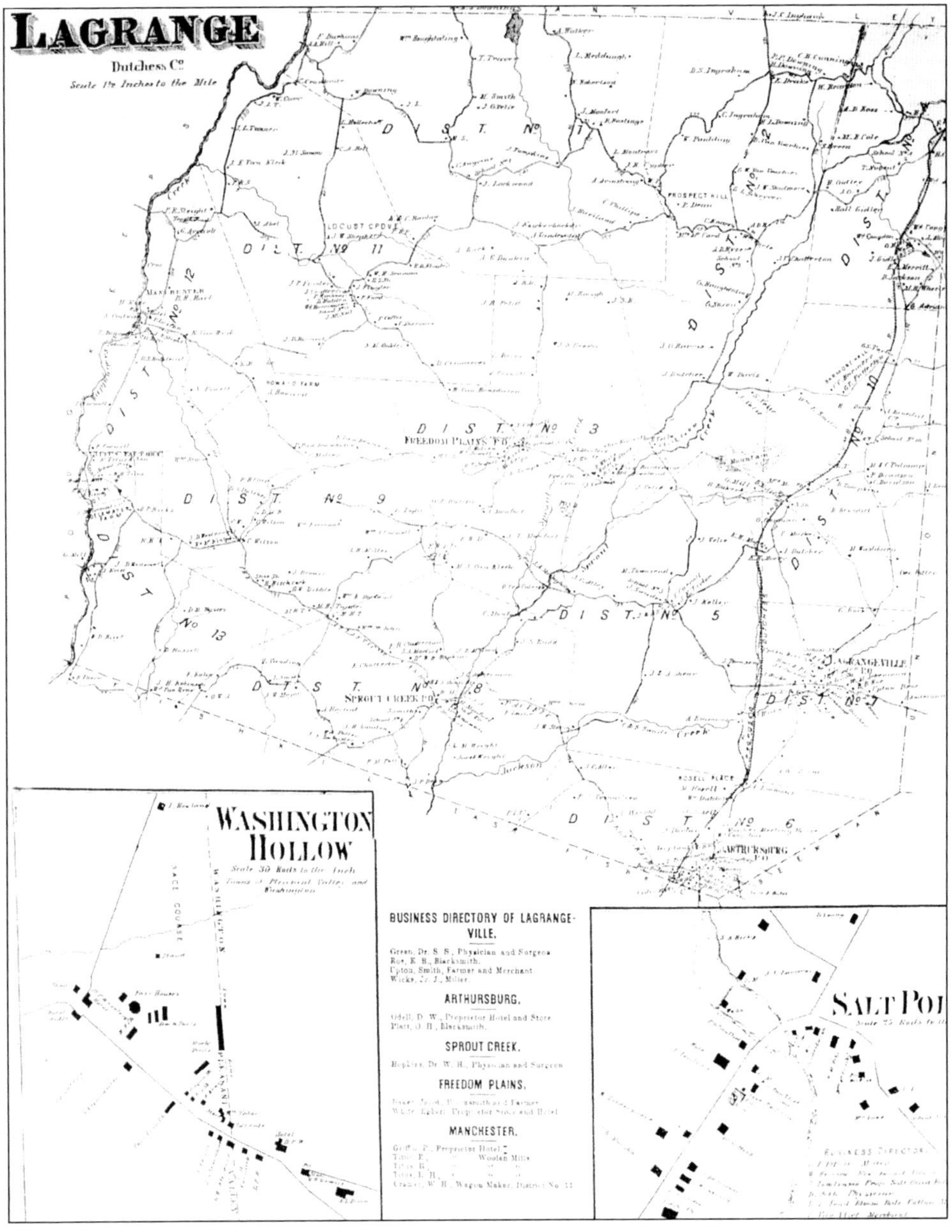

A Map of LaGrange, 1867. Then as now, the western boundary of the town is the Wappingers Creek. Two small hamlets existed along this creek in the 18th and 19th centuries—Manchester and "Titus Village," both of which had mills dependent on waterpower. In the very center of the town was and is Freedom Plains, which retains the original name of LaGrange. South and slightly east was the Sprout Creek Post Office, which was near the old Montfort Tavern, at which travelers used to stop as they wended their way toward Connecticut. To the east from north to south were Moores Mills, LaGrangeville, and Arthursburg, which were along the proposed railroad, first named the Dutchess & Columbia Railroad and later the Newburgh, Dutchess, & Connecticut Railroad. The rest of the town was covered by farms and orchards. The districts refer to school districts, each having its own one- or two-room schoolhouse. (DCHS.)

Four

LaGrange

The area that became the town of LaGrange was in the Rombout and Beekman Patents. From 1770 to 1780, it was called Oswego; in 1778, it became part of Fishkill and Beekman. In 1821, the town of Freedom was formed, and in 1827 part of it became part of Union Vale. The board of supervisors changed the name to LaGrange in 1829.

Early settlers in the western part of the town tended to be Dutch while those to the east came from the Palatine and New England. Hamlets grew up around mills and near railroad stations. Farms covered most of the land, which for at least the first half of the 19th century were self-sustaining. Later, grain and hay were grown for sale, and there were some sheep raised for wool until the 1840s. Then, sheep pastures became dairy farms, almost all having a "home orchard." The first commercial orchard was planted *c.* 1840. Today, many of the orchards have been replaced by housing developments.

Throughout the years, the relative importance of the hamlets has changed because water was no longer needed as a source of power, and the impact brought by the railroads surged and then faded. In the late 1960s, the decision was made to create a town center at Freedom Plains. It has become a linear hamlet accessible by the automobile.

LaGrange continues to grow. It has been a long time since children used to sit on their bikes beside the Taconic Parkway and count the cars going by. The parkway has brought many visitors to LaGrange, some of whom have become residents. Today, it is used by commuters as they drive to work—sometimes near, but sometimes far away.

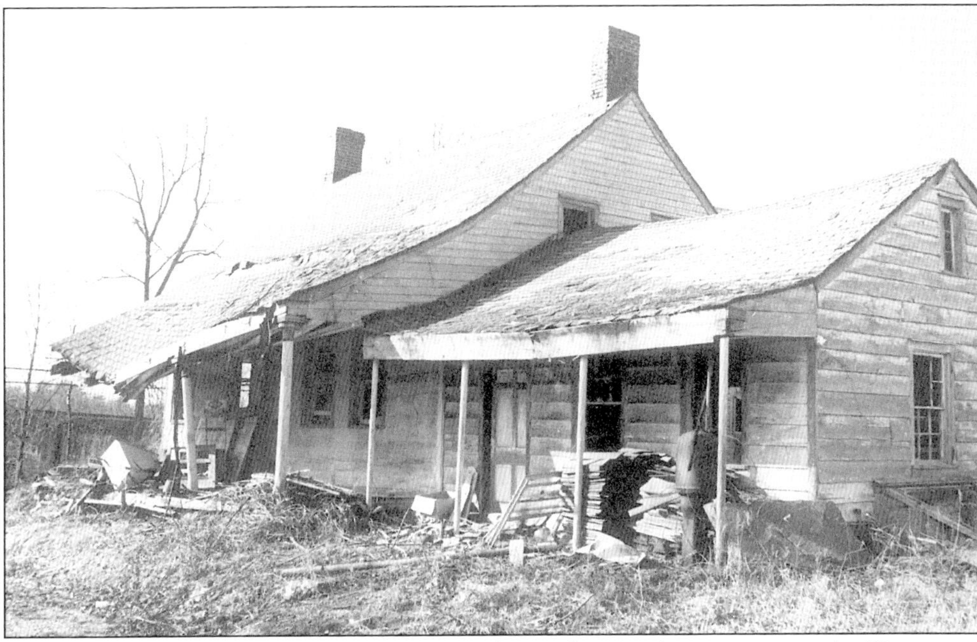

DeGroff Tavern, 1970s. Among the early settlers in the Manchester area near the Wappingers Creek were the DeGroffs. Replacing their original stone house was this wooden structure that served as a tavern and store for many years. When it faced the bulldozer in the 1970s, some town residents including Joe Genovese, the Lions, a Dutchess Community College teacher and students, and town historian Emily Johnson succeeded in saving some of the elements of the building, including a fireplace feature called an overmantle. (EJTH.)

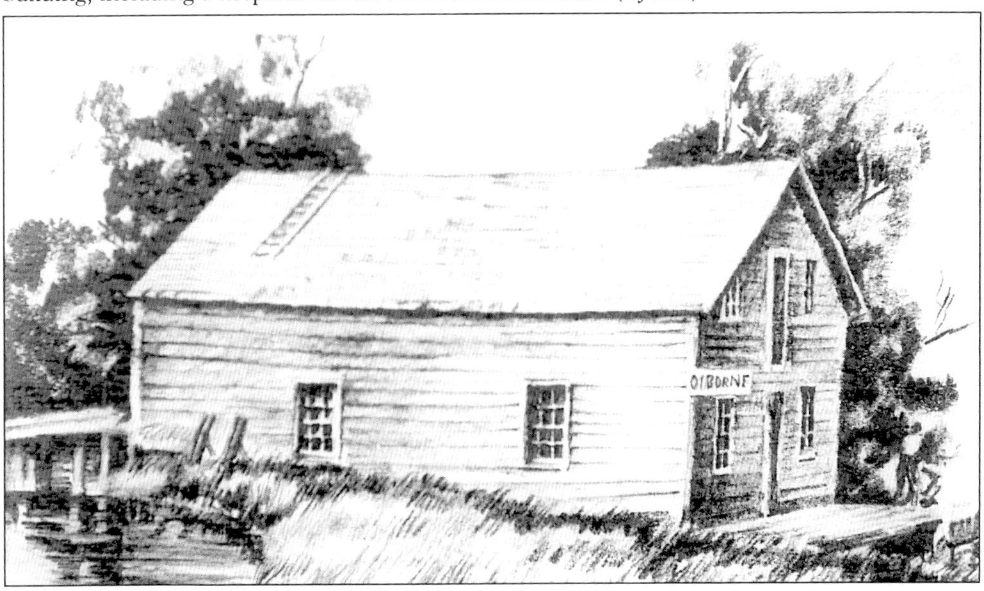

The Old Mill at Manchester. As early as 1766, this gristmill and flour mill was run by the De Groff family. Its power was provided by a ten o'clock wheel. When the railroad was built through the millpond in the early 1900s, thereby decreasing the volume of water available, there was not enough power to run the wheel. The last owners, the Coffees, tried a turbine wheel and later a gasoline engine, but the mill was discontinued and torn down. (LHS.)

Elias Titus, c. 1860s. About 1828, Titus left the town of Washington to locate a woolen business on the east side on the Wappingers Creek in LaGrange. He operated textile mills here and in Rochdale with his sons, using wool from his family's sheep ranch in Ohio. Business boomed, especially during the Civil War, when the factory produced blankets for the Union Army. (MDT/BL.)

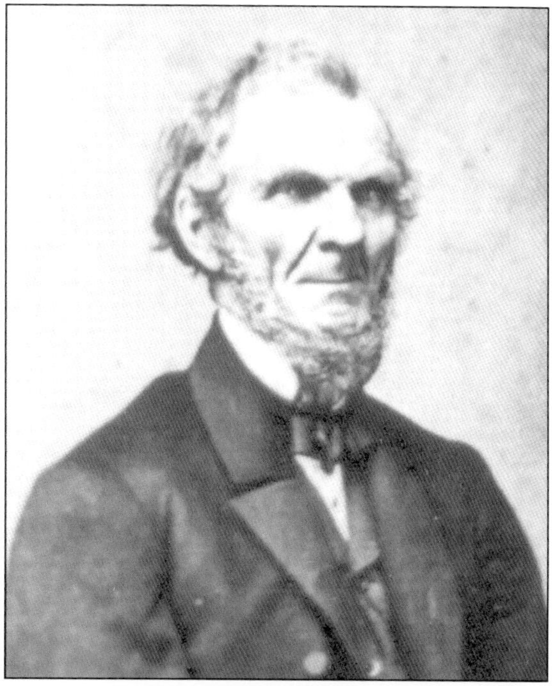

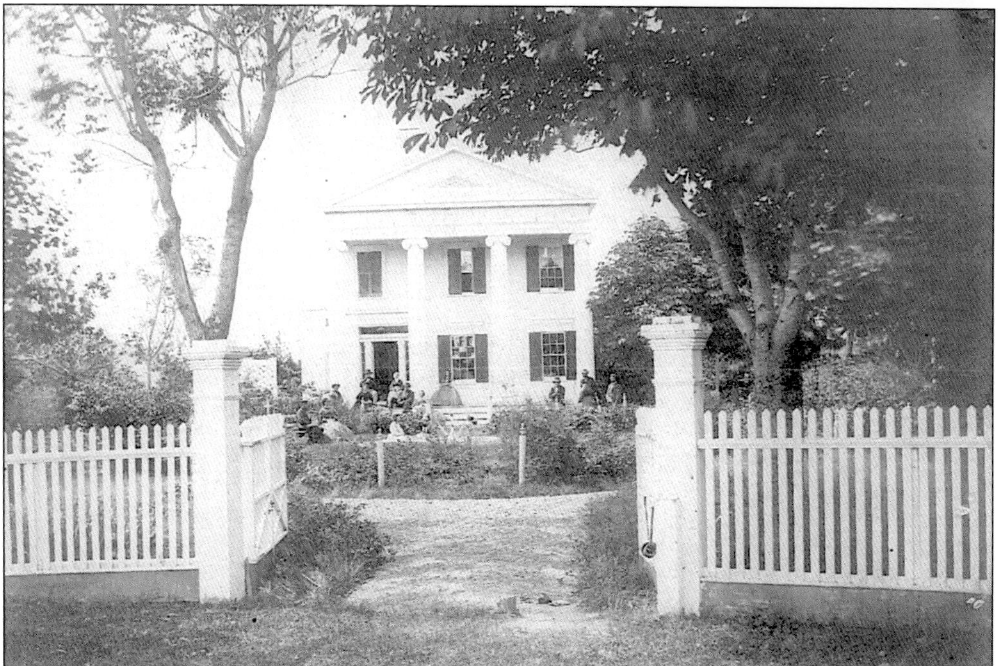

Titus Family Home, c. 1870s. Elias and his wife, Mary Annette Hoag Titus, built this stately home in the 1830s on what became known as Titusville Road. A small hamlet, "Titusville" grew up around the mill with a school, the Titus homes and company houses for the workers. The 1880 census of the "village of Titusville" indicates that about 80 people lived there. Sons Robert, Richard, and Henry carried on the business until the 1890s, when the mill was struck by lightning and burned. (MDT/BL.)

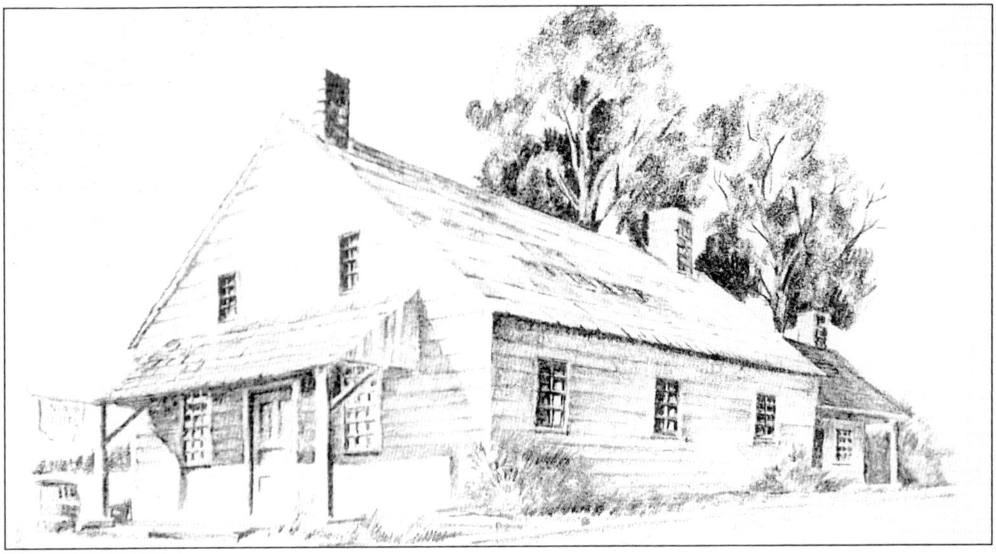

MONTFORT TAVERN'S IN SPROUT CREEK. According to the 1867 map of LaGrange, there were a number of Montforts located near the corner of Robinson and Noxon Roads. In the 18th century, the inn had been a stop on the way to Connecticut. Emile Walters, explorer and painter, made it his home and studio during the 20th century. (LHS.)

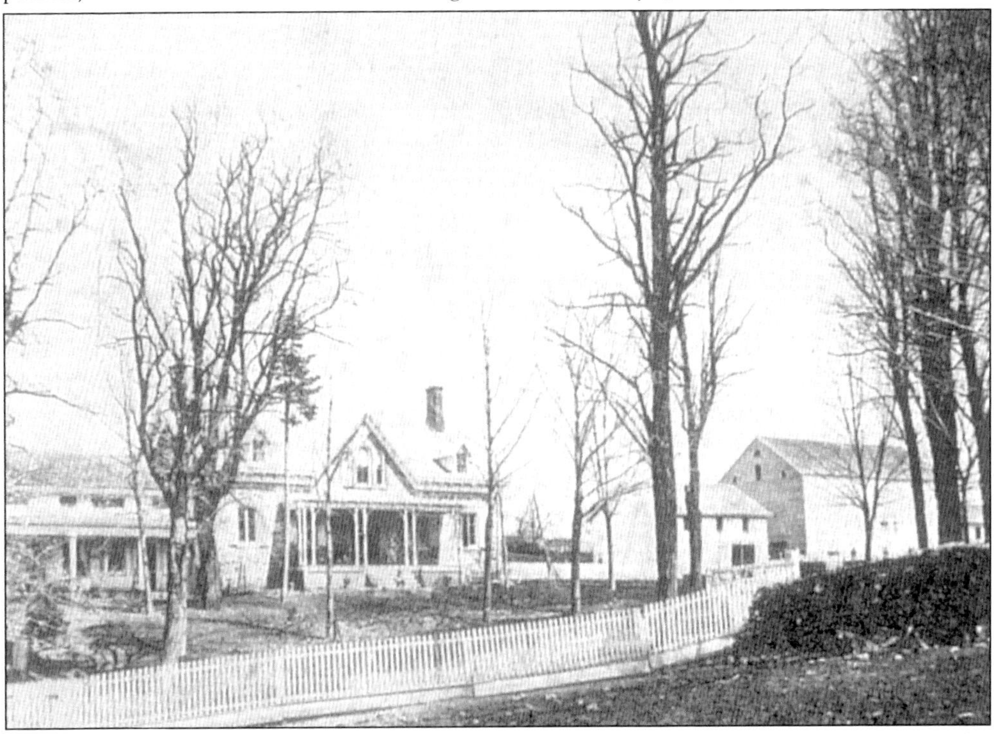

THE SLEIGHT FARM. The Sleight farm dates from the 18th century; a boundary marker on the property bears the date 1730. Other farms of this period were Prospect Hill off Barmore Road owned by Gilbert Livingston, the Buck farm on Freedom Road, and the Cornell Farm on Titusville Road. The Ayrault farm at the corner of County Route 43 and De Garmo Road had the distinction in 1870 of producing the largest beef cattle ever raised on an American farm. (CNS.)

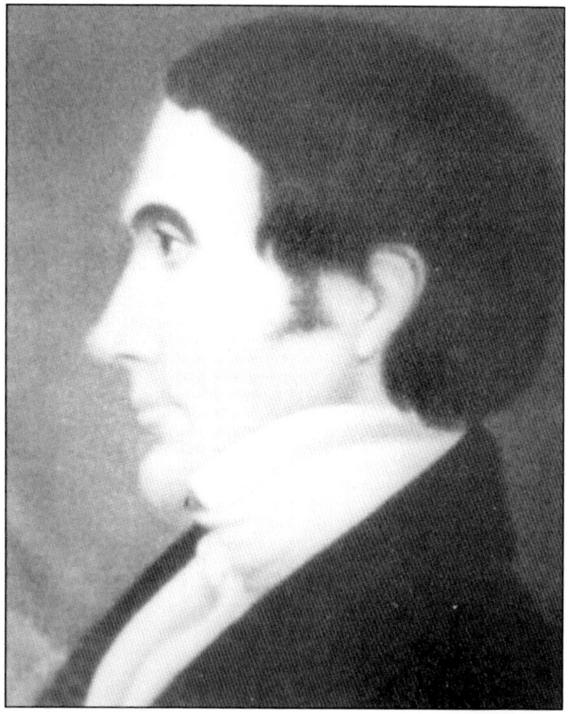

JOHN WILKINSON III, SUPERVISOR OF THREE TOWNS, EARLY 19TH CENTURY. Born in Oswego, Wilkinson was elected the first supervisor of Freedom in 1821. The year before, he had been supervisor of Beekman. In 1828, he became supervisor of Union Vale. As a young man, he received a commission in the Artillery Corps signed by Gen. George Clinton. This portrait by an unknown painter was featured in *Nineteenth Century Art in Dutchess County*, a publication of the the Dutchess County Bicentennial Committee. (EJTH.)

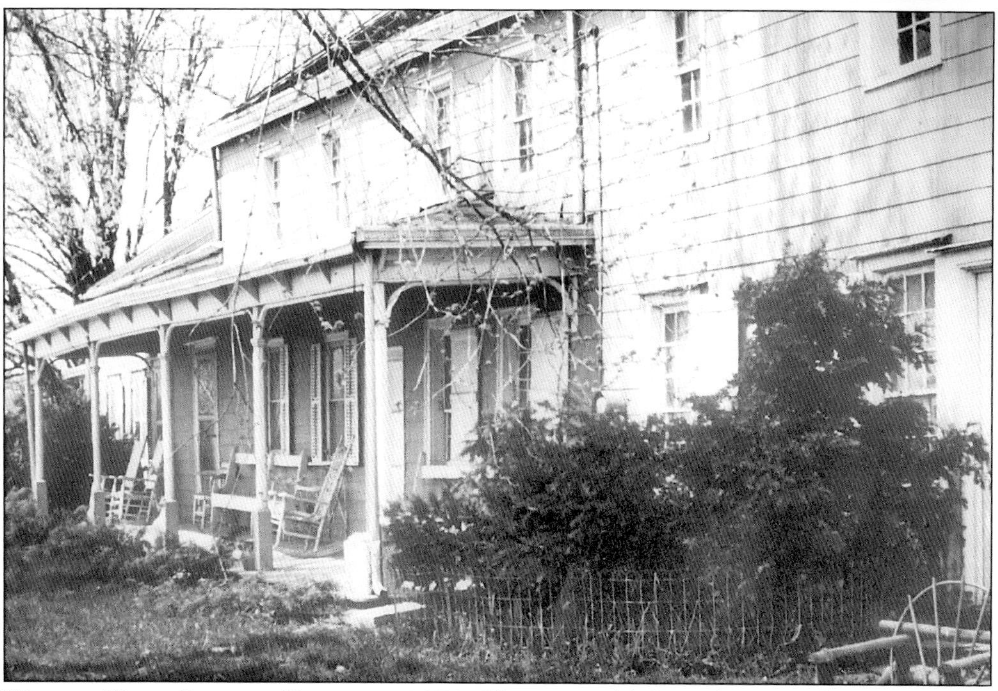

WOLVEN HALL, FREEDOM PLAINS, C. 1970. The act establishing the town directed that the first meeting be held in "the house of William Wolven." The building served as an inn, a store, voting place, tavern, courthouse, post office, and the site of church socials. For many years, it was the unofficial town hall. In her ongoing efforts to document the town's buildings, Rosemary Christ photographed Wolven Hall near the end of its long life. (RC/EJ.)

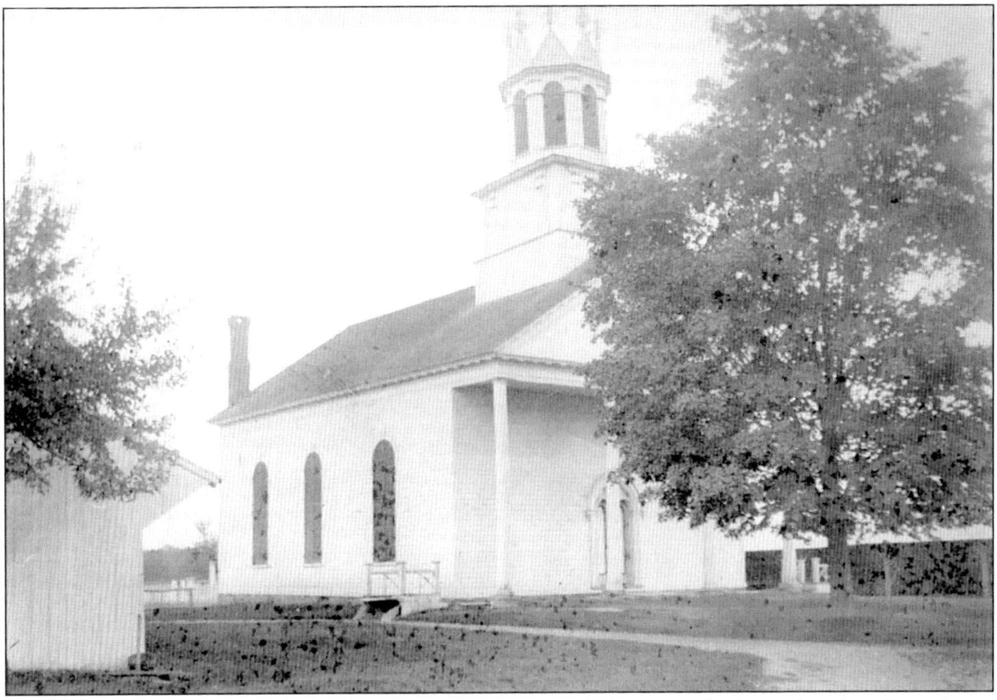

The Freedom Plains Presbyterian Church, c. 1910. The ground where the church and part of its graveyard stand was purchased from William Wolven in 1827. The church was dedicated in 1829. In 1914, a chapel named for Mark Wheeler, one of the elders, was added to the back, and in 1956 an educational unit and fellowship hall were constructed. Note the horse barns in the lower left where churchgoers left their horses. (GW.)

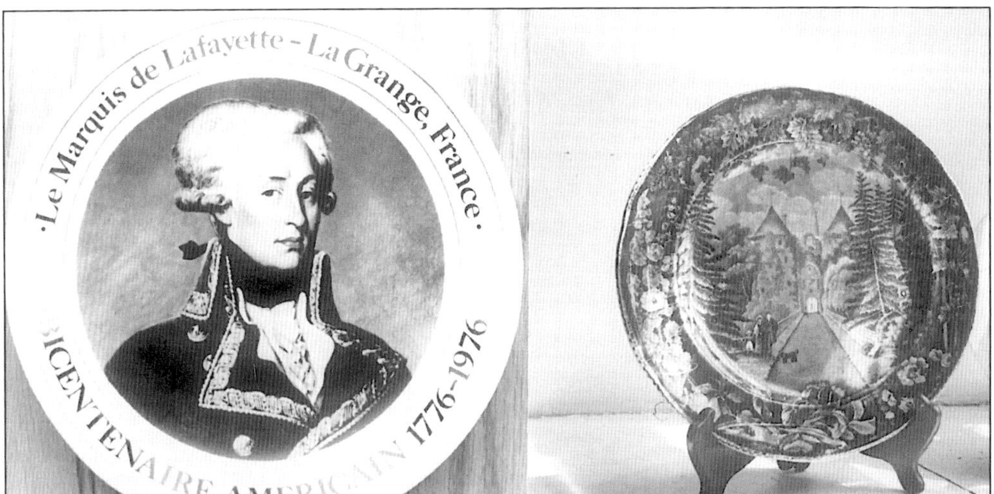

A Comment That Changed a Name, 1820s. The bicentennial commemorative plate on the left, created by the LaGrange Historical Society, celebrates the Marquis de LaFayette, who on his visit to the area in 1824 remarked that the town's landscape resembled that of his home, LaGrange. The 1830s Staffordshire plate on the right, owned by Doris Washburn, former president of the historical society, shows his farm in France. *Et voila,* the town of Freedom became LaGrange. (LHS/DW.)

LaGrange Nurseries, 1872. Benjamin Hart planted the first commercial orchard in LaGrange *c.* 1840. Soon, the family sold not only fruit, but also the trees. Hart's grandson, E. Stuart Hubbard, continued the family business, inviting people from the city to the country to "come and enjoy the apple blossoms." Hubbard was one of the founders of the New York and New England Apple Institute as well as a director and president of the New York State Horticultural Society. The family went out of the apple-growing business in 1961. (MBH.)

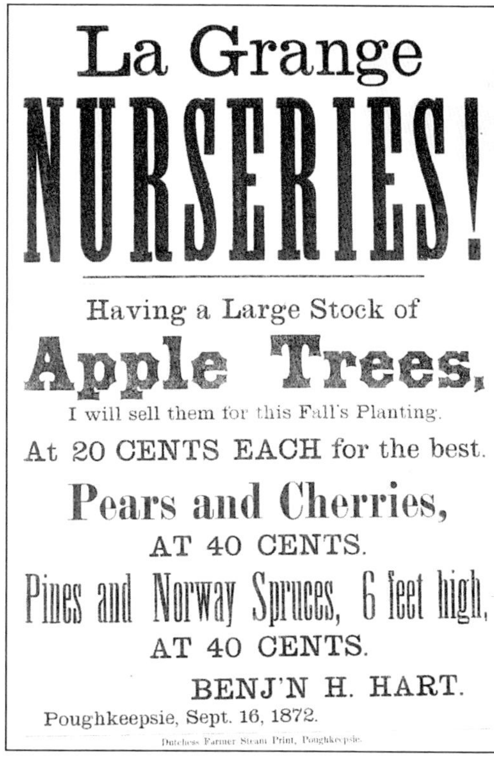

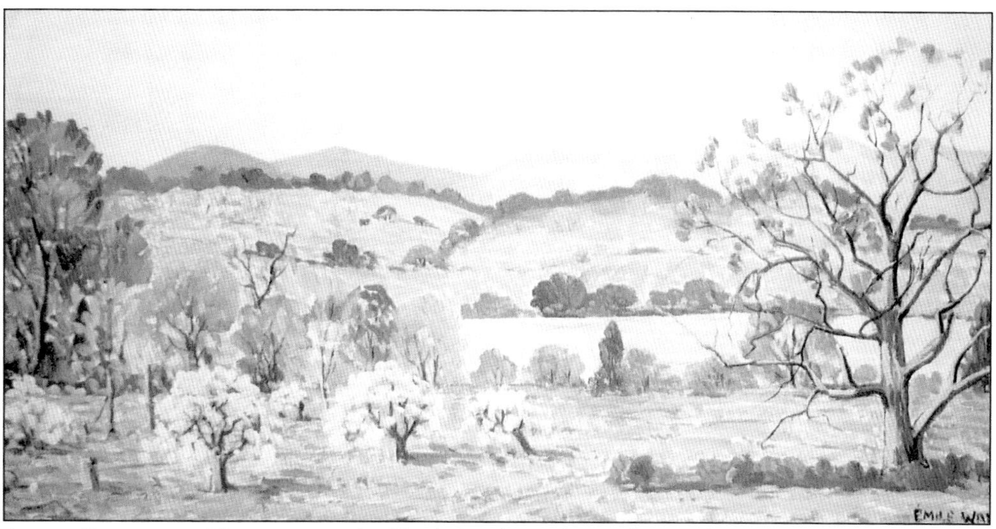

Apple Orchards. This painting by Emile Walters shows the apple orchards, some of which once lined Noxon Road. There were also other fruit trees. George Reid, town supervisor in the 1950s and chairman of the board of representatives in the 1970s, produced mainly apples, but also exceptionally fine peaches. A reminder today is the Apple Core, owned by the Barton family, who also has orchards in Beekman. (JG.)

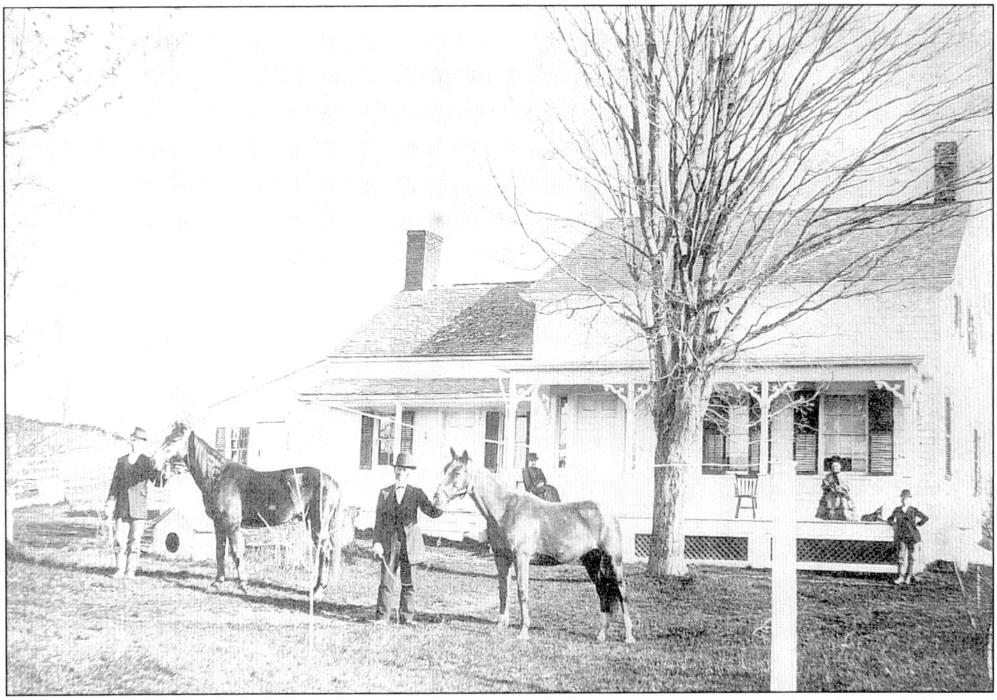

THE JEWELL HOUSE, WEST OF LAUER ROAD ON ROUTE 55, 19TH CENTURY. This house belonged to the Jewell family. Once a farm with two barns, the property was inherited in 1930 by Chester Phillips from his great uncle, Sherman Jewell. Mr. Phillips's daughter, Betty Lundewall, attended the "Little Red Schoolhouse" (when it was white) and served as the tax collector in LaGrange for 16 years. The small chair seen on the porch is in her barn. (BAL/VQ.)

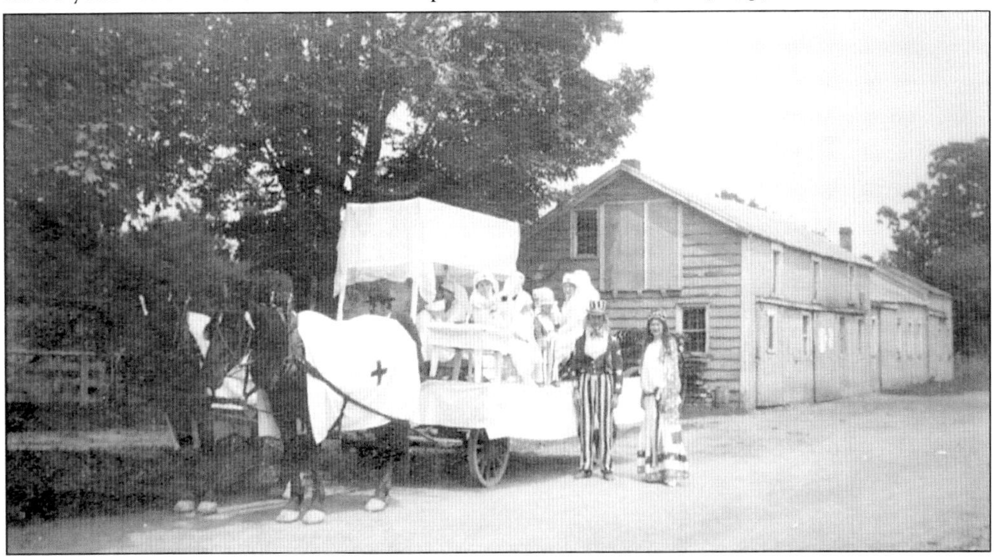

PAUL BERGER'S BLACKSMITH SHOP, 1917. The Red Cross float in the LaGrange 1917 parade is in front of the blacksmith shop owned by Paul Berger, a Prussian émigré who had learned this trade from the Bakers, also blacksmiths in Freedom Plains. The shop became the site of the Diamond Horseshoe, the name of which at least recalls the importance of horses to this former farming community. Berger was also an active member of the nearby Presbyterian Church. (GW.)

Mr. and Mrs. Robert Smith, 1894. This formal portrait of the Smiths captures the quiet dignity of a couple living in the late Victorian era. Posed before an elaborately patterned curtain, the Smiths stare out calmly at the world. Their homestead was on Smith Road. The Smith's daughter, Margaret, married Montfort Wade. (GW.)

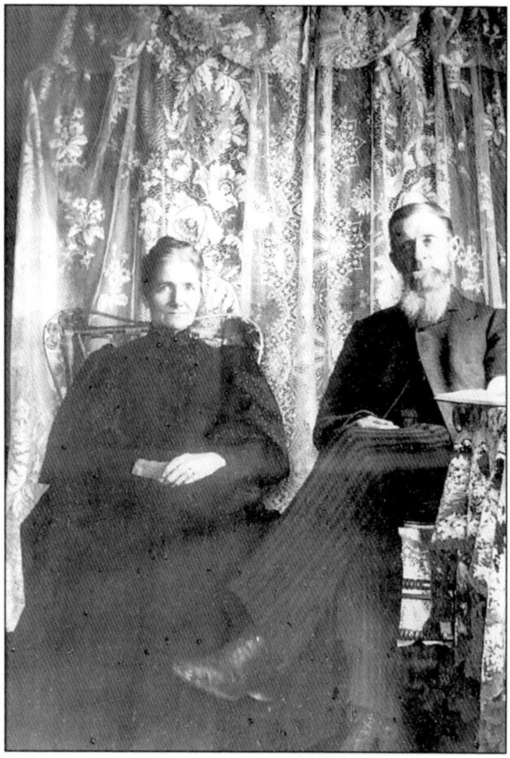

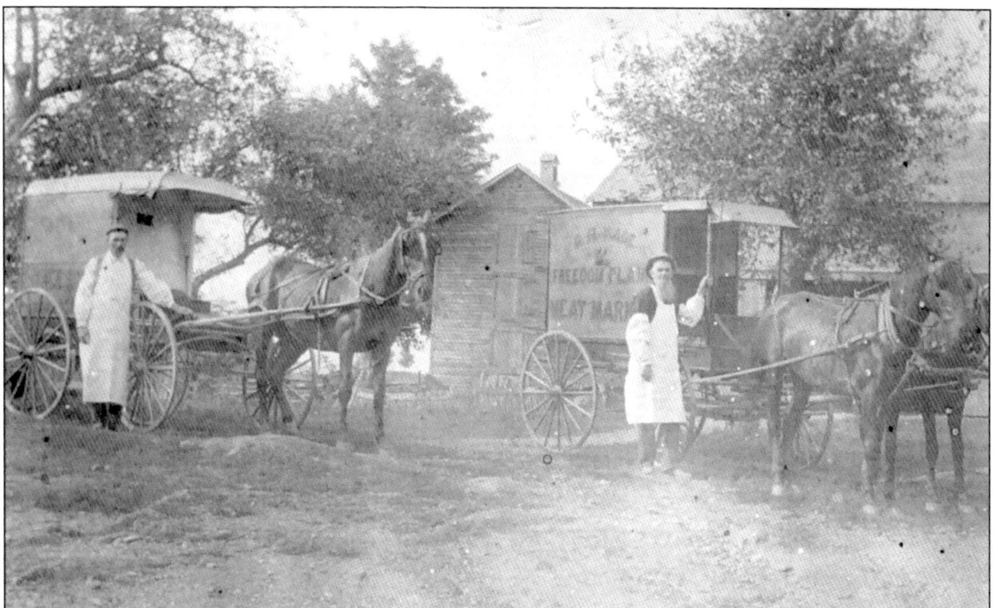

The Wade Meat Market Wagon, c. 1900. According to a 1946 article by Helen Myers in the *Poughkeepsie New Yorker*, the Wades had then been in the meat-peddling business for 106 years. They had four routes, which covered all of LaGrange and some of Beekman, Poughkeepsie, and Fishkill. Until electricity arrived, they stored meat in a cooler filled with ice that was harvested by 17 or 18 men during the winter. (GW.)

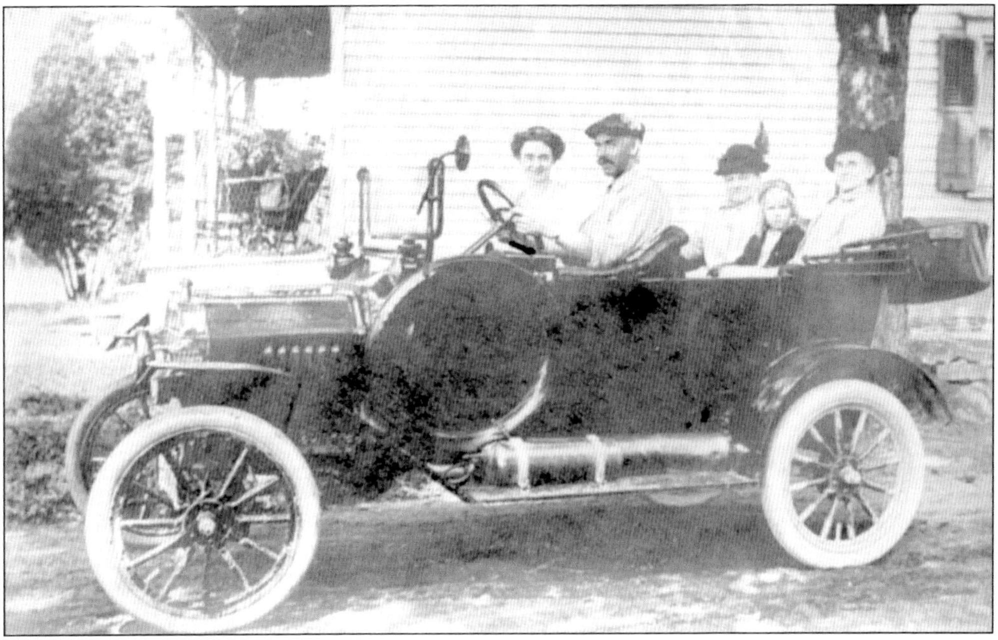

The Wade's First Car, c. WWI. The Wades used both horses, carts, and motorized vehicles to deliver their meat. While this was a family car, the Wades also had a truck. Montfort Wade, the grandfather of George Wade, the present town supervisor, preferred the horse as it needed no instructions of where to go, while his son, like all young men, opted for the latest technology. (GW.)

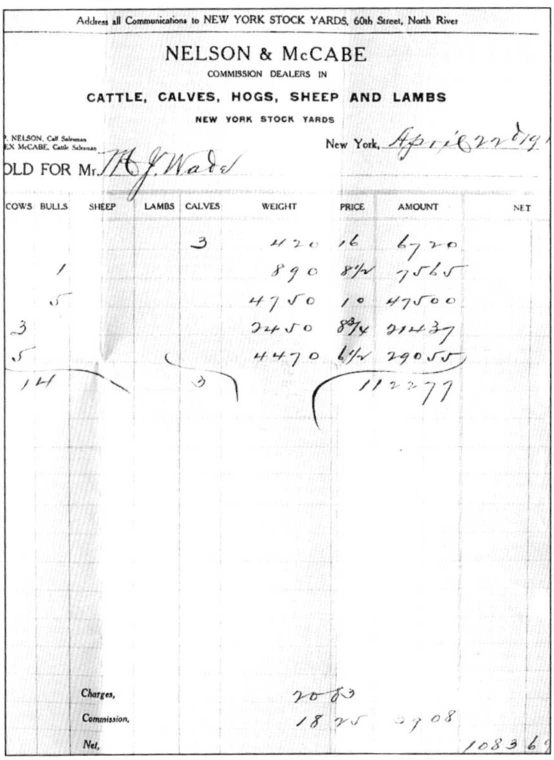

Address all Communications to NEW YORK STOCK YARDS, 60th Street, North River

NELSON & McCABE
COMMISSION DEALERS IN
CATTLE, CALVES, HOGS, SHEEP AND LAMBS
NEW YORK STOCK YARDS

. NELSON, Calf Salesman
EX McCABE, Cattle Salesman

New York, April 22nd 191

OLD FOR Mr. M. J. Wade

COWS	BULLS	SHEEP	LAMBS	CALVES	WEIGHT	PRICE	AMOUNT	NET
				3	420	16	6720	
	1				890	8½	7565	
	5				4750	10	47500	
3					2450	8¾	21437	
5					4470	6½	29055	
14				3			112277	

Charges, 20 83
Commission, 18 25 3908
Net, 108369

A Wade Bill, 1918. The Wades had a local business and a relationship with a New York City business—Nelson and McCabe Commission Dealers, which sold calves, bulls, and cows for the Wades. The price per calf (16¢ per pound) was higher than the price for bulls and cows. The price for bulls and cows differed according to factors, such as age. (GW.)

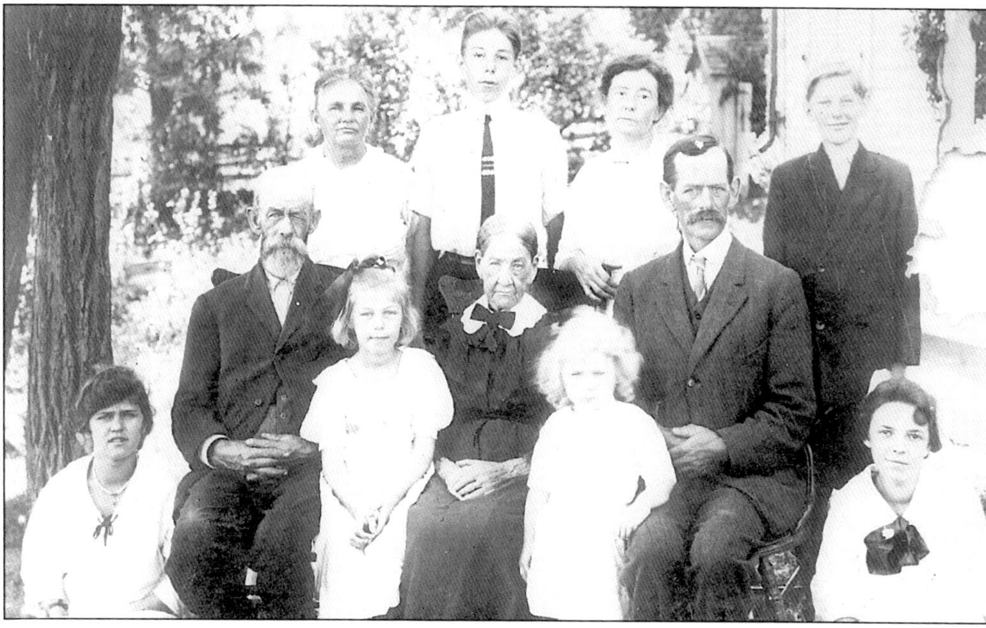

DUNCAN FAMILY, 1915. This 1915 photograph of the Duncan family was taken by Henry Townsend, a local photographer. It is from the collection of Dom O. Napoleon and was published in 1987 as an anonymous portrait of "an American family." When Grace Duncan—the little girl wearing the bow who later became Grace Meddaugh—saw the picture, she called the newspaper to identify all the people in the photograph. Mrs. Meddaugh's daughter, Nancy, married George Wade. (DON.)

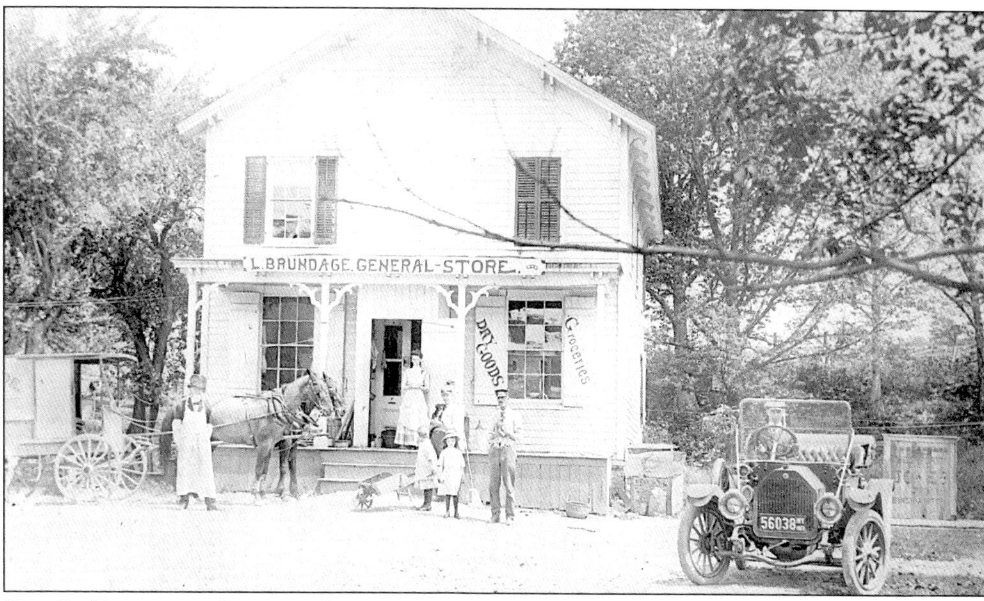

THE L. BRUNDAGE GENERAL STORE, EARLY 1900S. Note the Wade wagon on the left. This store, which also served as a post office, was in Billings, a small hamlet with a railroad flag station. The Locust Farm Company built a milk station in 1910; in 1917, the company merged with the Sheffield Plant, which sent the milk to New York City. The milk plant remained in business until 1953. Today, Ryan Oil occupies the site. (GW.)

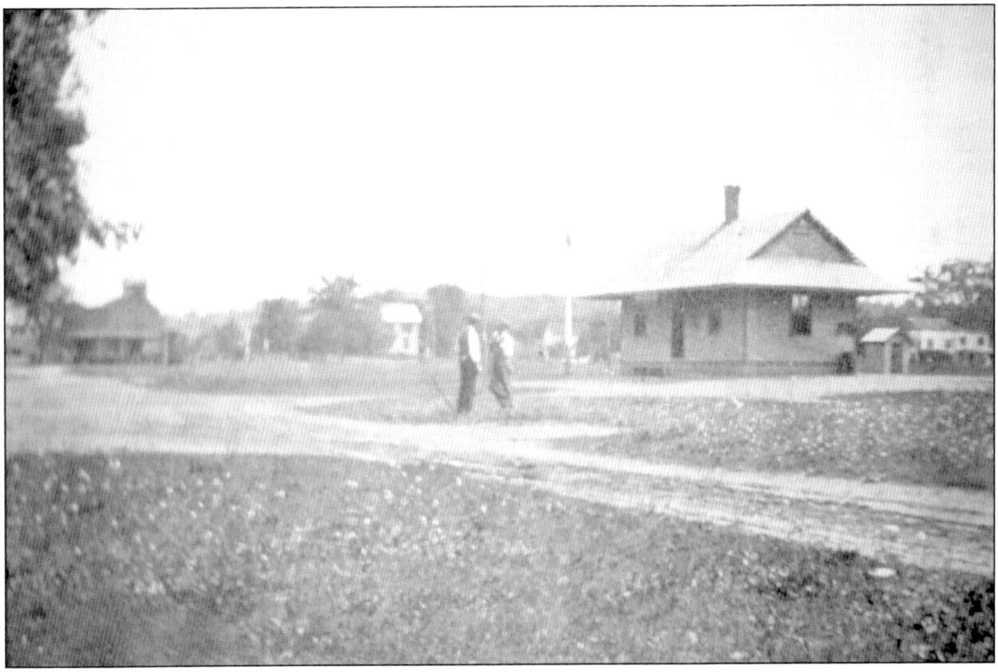

The LaGrangeville Railroad Station, early 1900s. Today, it is perhaps difficult to understand the impact the arrival of the railroad had on a small hamlet. The very existence of this hamlet was due to the coming of the Dutchess & Columbia Railroad. The business center left Morey's Corners and moved to this hamlet, where there came to be about 25 houses, a school, a store, and a post office. (VV.)

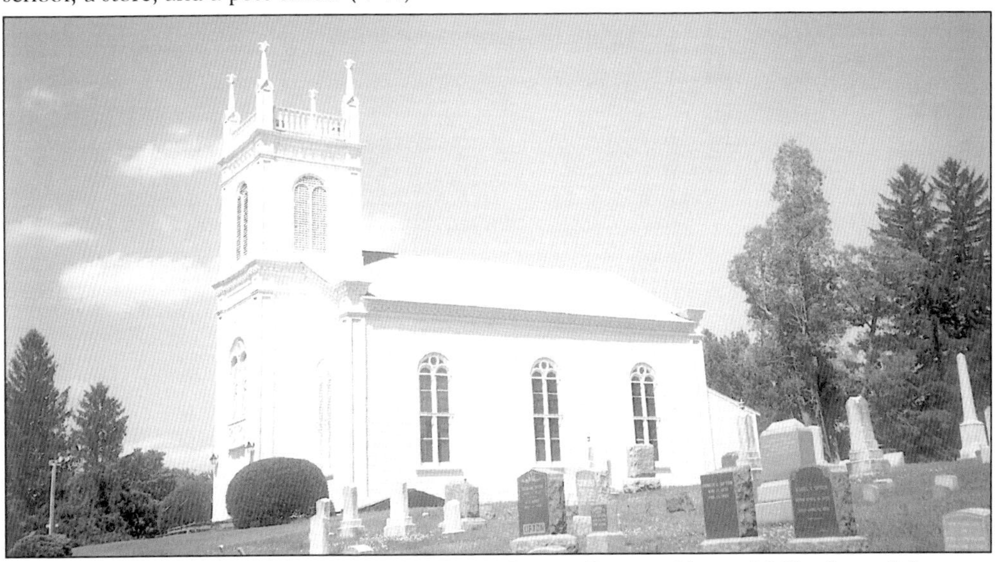

The Trinity United Methodist Church, Cross Road. About 1863, this edifice was removed from Potters' Corners in Union Vale and was reconstructed on its present site on Cross Road just off Noxon Road. Originally, Methodists from Morey's Mills had attended church at Potters' Corners, but in 1849 they evidently decided to form their own congregation. In the church's burial ground is the grave of Dr. George Huntington—after whom Huntington's Disease is named. (JS.)

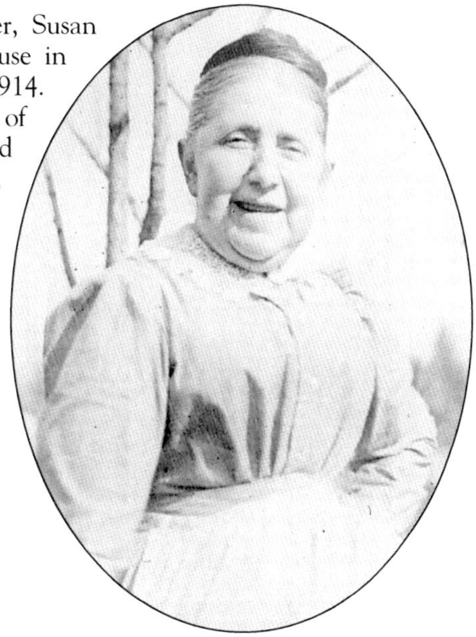

SUSAN MOORE C. LATE 1800S. A gentle Quaker, Susan Moore presided over Floral Home, a boardinghouse in Moore's Mills, for 50 years until her death in 1914. Visitors came to enjoy the beauty and tranquillity of the countryside as well as to walk, play games and charades, skate, read, and play croquet. The house, built in mid-18th century, still stands. (GW.)

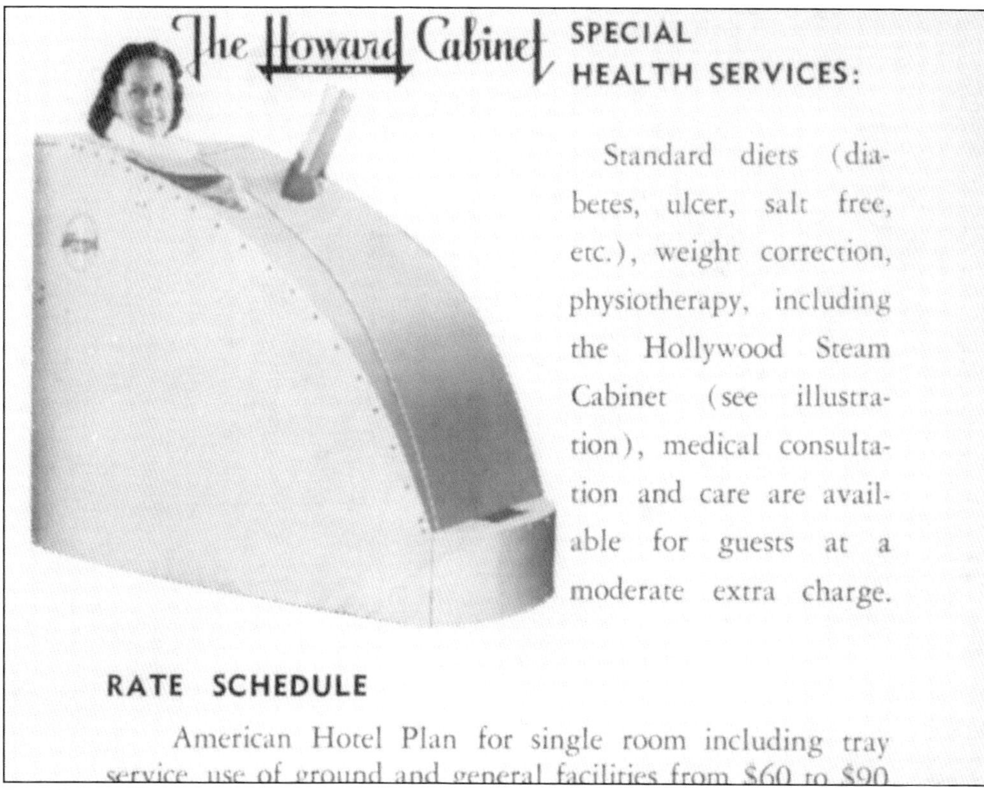

THE PARKWAY HEALTH RESORT, C. 1950. Two world wars later, the Parkway Health Resort, once Floral Home, advertised its proximity to the Taconic State Parkway, making it easily accessible from New York City. The resort touted its "special health services," which included use of this machine that the advertisement writer called "Hollywood" rather than "Howard." Perhaps the glamour of Hollywood had already bewitched the writer. (MF/MB.)

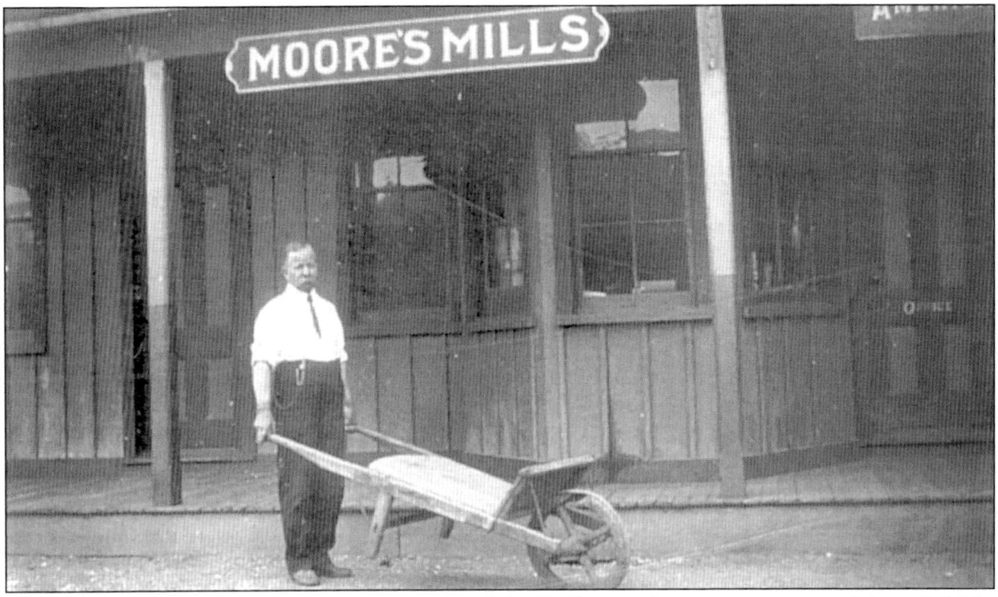

MOORE'S MILL RAILROAD STATION, c. 1920s. Mr. Wells was the station agent at Moore's Mills on the Dutchess & Columbia Railroad, which was built in the 1870s from Beacon to Millerton by Millbrook entrepreneur George Brown. In the days when few people had telephones, the station agent, who had access to the telegraph, functioned as a center of communications. He could also arrange for the delivery of parcels arriving by train, as he would often know who would be going in the right direction. (HC.)

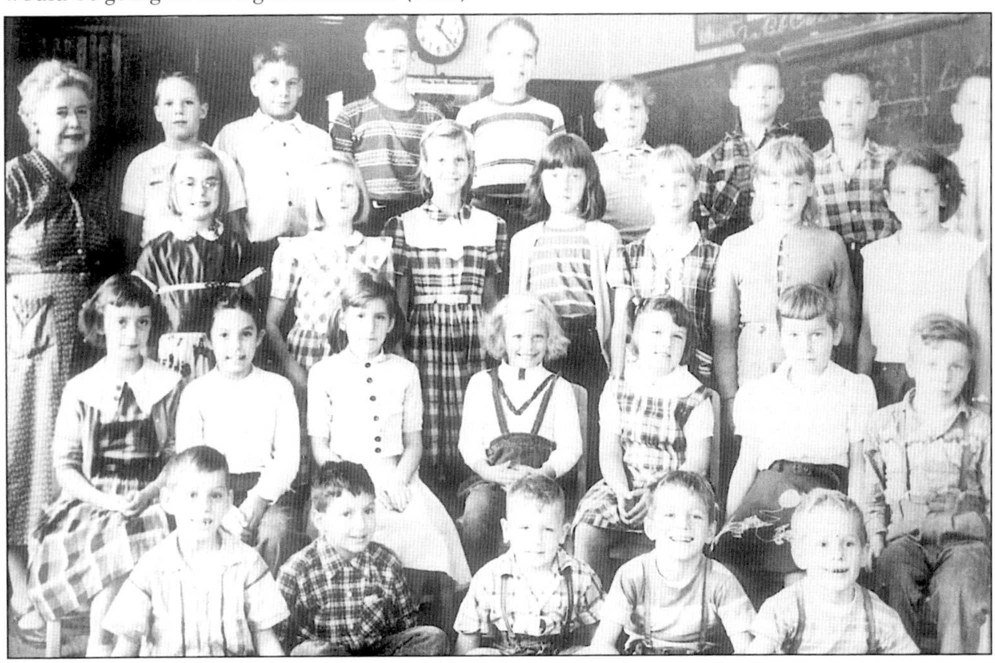

MOORES MILL SCHOOL, c. 1957. Sara Belle Wells, the teacher, was the daughter of the railroad station agent. While Floral Home had become the Parkway Health Resort, this one-room schoolhouse in Moores Mills located on Oswego Road remained much as it had been until it was dismantled about 1967 and rebuilt as a residence on Route 82. (EJTH.)

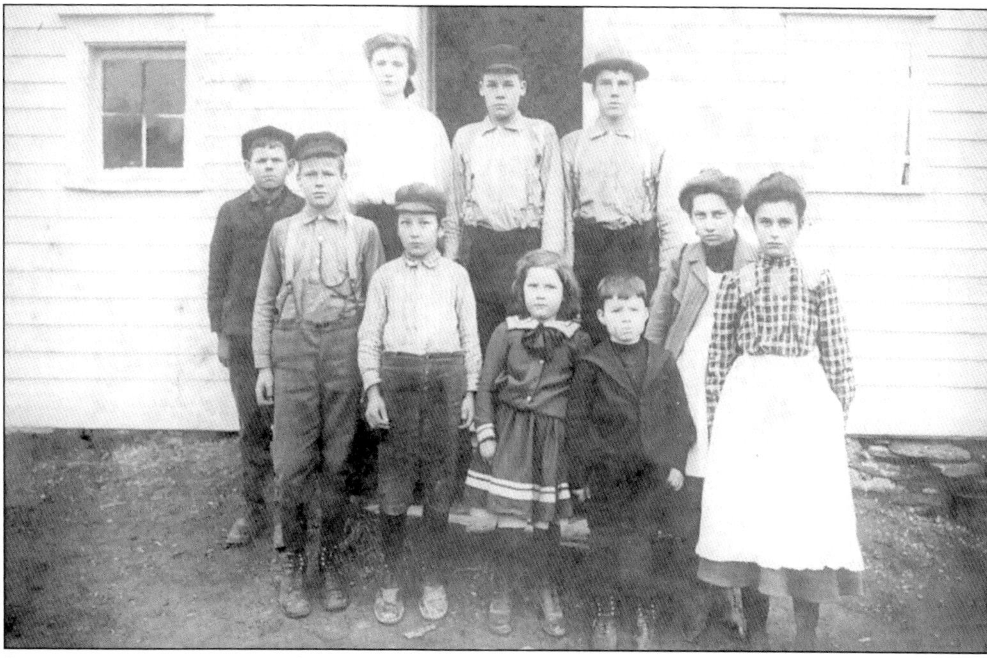

SCHOOL NO. 1, C. 1900S. This school, located in the northwest corner of the town, was called the Lockwood School, the name of the adjoining property owners. Clifford Buck, the donor of the photograph to the LaGrange Historical Society, attended this school from 1906 to 1914, when it had 15 to 20 pupils. Some of the pupils look almost as old as the young woman in the back row, who is presumably the teacher. (LHS.)

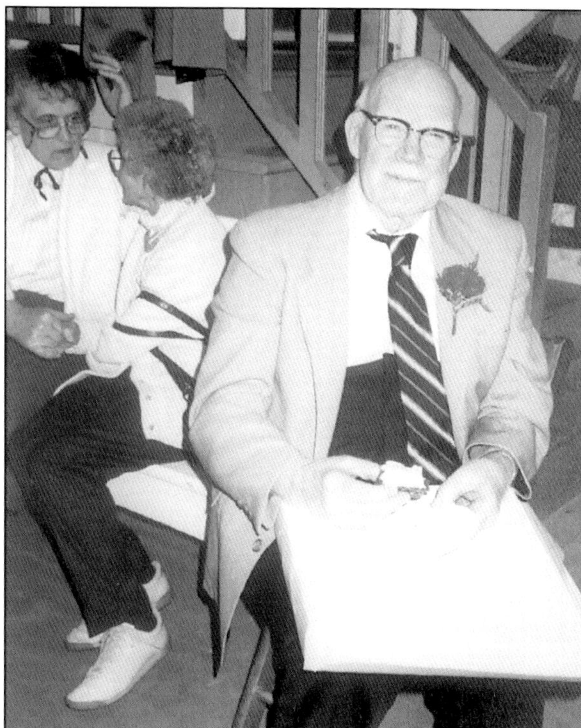

CLIFFORD BUCK, 1989. Clifford Buck was recognized for his 25 years on the board of the Friends Cemetery, just one of his many community activities. A farmer, respected local historian, genealogist, researcher, and author, and characterized by the *Poughkeepsie Journal* as "gentle, genial and generous," he was always willing to share his phenomenal knowledge of Dutchess County, which was based on meticulous research. Whenever there was a question about land deeds or other historical matters, Clifford Buck could always provide the answer. (LMcD.)

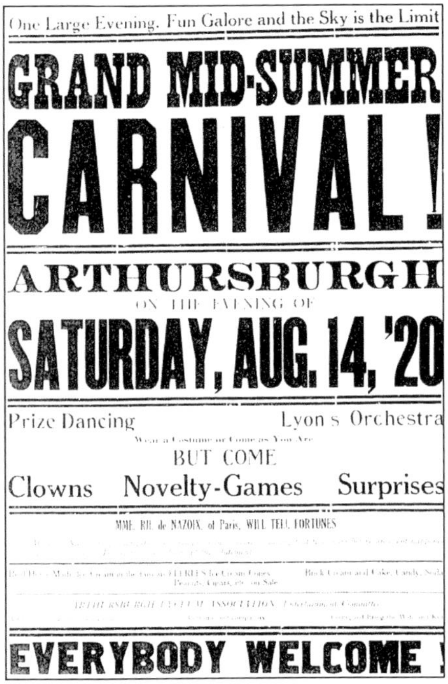

"FUN GALORE," 1920. This is a poster for a carnival at Arthursburg, another small hamlet, located in the southeast corner of town. It must have been hard to resist Mme. Ril de Nazoix of Paris telling fortunes, the homemade ice cream, and the prize dancing. After all, "the sky is the limit!" The program was put together by the Entertainment Committee of the Arthursburg Lyceum Association, an example of how people created their entertainment before television and videos. (EJTH.)

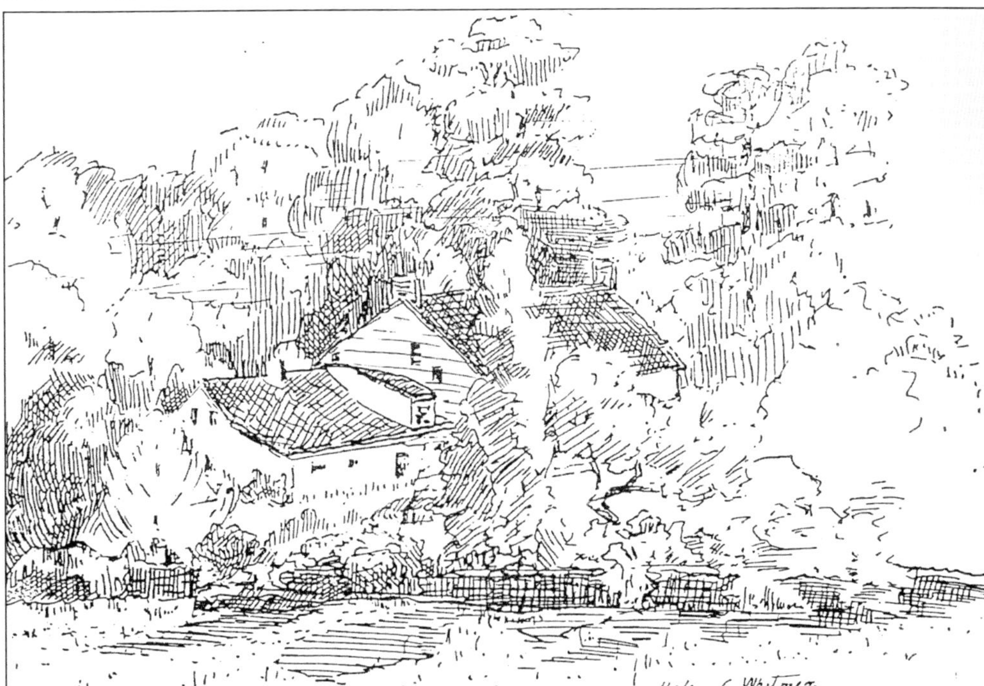

DRAMAMOUNT, c. 1920s. Helen C. Whitmer sketched the farm in LaGrange that she purchased in 1923 with her husband, T. Carl Whitmer, noted composer of orchestral, chamber, and choral works. Attracted by its beauty and natural amphitheater as well as by its proximity to New York, the Whitmers established Dramamount to further his musical dramas as well as to provide a summer home where students and fellow artists could come to work and study. Helen Whitmer taught landscape painting, and Edward Harris taught dance. (EJTH.)

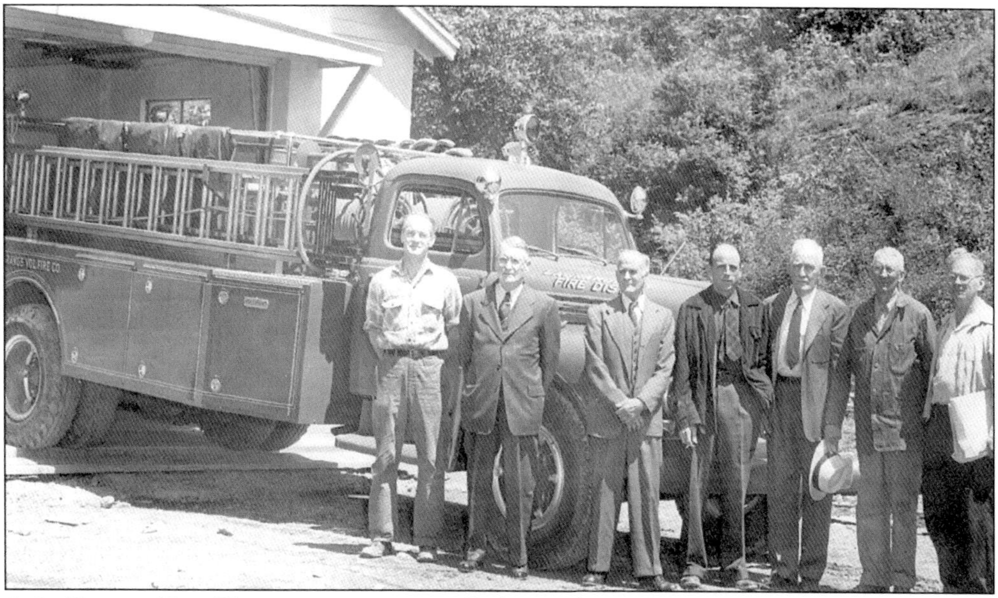

A LaGrange Fire Truck, early 1940s. Early members of the LaGrange Fire Department, which held its first meeting in the Freedom Plains Grange Hall in 1941, stand proudly in front of the first fire truck. The truck went into service in 1943. On the left is E. Stuart Hubbard Jr., who later became town supervisor. Also pictured, sixth from the left, is Edmund Van Wyck, the town historian who wrote many articles on the history of LaGrange. (MBH.)

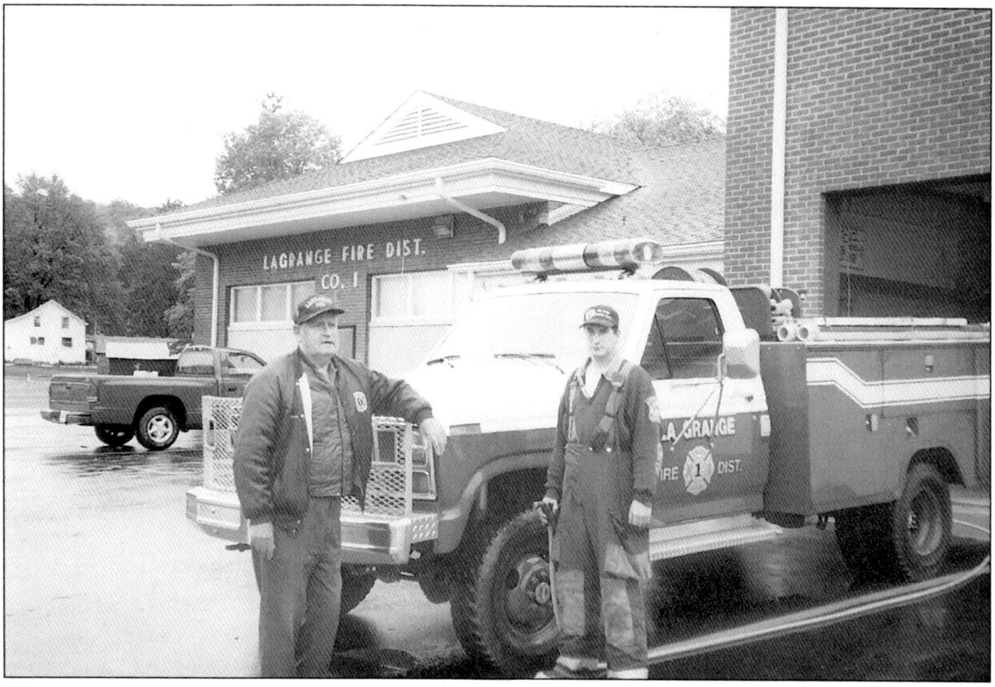

Washing the Engine, 2000. Sonny Phelps, one of 22 charter members of the LaGrange Fire Company No. 1, and Andy McGarry continue the tradition of maintaining the equipment. Sonny recalls responding to the first alarm that the company ever had on the Howard Michaels farm on Freedom Road. Andy has been a volunteer firefighter in LaGrange for two years. (JS.)

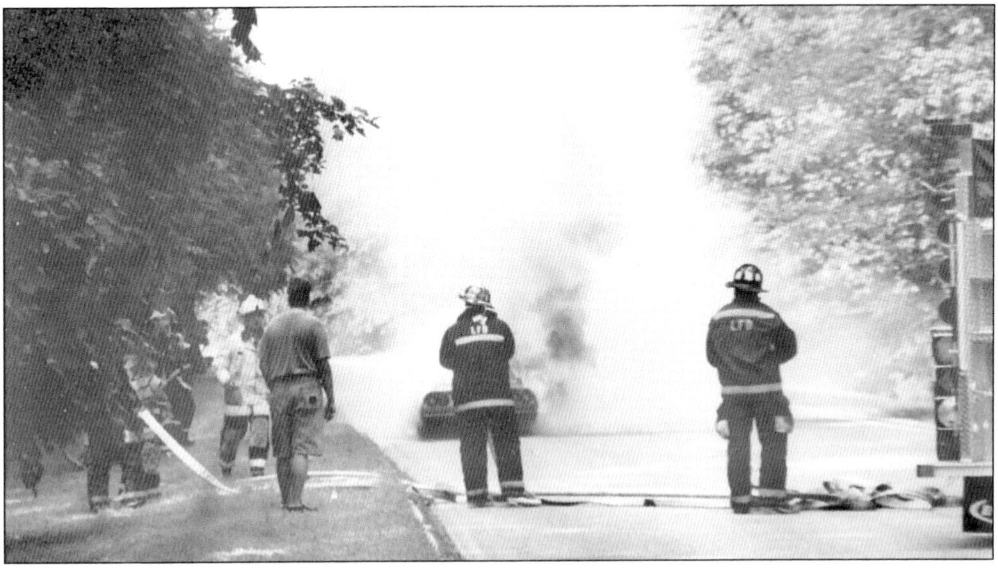

A Car Fire on the Taconic State Parkway. The impact of the Taconic State Parkway on LaGrange firefighters is not limited to responding to fires. Jeff Kaiser explained that paid firefighters have been added to the volunteers at Station No. 2, as many residents face long commutes and increasing family demands. Originally next to the Van Wyck homestead on Route 55, Station No. 2 burned in 1978 and was rebuilt on land donated by Henry Page. Station No. 3 on Red Oaks Mill Road was established in 1956. (LaGFD.)

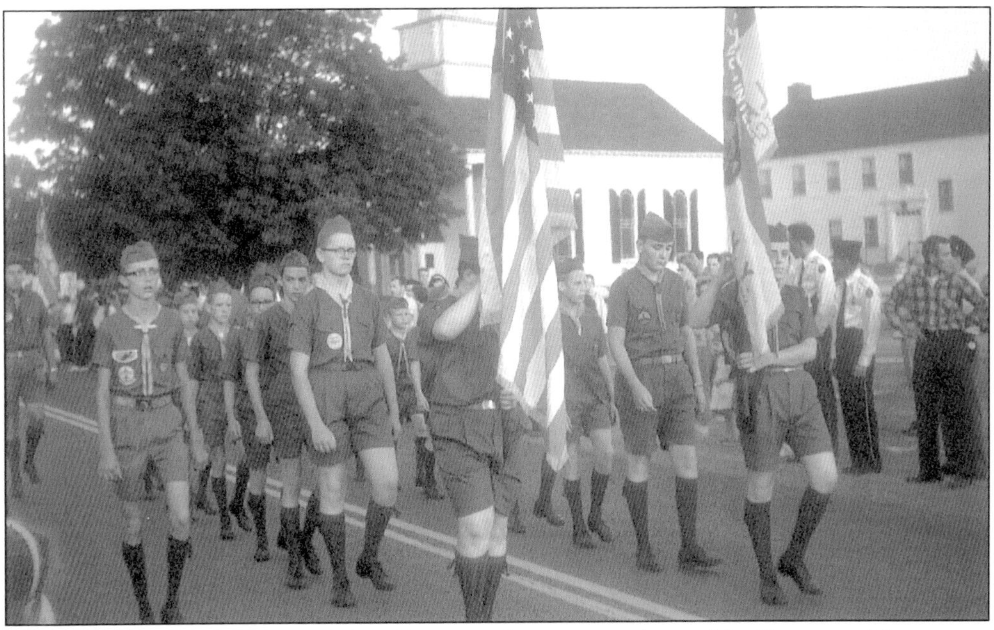

Boy Scouts Marching, c. 1960s. Everyone loves a parade, and LaGrange residents were no exception as they watched the Boy Scouts marching by the Freedom Plains Presbyterian Church. In 1959, Irving Rymph had predicted that the town would grow, and it did, as IBM continued to expand in the country. Housing subdivisions seemed to spring up overnight. New residents joined with longtime residents in community activities such as Boy Scouts, 4-H, and others. (PJC.)

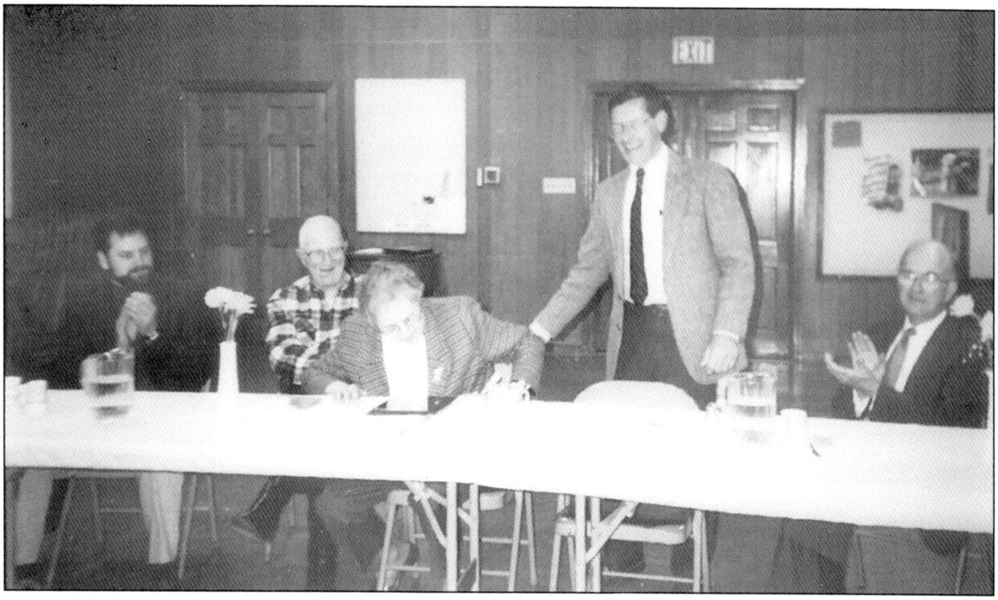

CELEBRATING COMMUNITY SERVICE, 1992. On the left, Jim Gell, superintendent at Baird Park, and Tom Jacob look on as county legislator Joe Lombardi presents Fran Jacob with an award for "tireless devotion to the LaGrange Historical Society and to the community." The Reverend Boak, long-term minister at the Freedom Plains Presbyterian Church, is applauding. The event took place in the Fellowship Hall of the church. (FJ.)

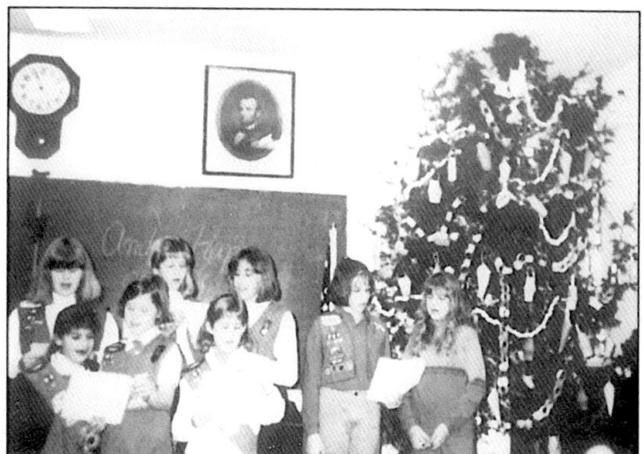

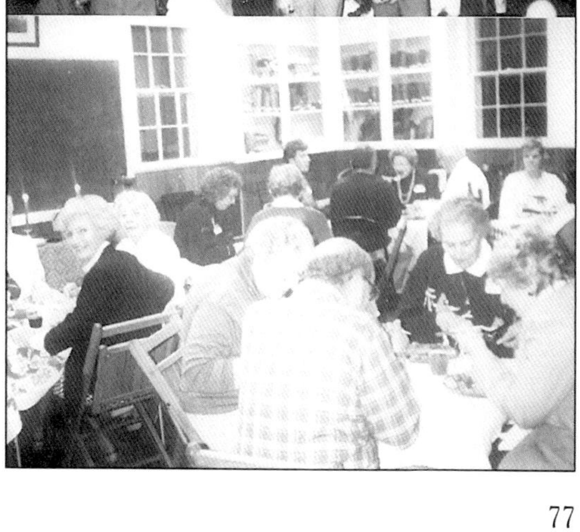

LITTLE RED SCHOOLHOUSE HALLOWEEN AND CHRISTMAS PARTIES, 1990S. Since the LaGrange Historical Society acquired the schoolhouse in 1962 from the Arlington School District to use as a meeting place and museum, it has been the scene of school programs, meetings, and other occasions. Originally built c. 1860s, it was closed in 1941 when the Arlington Central District was formed. It has also served as the LaGrange branch of Adriance Memorial Library. (FJ.)

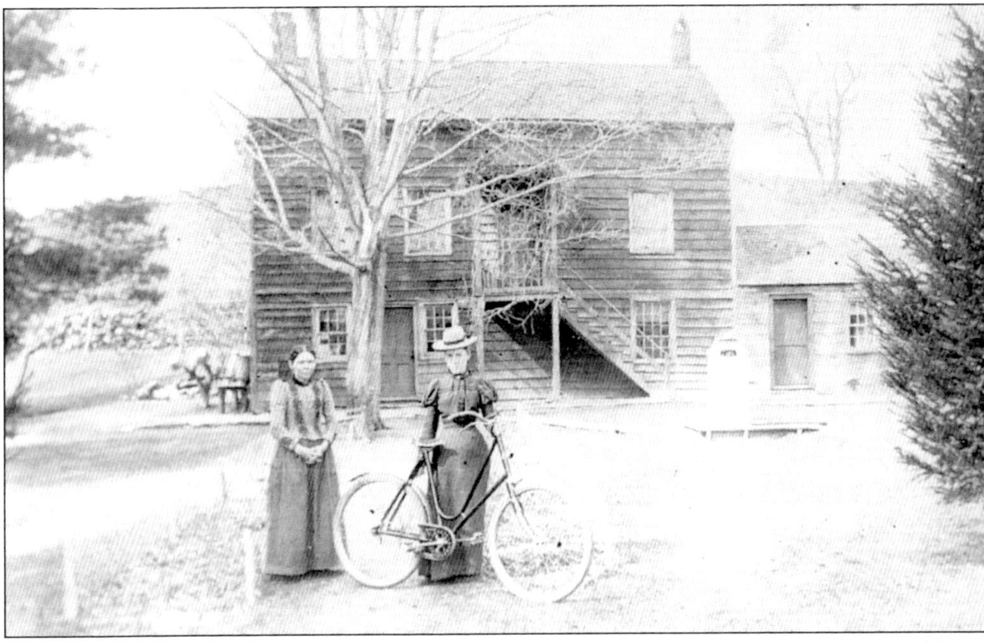

Rebecca Jewell Gidley and her Daughter, Susie, c. 1890s. Susie, who later married F. Jay Skidmore and became the mother of Hazel, stands with a bicycle in front of her family home on Gidley Road. Susie's home was described in a rhyme written by Rebecca Jewell Gidley in 1900 as "ancient and tall, with clapboards of red." The Gidleys and Skidmores were among the earlier settlers of the town. (EJTH.)

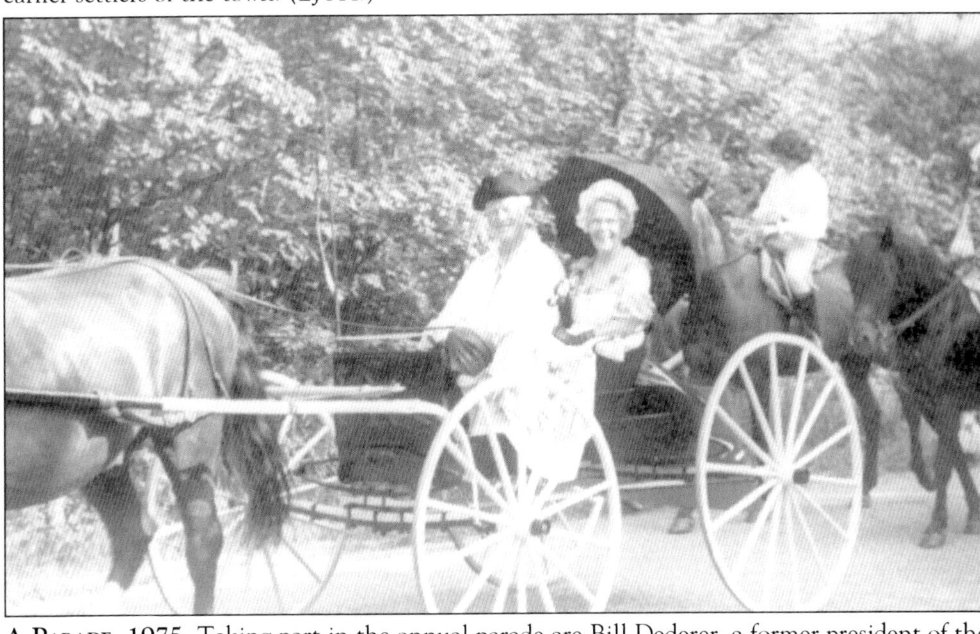

A Parade, 1975. Taking part in the annual parade are Bill Dederer, a former president of the LaGrange Historical Society; Hazel Skidmore, who grew up on the Skidmore farm and taught at the "little red schoolhouse;" and Ethan the horse, obviously camera shy. Unlike her mother Susie, who used one of the latest means of transportation of her time, Miss Skidmore seems content to return to the days of horses and carts, at least for the parade. (FJ.)

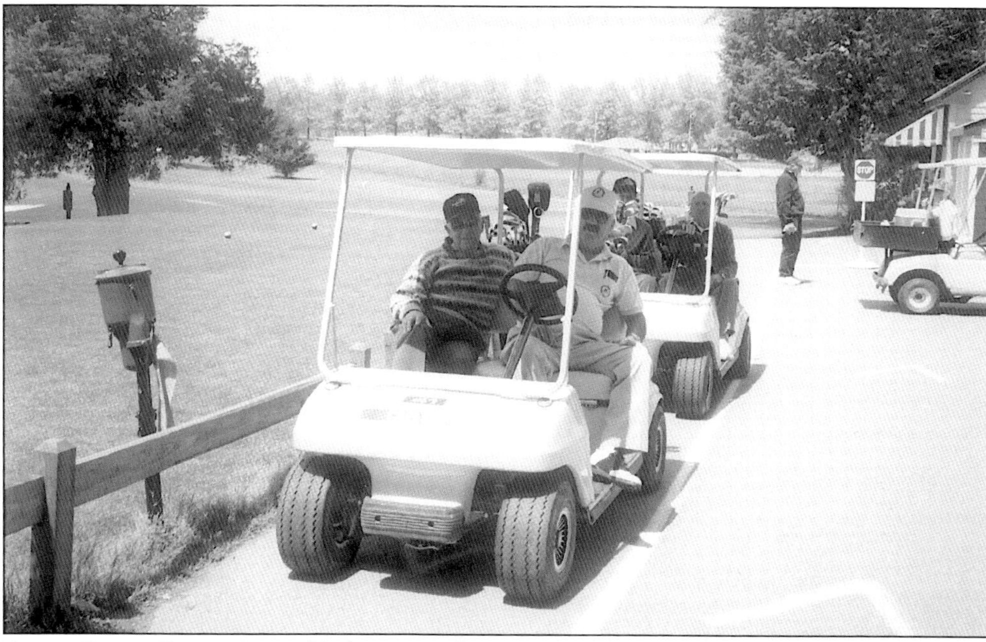

BAIRD STATE PARK, 2000. Today, even leisure activities are motorized. James Baird, who directed the construction of the Lincoln Memorial in Washington, gave his LaGrange farm of 600 acres for use as a park to the State of New York in 1939. A man of vision, he wrote, "The important thing is how the entire plant [park] is to be 10 or 20 or 100 years from now." More than 50 years after its opening in 1948, the golf course continues to be popular. (JS.)

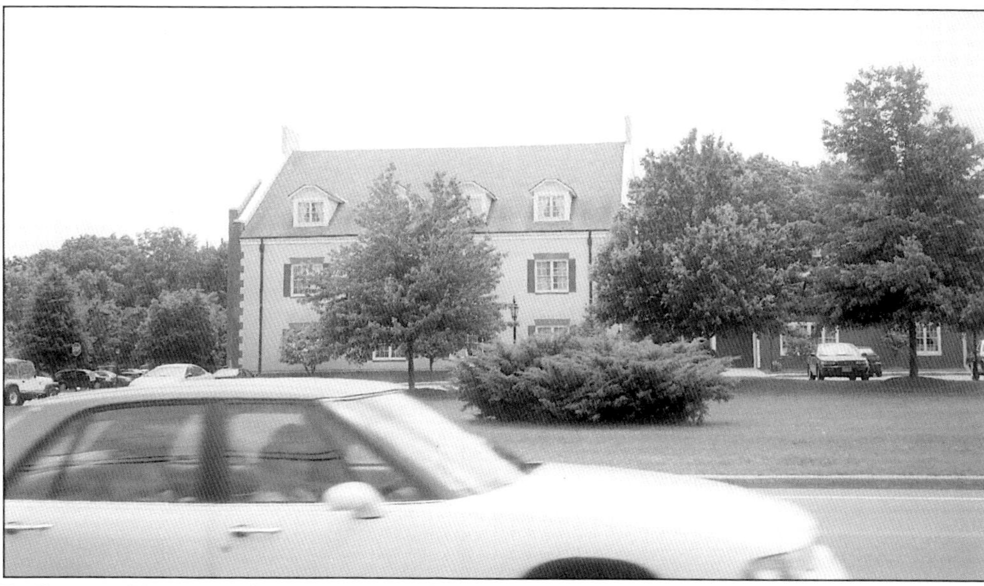

LAGRANGE TODAY. In the 1960s, it was decided that Freedom Plains would be promoted as the town center. The town hall was built on Stringham Road, and the post office was constructed on Route 55. With Arlington High School, the Freedom Plains Presbyterian church, a bank, offices, and stores, a linear hamlet has been established that has available many of the services once provided in small hamlets throughout the town. The difference is, of course, its reliance on the automobile. (JS.)

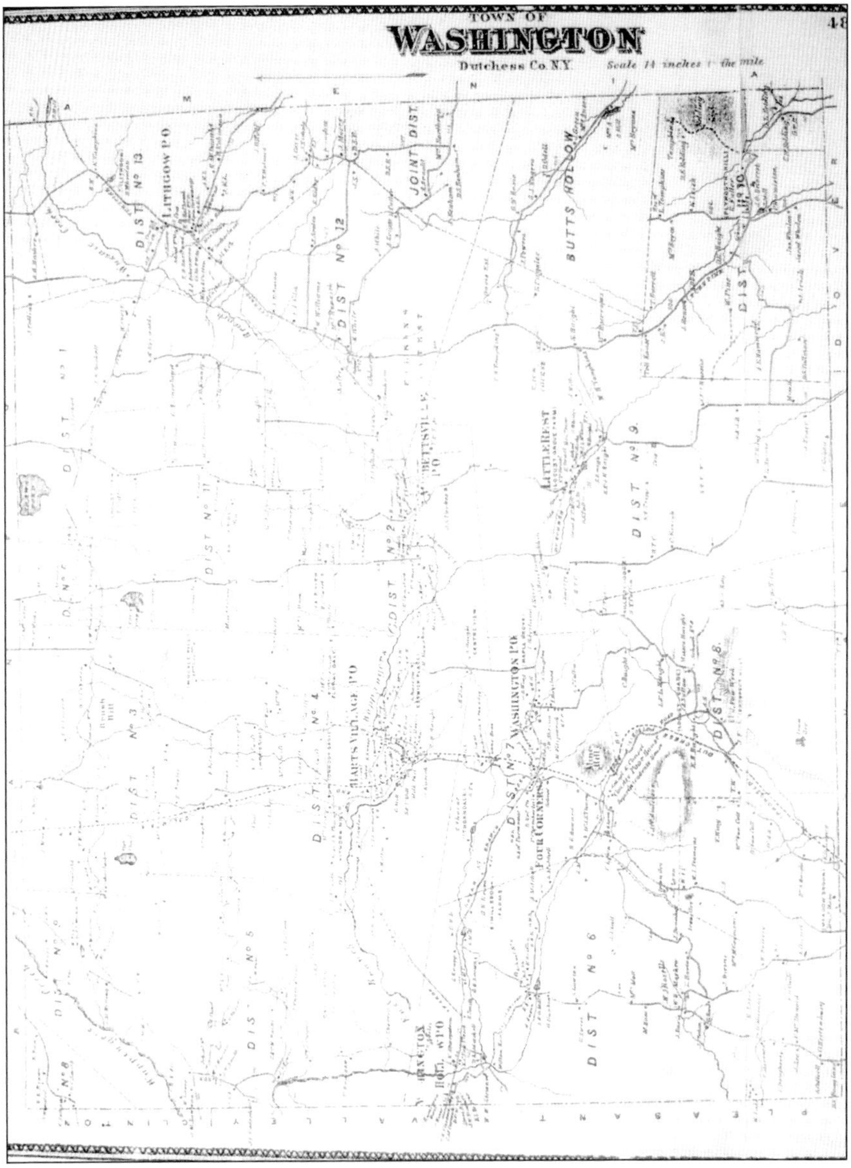

An 1867 Map of Washington. Beers municipal maps, published cyclically in large, bound booklets, can be found in the collections of the Dutchess County Historical Society. They addressed many physical and social aspects of 19th-century communities within New York State that are useful to current day researchers. Geographical features such as rivers, streams, wetlands, and mountains are defined. Township, village, and school district lines denote the respective jurisdictions. Major roadways are drawn and public institutions are noted as well as the names of hamlets, commonly known neighborhoods, and property owners. Some of the most useful information comes from inset promotional sponsorship lists concerning commercial and professional activity in primary centers. While the 1867 Washington map does not identify Millbrook, it does identify "Millbrook Farms," a nearby estate, and three hamlets—Harts Village, Four Corners, and Washington Post Office—that encircle the area that within a generation became the heart of Washington. Little Rest hamlet has become even littler, and Washington Hollow is recognized as being primarily in the town of Pleasant Valley. (DCHS.)

Five

WASHINGTON

Rolling hills, stone fences protecting grazing cattle and horses, and prosperous estates greet those entering Washington on Route 44 east of the Taconic State Parkway. One of Dutchess's original towns, it was founded in 1788 from a portion of the Great Nine Partners Crown Patent. Named to honor George Washington, it originally encompassed all of Stanford lands. Apart from rocky portions of Chestnut Ridge along the Harlem Valley line, this is rich farmland, prized by 18th-century immigrants: Quakers, other New Englanders, and Long Islanders. Descendants of 18th-century purchasers—Thornes, Hams, and Harts among them—still reside here.

Separated from New England by the ridge and from the Hudson by a lack of good roads, a self-sufficient agrarian economy prospered. Hamlets providing needs and services not originating at home grew around houses of worship, businesses, postal stops, and mills at Harts Village, Mechanic, Mabbetsville, Lithgow, and Little Rest. Trade in pelts and farm products linked town entrepreneurs to New York City. However, the town's isolation ended with the construction of the Dutchess Turnpike from Poughkeepsie to Connecticut after 1804. West of Harts Village, the road split into branches, north to Sharon, Connecticut, and south to Dover.

Post–Civil War railroad construction linked Washington with Poughkeepsie and New York commerce while creating Millbrook Station as the new town center. Millbrook Village, named for a nearby estate, emerged from economic development around the station itself that spilled over into several hamlets.

The latter 19th century marked the evolution of large farms to estate status and the redefinition of the area as a vacation venue, promoted by popular hotels and boardinghouses. Personal relationships nurtured by generations of successful business ties to New York City fed a new cultural migration still prevalent today—the well-to-do weekender for whom this is home.

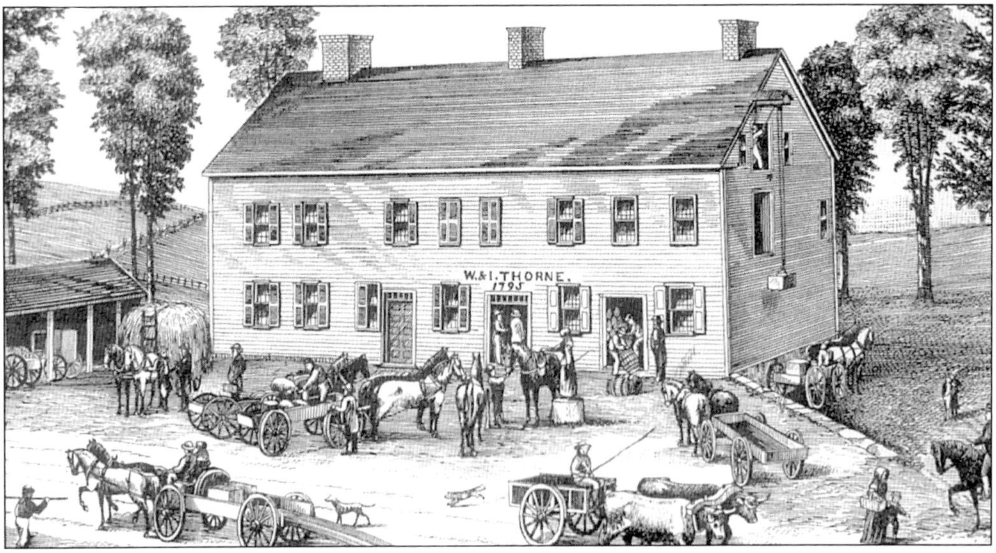

The Thorne's Store in Mechanic. Among the earliest to settle in Nine Partners was the Thorne family, Long Island expatriates. Public records show a growth of Thorne investments and land transactions after 1740. William and Isaac Thorne's successful store and trading post, opened in Mechanic in 1795, was still operating when James Smith wrote his 1882 county history. William's son, Samuel, continued the businesses and land purchases, expanding into imports until he retired. Successive generations, although focused on broader city markets, have remained devoted to Thorndale, the family residence here. (DCHS.)

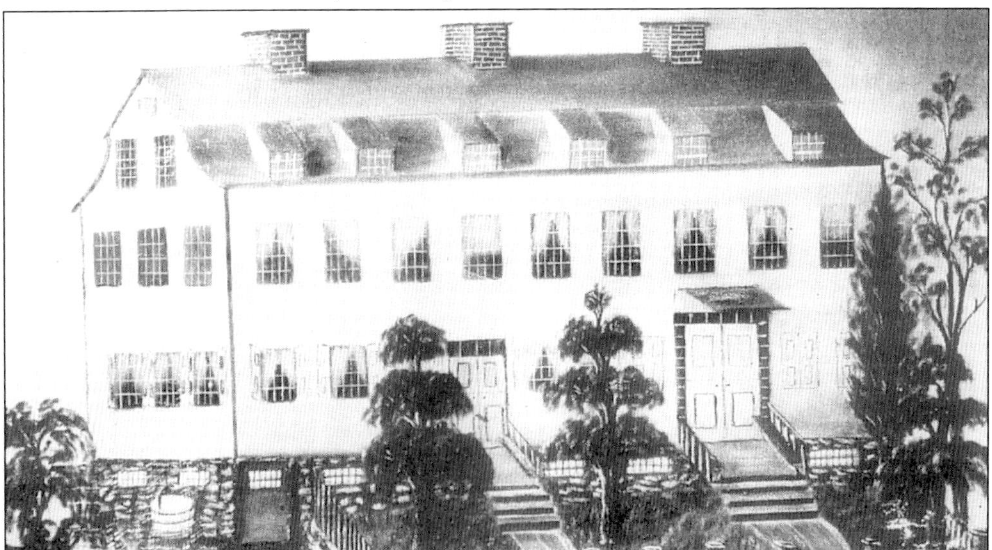

The Nine Partners Quaker School, Mechanic. Within 50 years of settling, Friends had established important community institutions. A boarding school recognized for renowned faculty members, such as Jacob and Deborah Willets, it was an early model for co-education. Joseph Mabbett's store and tavern, built c.1762, was purchased by Yearly Meeting leaders in 1795 for the new school. Despite divisions of the Hicksite Separation and several moves, it continues today as Oakwood School in Poughkeepsie. An itinerant painter of the early 19th century captured its earliest incarnation. (DCHS.)

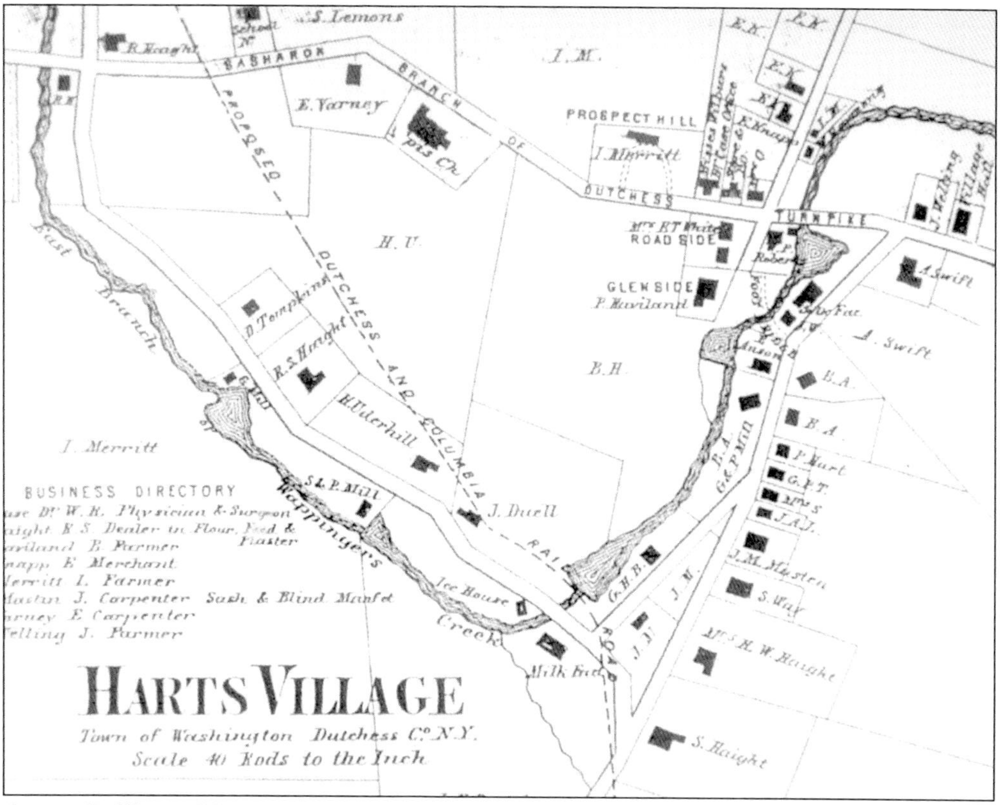

AN 1867 HARTS VILLAGE MAP. Successful commerce and milling at the intersection of the Sharon Branch of the Dutchess Turnpike and the East Branch of the Wappingers Creek made Philip Hart's family wealthy before the turn of the 18th century. The swift waters that ran through the gorge directly in front of the family homestead also attracted other industries in need of waterpower and a way to market along good roads. For more than a century before this map was drawn, Harts Village was the town center. (DCHS.)

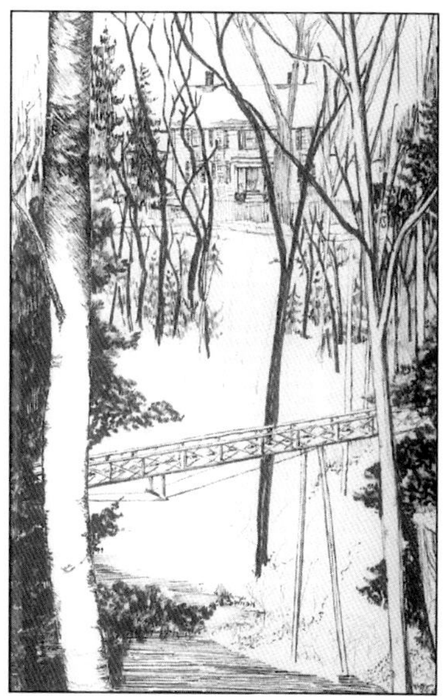

THE PHILIP HART HOUSE. Around 1769, Philip Hart bought land along the East Branch of the Wappingers Creek, where he built his gristmill. A fine house for his Quaker wife marked the center of a family compound, giving rise to the settlement's name. This handsome Georgian home opposite the footbridge to the mills is cherished by present owners, artist and town historian David Greenwood and his wife, Nan. Greenwood's drawing records the footbridge destroyed in 1999. (DG.)

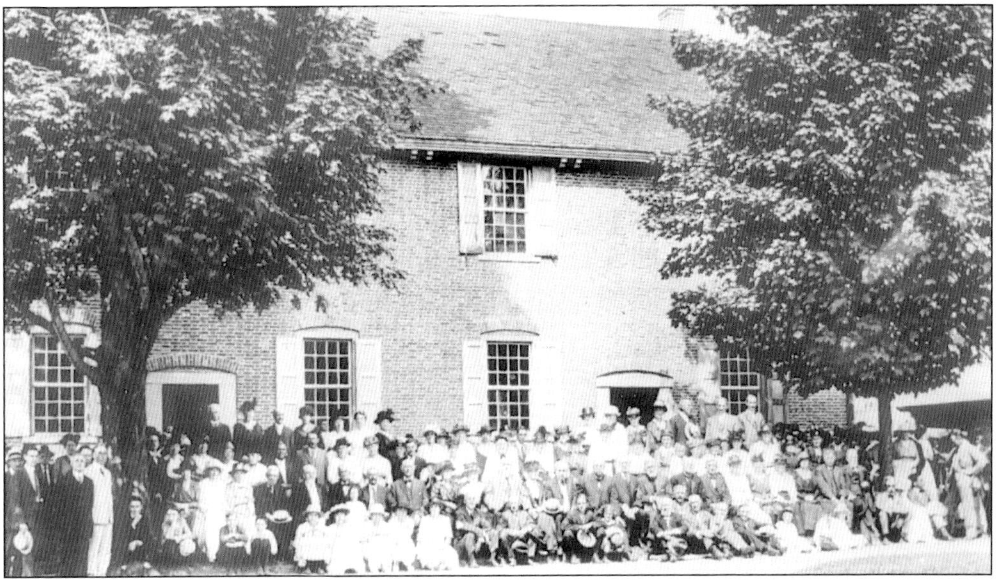

Nine Partners–Brick Meetinghouse. By 1750, Long Islanders and New England Quakers had settled Mechanic along present-day NYS Route 343. Weekly and monthly meetings in this second meetinghouse, built *c.* 1780, brought all together until a division in thought in 1828 separated Elias Hicks's followers ("Hicksites") from Orthodox Friends. This led to an amicable division of property with the brick meetinghouse going to the Hicksites and Orthodox Quakers building nearby. Members of the Brick Meeting are shown at a late-19th-century gathering. (DG.)

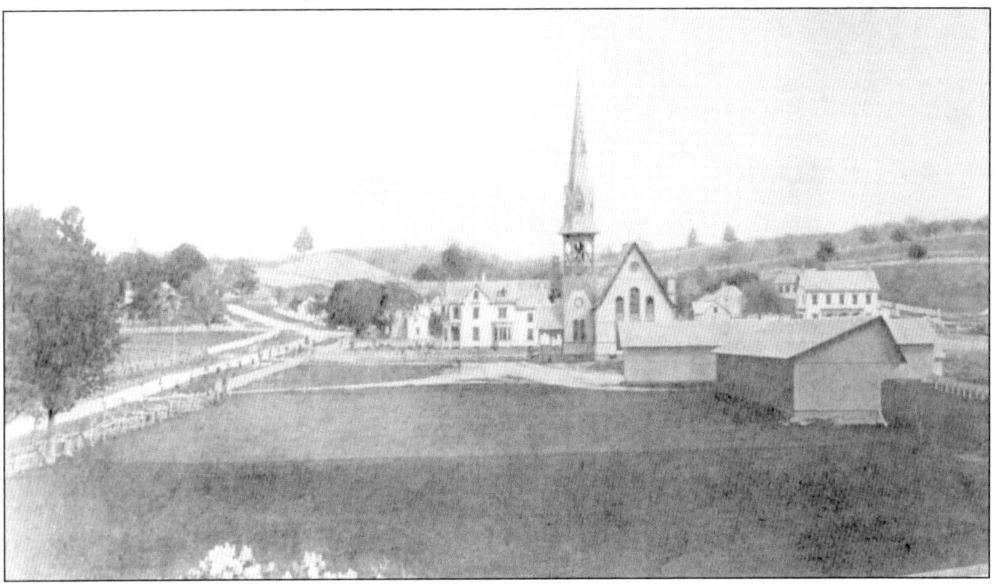

The Old Reformed Church at Four Corners. Thiss mid-19th century photograph shows the Reformed church that formerly marked the center of Four Corners. Although this congregation long ago moved, church steeples along the Dover and Sharon branches of the Dutchess Turnpike were settlement beacons. The Routes 82 and 44 traffic light and the monument at County Road 111 identify today's neighborhood, now within Millbrook Village where Lyall Memorial Federated and Grace Churches serve Protestants and St. Joseph's ministers to Catholics. (DCHS.)

ST. PETER'S EPISCOPAL CHURCH, LITHGOW. Its 1801 charter marks St. Peter's as among New York's earliest Episcopal congregations. Its second building is a charming Victorian chapel that was erected in 1880 after a fire claimed the first building. It is the heart of a lively, diverse community of old families and Washington-loving weekenders meeting at Deep Hollow Road. The hamlet's name derives, like that of a nearby 18th-century estate, from Linlithgow, a Johnstone family seat in Scotland. Grace Church in Millbrook, which was formed in the 1860s, was a mission church of St. Peter's. (SB.)

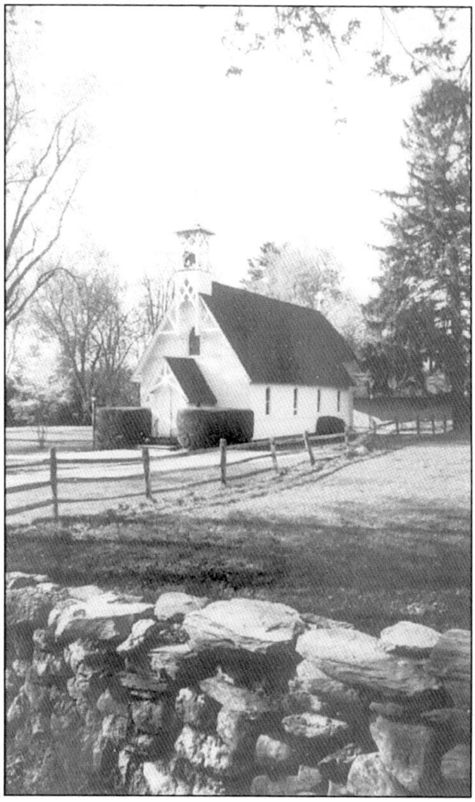

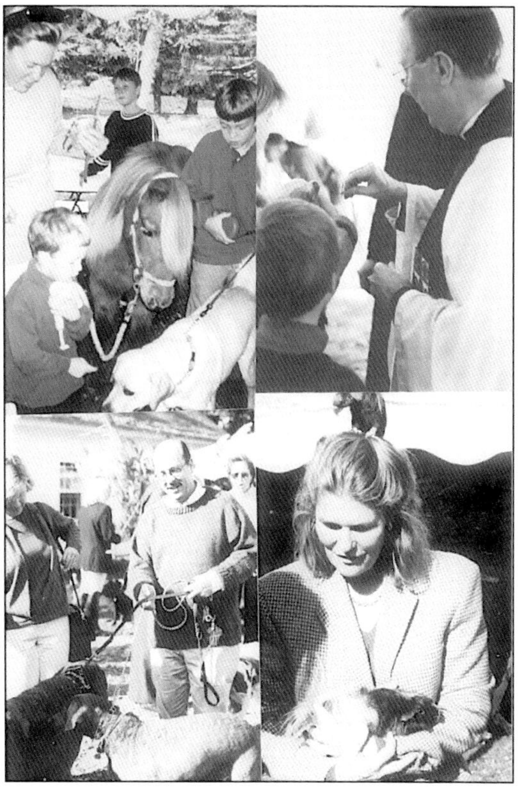

THE BLESSING OF THE ANIMALS. Two annual events bring the members of St. Peter's together—fall leaf raking and a service to bless animals. Rev. Edward Johnston welcomes parish friends, families, and pets to this joyous service. It is a delightful event shared by cats, dogs, hamsters, parakeets, ponies, sheep, or any creature loved by a household. The animals are a well-behaved lot, sometimes less boisterous than the children recruited for the fall leaf raking. (DNG.)

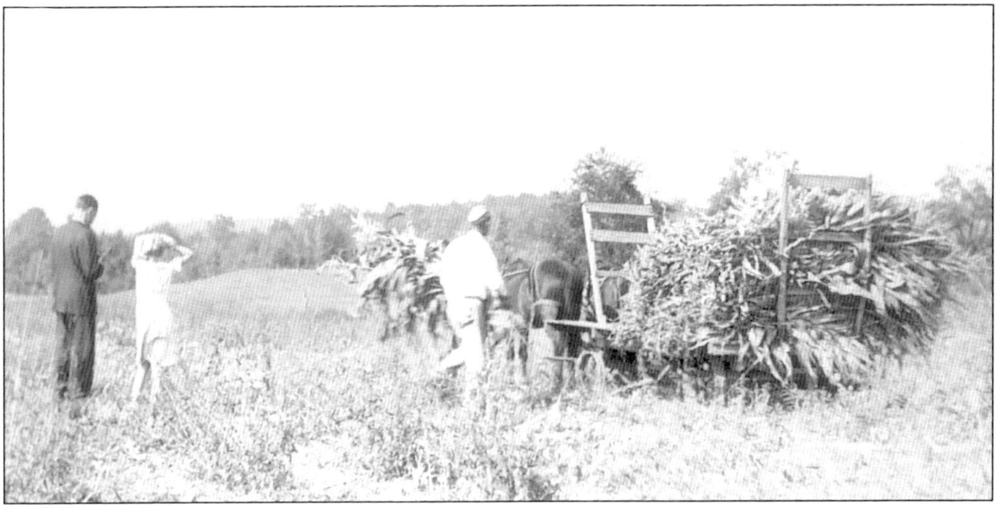

THE VAN TASSELL FARM. Farmers have a commitment to hard work, whether the farm is 100 or 1,000 acres. The adjoining Van Tassell and Dyson farms on Verbank Road represent devotion to land and family values. Stock broker Wilbur Fisk Van Tassell bought the dairy farm in the 1920s and was experientially trained by neighbors. Three generations shared home and work, including grandchildren Henry, Wilbur Fisk, Marian, and Margaret Van Tassell (Fettes), who watches with Uncle Charles as grandfather harvests corn for cattle feed in this photograph taken in the fall of 1936. (MB/MF.)

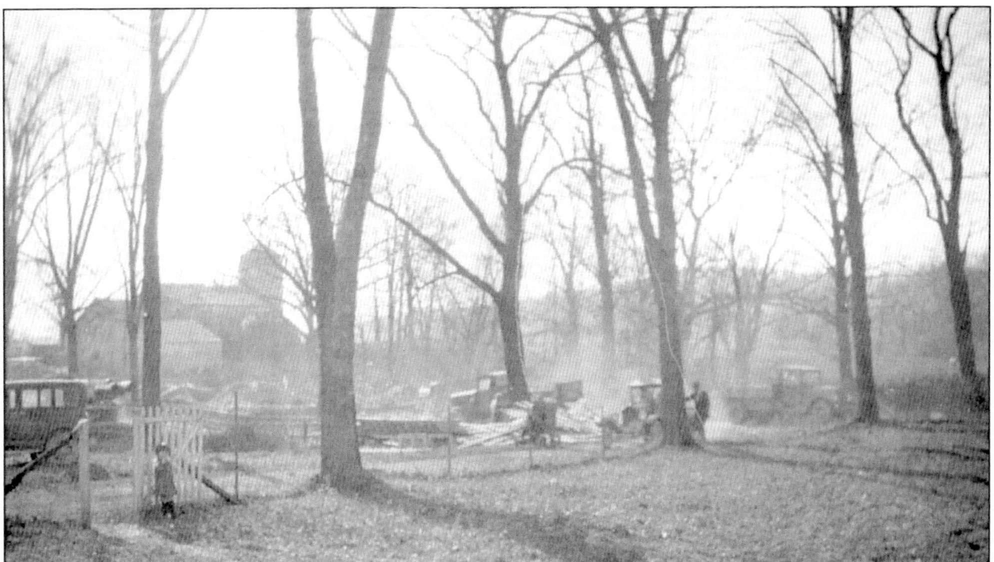

THE BENHAM FARM MEETS NYS ROUTE 82. Before construction began on the Taconic State Parkway, meandering unpaved lanes connected outlying farms, hamlets, and post offices, serving as the only central county roadways. Plans for state and municipal road improvement projects by 1926 followed existing roads when feasible, and paved farm fields when necessary, to construct NYS Route 82, connecting central Dutchess with east–west highways. The Shunpike, amazingly, remained untouched by progress. A small member of Stanley Benham's family watched a new bridge between Stanford and Washington take form as daily farm chores continued unabated. (SB/SSB.)

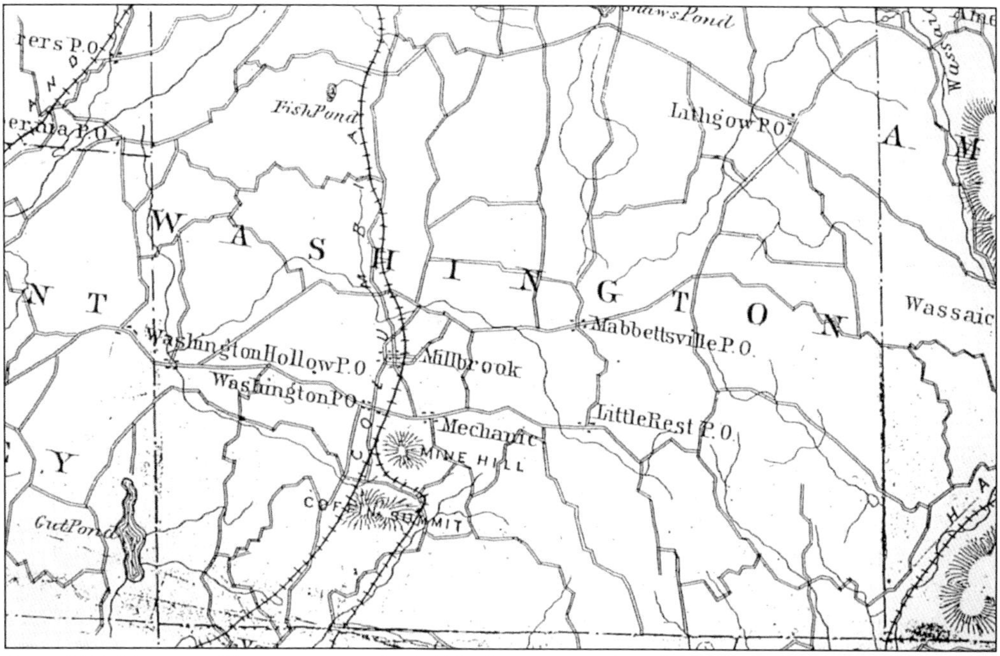

AN 1876 MAP OF WASHINGTON. By 1876, the proposed path of the Dutchess & Columbia Railroad was a *fait accompli.* The town map shows the line going past the county home, crossing the Dover branch of the turnpike and passing directly through a new community identified as Millbrook, on the way north to Columbia County. Other maps call the unincorporated hamlet Millbrook Station. Harts Village, no longer shown on the map, has been displaced as the commercial center. (DCHS.)

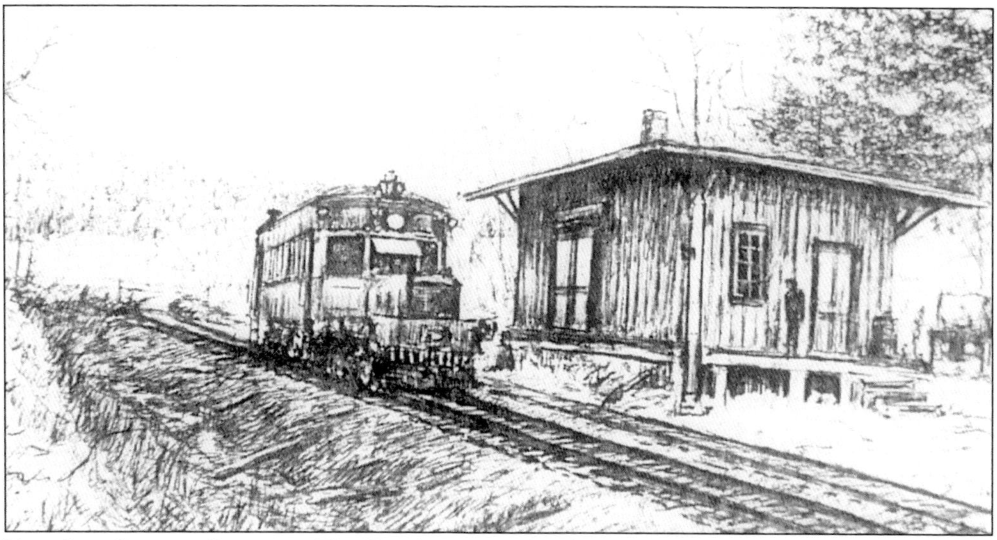

THE OAK SUMMIT STATION. The Dutchess & Columbia Railroad signaled great physical and economic change for many hamlets after 1869. It would turn Millbrook Station into a town center and ease travel to and from the smallest whistle stop. A few years earlier, in 1863, Oak Summit, south of the village, had been designated by the New York state legislature as the site for a county poor farm to shelter the needy. Retired railroader Victor Westman's drawing shows the tiny station where farm visitors could wait for a train to almost anywhere. (VGW.)

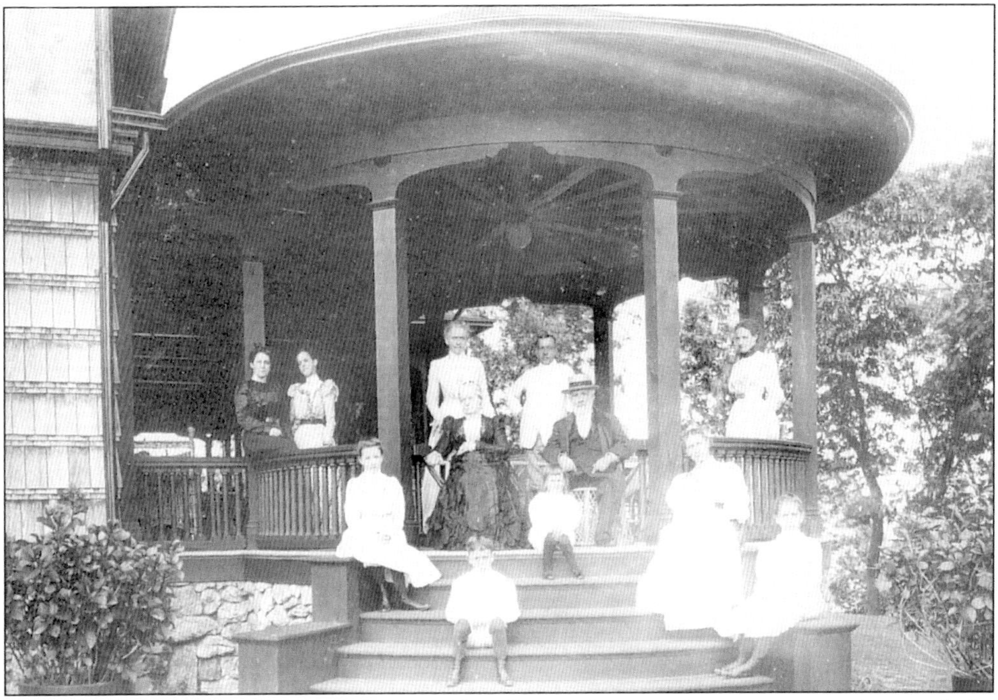

The Wing Family at Sandanona, c. 1890. County historical society materials record the fortunes and daily lives of the Wings, early settlers here. Turn-of-the-century photographs capture social highlights of a closely knit family enjoying Sandanona, the splendid 19th-century John Wing estate built on the site of the Orthodox Quaker Meeting. Noted for its elegant gardens and hospitality, it was simply home to Wing children. Sandanona is also the name given a nearby gentlemen's hunting preserve, the oldest in the United States. (DCHS.)

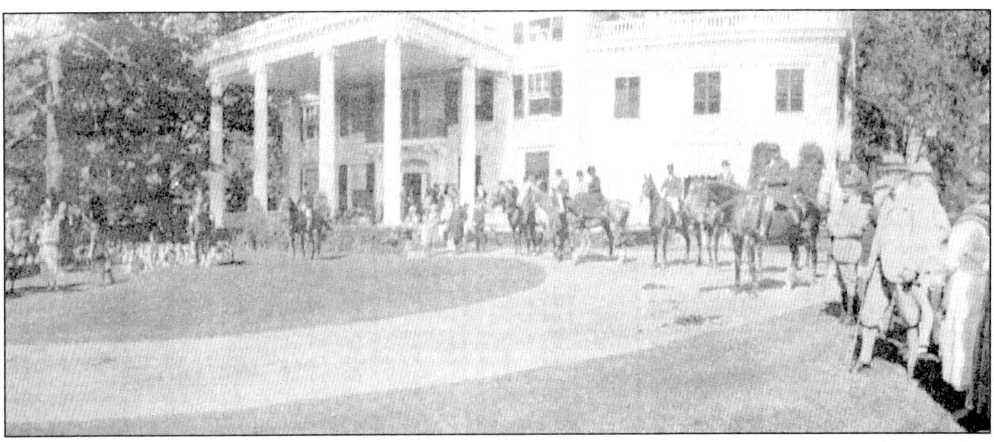

A Hunt Meet at Thorndale, Early 1900s. Descendants of early Thorne settlers in the patent established their commitment to the town and ability to gather wealth long before the railroad arrived. By 1850, Jonathan Thorne had turned the farm into a year-round residence. Son Samuel and grandson Edwin concentrated on improving cattle and race horse breeding stock and made the house and gardens a showplace. Thorndale remains a treat for its fortunate visitors and for passers-by. Horse lovers still gather there. (DCHS.)

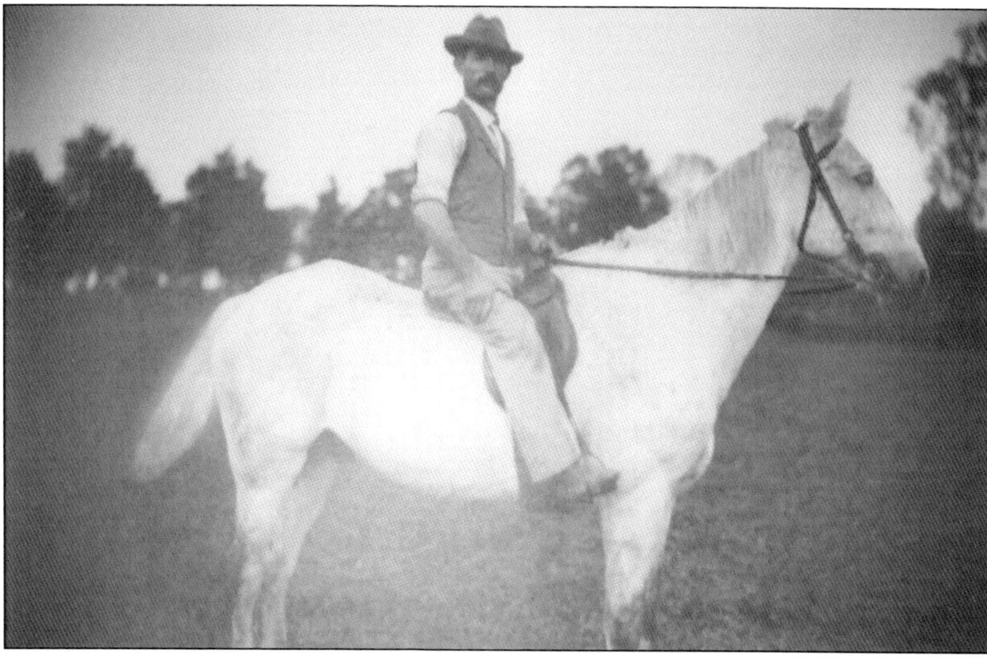

JAMES MURPHY, ESTATE SUPERINTENDENT. Murphy came to Millbrook at the end of the 19th century. Experience in overseeing farms combined with skill in handling horses made him a valued employee of the Dietrich family, owners of Daheim, north of Millbrook. As large estates proliferated in the town, finding skilled staff locally to handle household and farm tasks became a challenge to owners whose lives were taken up with far-flung business enterprises. Unlike their experience elsewhere, Irish immigrants found welcome in the community. (MM.)

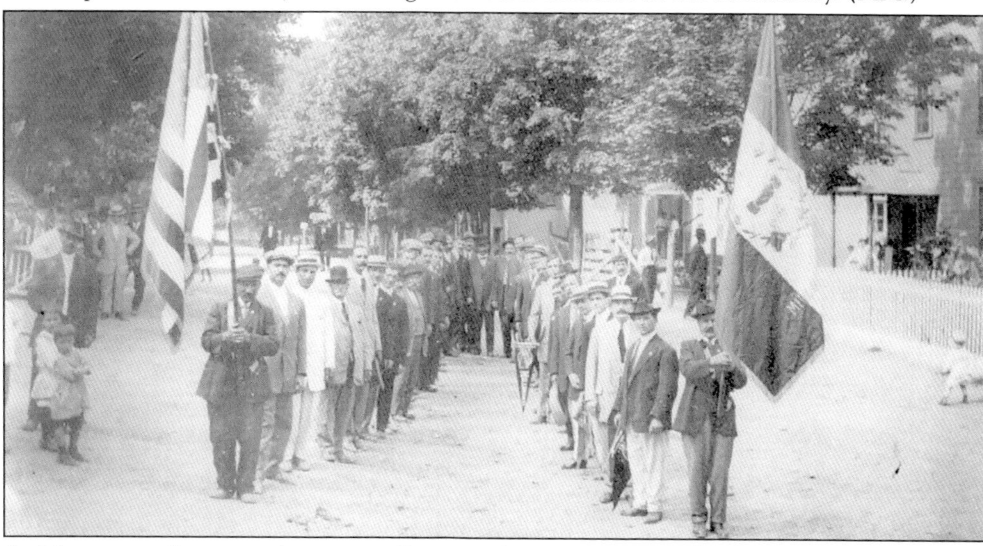

A MILLBROOK ITALIAN AMERICAN SOCIETY PARADE, 1930. The homogeneous nature of the town's population began to change with the railroad and the building of many estates. Irish immigrants were joined by Italians, whose building skills created most of the walls that distinguish the architecture here. They also were talented gardeners and sheep handlers. Velletris, Setaros, Sepes, Rotunnos, and other families used their talents to build an important place in local society and increase their own fortunes. (DGTH.)

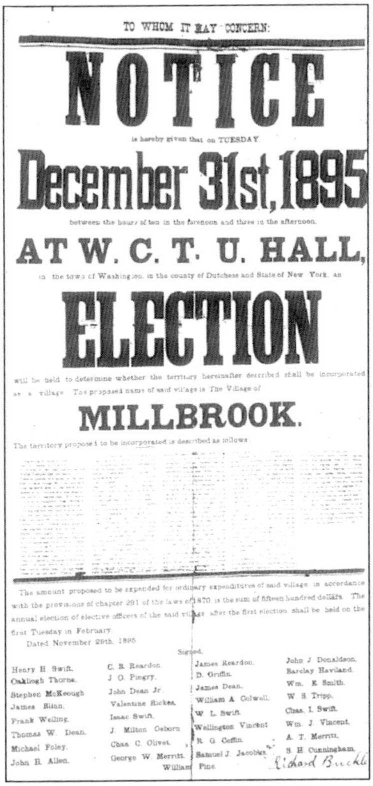

TO WHOM IT MAY CONCERN:

NOTICE

is hereby given that on TUESDAY

December 31st, 1895

between the hours of ten in the forenoon and three in the afternoon.

AT W. C. T. U. HALL,

in the town of Washington, in the county of Dutchess and State of New York, an

ELECTION

will be held to determine whether the territory hereinafter described shall be incorporated as a village. The proposed name of said village is The Village of

MILLBROOK.

The territory proposed to be incorporated is described as follows

[illegible]

The amount proposed to be expended for ordinary expenditures of said village in accordance with the provisions of chapter 291 of the laws of 1870 is the sum of fifteen hundred dollars. The annual election of elective officers of the said village after the first election shall be held on the first Tuesday in February.

Dated November 29th, 1895

Signed,

Henry H. Swift, Oakleigh Thorne, Stephen McKeough, James Binn, Frank Welling, Thomas W. Dean, Michael Foley, John H. Allen, C. B. Reardon, J. O. Pingry, John Dean Jr., Valentine Rickes, Isaac Swift, J. Milton Osborn, Chas. C. Olivet, George W. Merritt, William Pine, James Reardon, D. Griffin, James Dean, William A. Colwell, W. L. Swift, Wellington Vincent, R. G. Coffin, Samuel J. Jacobus, John J. Donaldson, Barclay Haviland, Wm. E. Smith, W. S. Tripp, Chas. I. Swift, Wm. J. Vincent, A. T. Merritt, S. H. Cunningham, Richard Buckle

VILLAGE REFERENDUM NOTICE, 1895. The Women's Christian Temperance Union Hall was the venue, and the time was New Year's Eve 1895. Hamlet residents were invited to an election to decide if the territory described in detail should become an incorporated village with a proposed budget of $1,500. One assumes the voters were all men, as women did not yet have the right to vote. Voters got another chance in February, 1896 to elect a village board of trustees. Its first president was Oakleigh Thorne. (DGTH.)

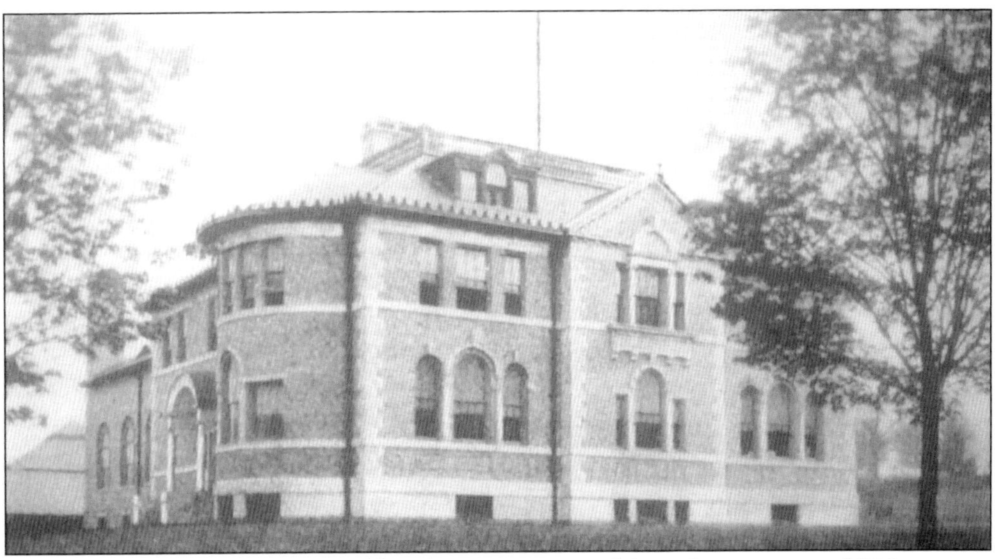

THE THORNE BUILDING, 1895. Millbrook Station emerged from the strategies of 19th-century industrialist and entrepreneur George Hunter Brown, who brought the Dutchess & Columbia Railroad here. The station became the center of a new hamlet named for Brown's nearby estate. The growing community needed schools and services. Village incorporation, immutable boundaries, and government came in 1895 as a side effect of Oakleigh Thorne's gift of a school and community center. The building could only be received by a bonafide municipality. Millbrook Village was formed. (VV.)

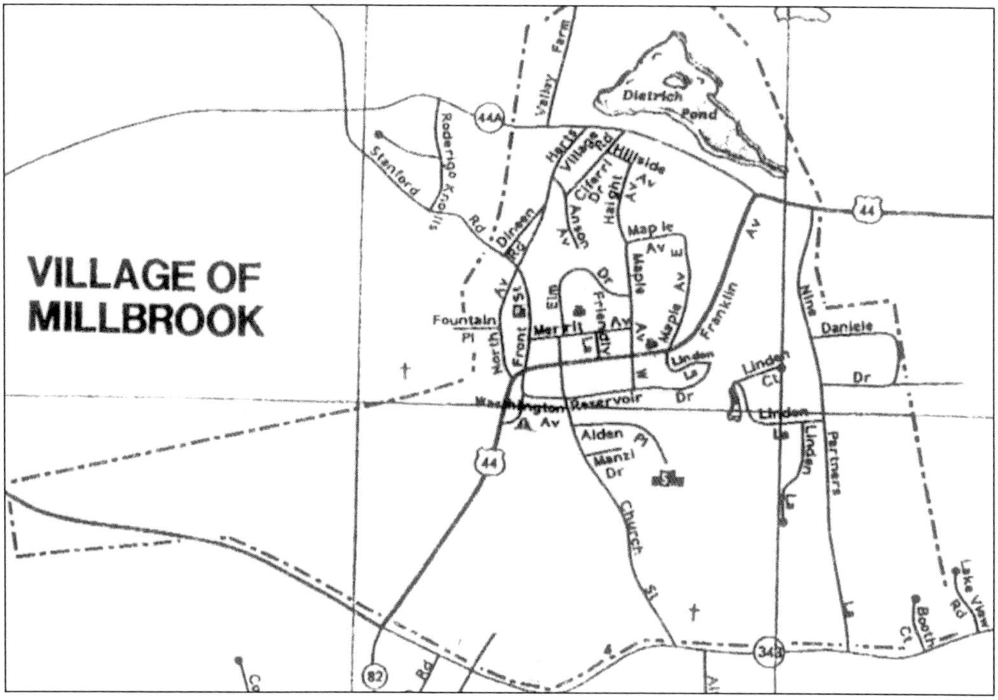

A Map of the Millbrook Village Area. A recent map of the village shows the unique outlines drawn in 1895 to define the municipality. By then, growth in population and commerce had already engulfed nearby hamlets. The scale and spaces surrounding residences, businesses, and public institutions around the village core along Franklin Avenue testify to the influence of major landowners—the Thornes, Flaglers, Wings, and Dietrichs, whose properties completely encircled the new municipality, confining growth within lines drawn to their liking and effectively controlling village expansion. (DCHS.)

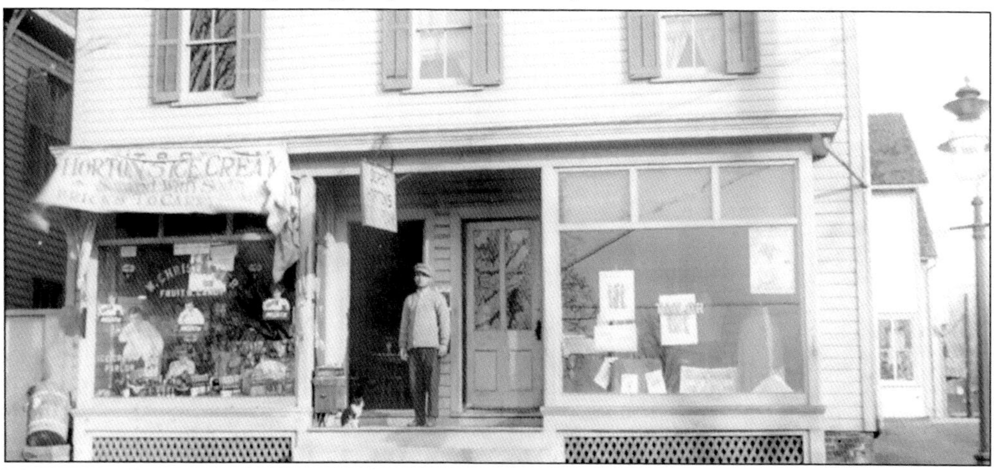

Millbrook Commerce. Areas near the railroad station saw growing commerce. Residents working at mills, estates, or in small hotels and boardinghouses found Millbrook convenient for business. In 1891, the Bank of Millbrook moved into the former offices of railroad builders. General stores gave way to specialty emporia and services. One of two shops in the Monfort Building specialized in foods needing refrigeration—oysters and ice cream. The other did tailoring and sold clothing. Millbrook is still the favorite shopping center for central Dutchess. (DGTH.)

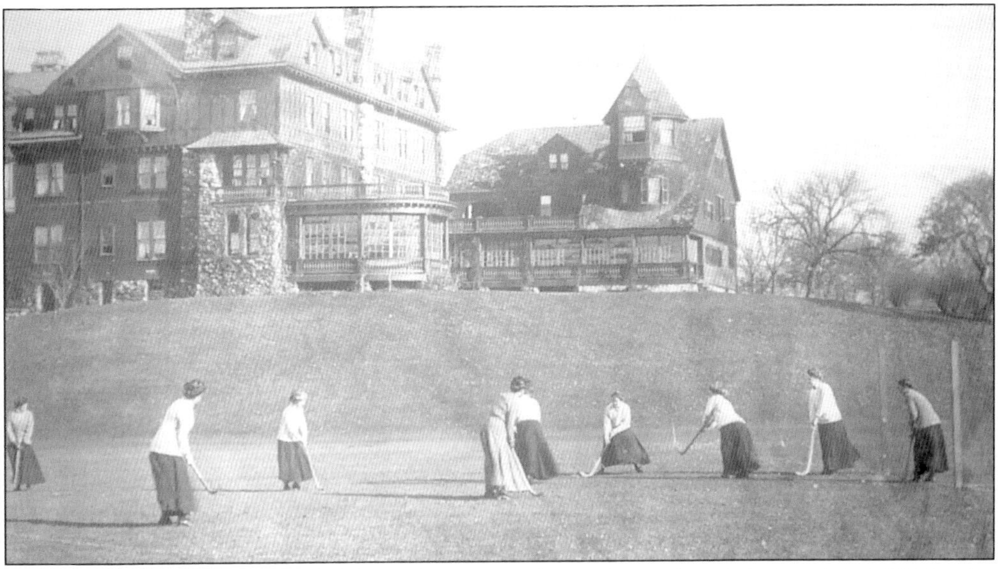

Halcyon Hall. Halcyon Hall, Henry James Davidson's luxury hotel designed in 1893 by the architects of Mohonk Mountain House, provided guests with every comfort: fine cuisine, sports, and the music of a Russian orchestra. However, it survived less than a decade. In 1907, May Friend Bennett saw the structure as ideal for her girls school. Bennett School, a prestigious finishing school, later became a junior college, which closed in the 1970s. Young ladies learned to hold up their end of a fierce field hockey game as well as a literary discussion. (ML.)

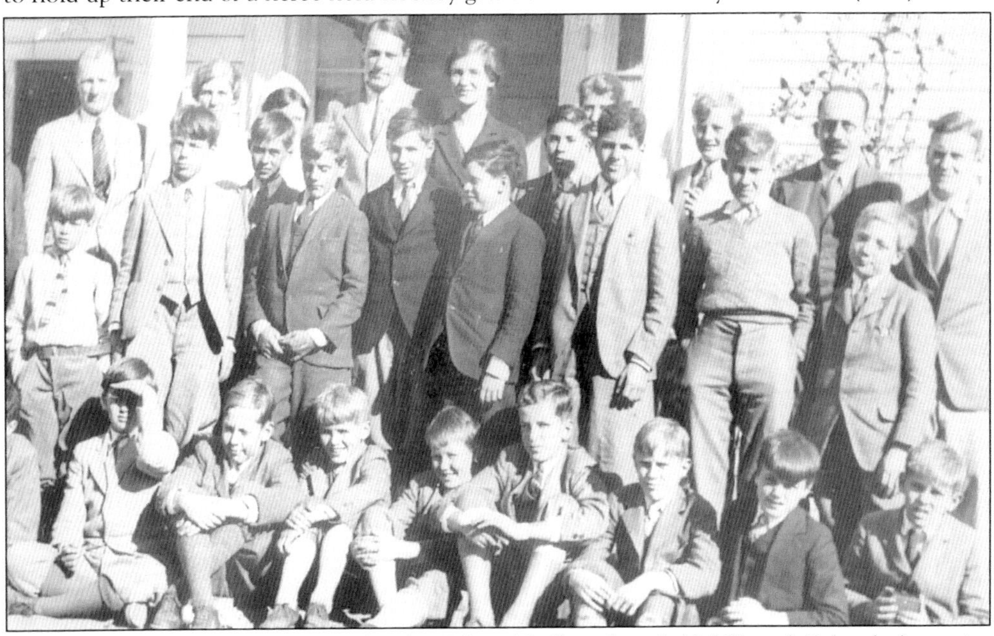

Millbrook School. In 1931, shortly after Edward Pulling founded Millbrook School, the entire enrollment of the private boys-only school fit into one snapshot. Despite advocacy of Hyde Park as a site by Gov. Franklin D. Roosevelt, Pulling's dream of a fine institution modeled on English preparatory schools was realized in the hills near Millbrook. It has been coeducational since 1971. With a current enrollment of 230, the school prides itself on producing well-rounded, academically superior students ready for life's challenges. (MS.)

The Boys and Men of the Wing Family. Those born around the turn of the 19th century witnessed incredible life-changing events. Wing boys Morgan, Jack, Bryce, and Stuart, nourished by family affection, experienced a childhood enriched by pet dogs and imaginary battles in Sandanona's fields. The advantages of wealth that provided the best of academic and physical training also prepared them for real wars that they faced as men. These touching photographs compare idyllic imaginary battles with the reality of their service in WWI. (DCHS.)

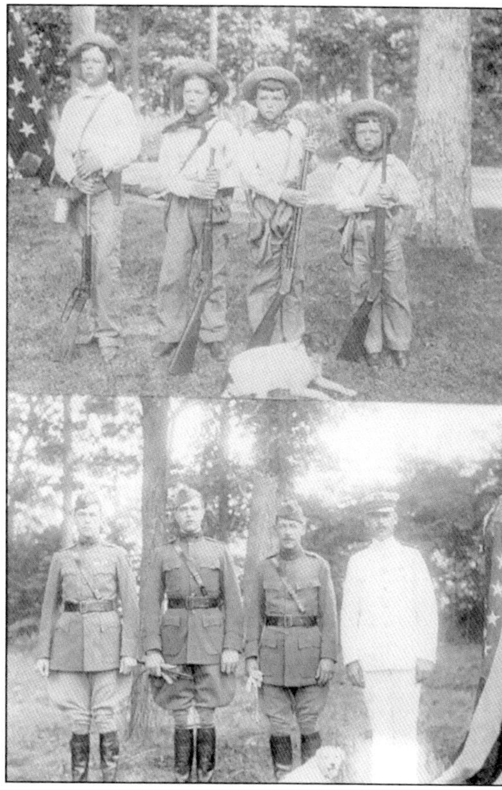

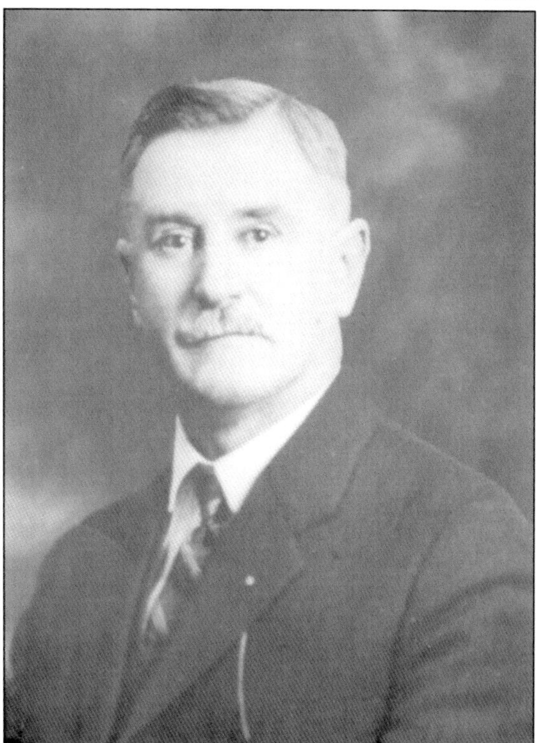

Supervisor Sidney Benham. By the 1920s, even rural towns like Washington were seeing the impacts of national and local economic changes. These town were also experiencing pressures from an increasingly diverse and vocal electorate. Those elected to public office could find themselves overwhelmed by complex political, legal, civil, financial, and social issues. Farmer Sidney Benham's political skills successfully led Washington through an era of major road building from 1922 to 1927 and again through the Depression years of 1934 to 1937. (SB/SSB.)

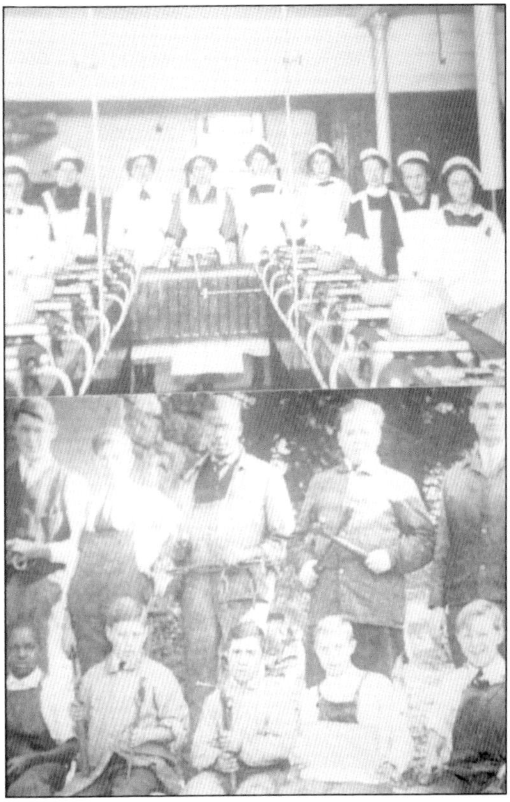

IRONWORKING AND HOME ECONOMICS AT MILLBROOK MEMORIAL SCHOOL. The memorial to Jonathan and Lydia Thorne prepared students for a different world than ours, but exceeded the expectations for early-1900s working classes, academically and vocationally. Iron and woodworking classes served young men seeking work on the estates or with local businesses. State-of-the-art kitchen and sewing facilities taught village girls the lifelong tasks they could expect to handle at home or "in service." No male would be caught attending home economics classes until the 1960s. (DGTH.)

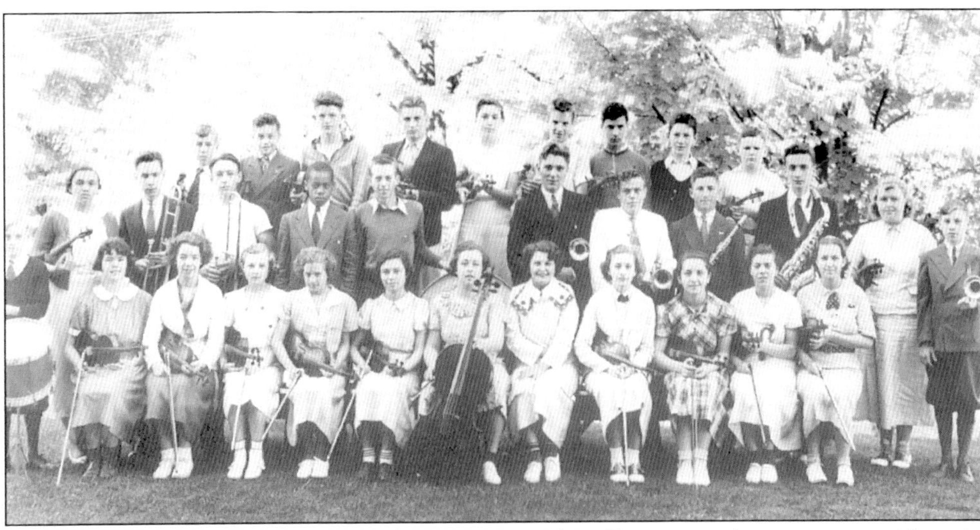

THE MILLBROOK MEMORIAL SCHOOL ORCHESTRA, 1930S. Even as reading, writing, arithmetic, and traditional vocational education continued to be seen as important foundations of curriculum, young people were becoming exposed to new cultural avenues. Millbrook Memorial School's music program provided both girls and boys an opportunity to learn an instrument and perform ensemble music. The arts were accepted as essential elements of a publicly supported education. (DGTH.)

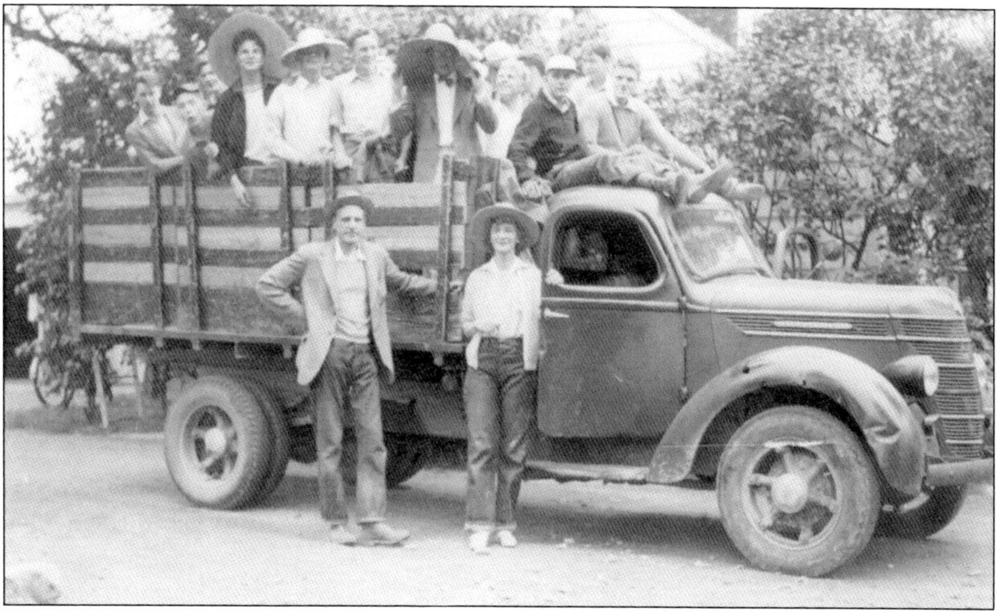

A Millbrook School Trip, 1942. In this photograph taken during WWII, boys from Millbrook School—accompanied by headmaster Pulling and his wife, Lucy—prepare for a school trip in a truck. A curriculum already rich in the arts was enhanced by a program of community service and stewardship of the natural world, which among other results produced a campus vegetable garden and trained boys as airplane spotters. While nearby public school students sought personal expression in the arts, these youngsters found service to others rewarding. (MS.)

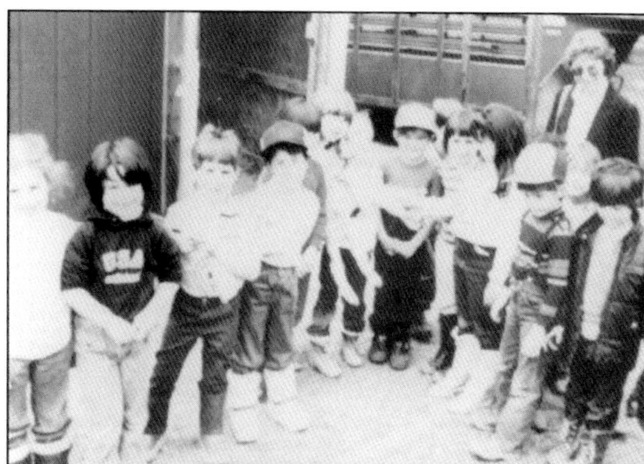

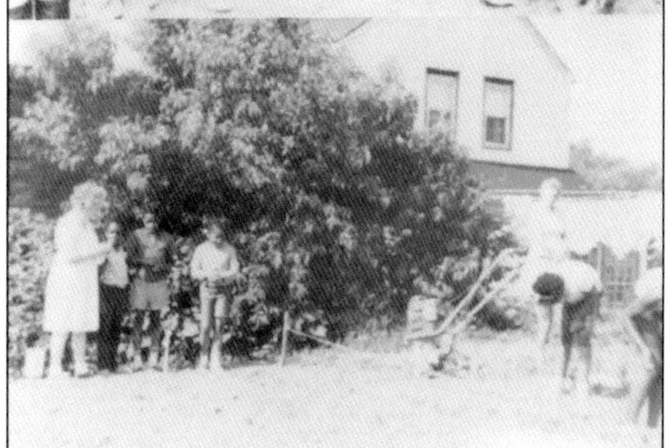

School Trips as Kids' Vacations. For children, school is work. A day out of the classroom, even if it involves hands-on education, is like a vacation. John Kading's sheep farm on Route 44 hosted elementary school students who thrill to handling and feeding lambs and learning about how wool becomes a sweater. Susan Van Tassell's third graders from Greer School in 1966 were just as enthusiastic about a day spent learning to plant a garden on the Van Tassell farm. (JK/MB.)

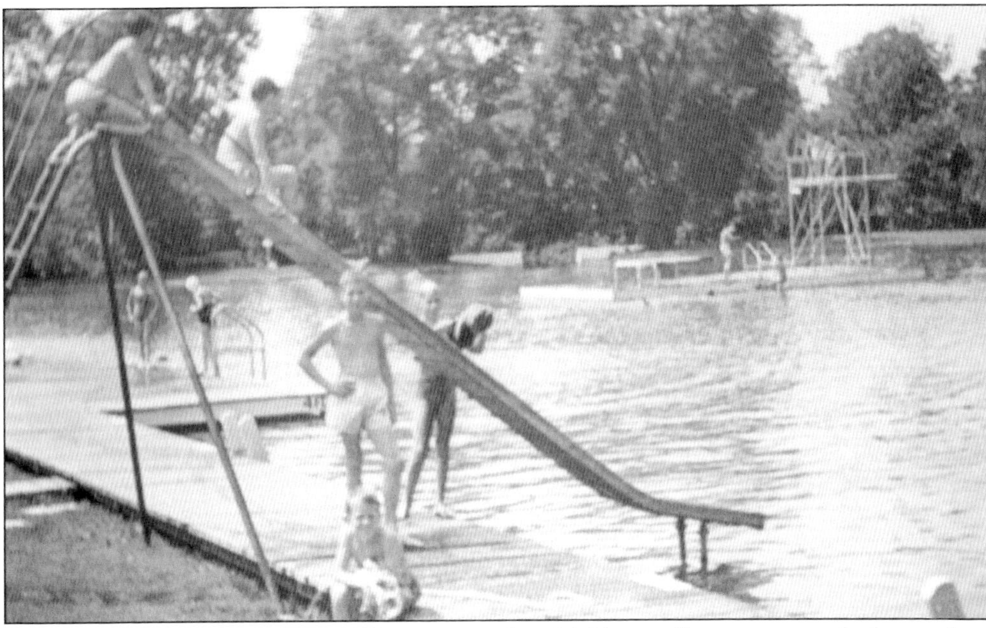

The Washington Town Pool. The town pool in Mabbettsville was once a feeder creek to the Shaw and Mill Brooks—summer territory of boys in birthday suits. The surrounding former farmland has become parkland. The creek is dammed and divided into safe beach areas for tots, waders, and swimmers. After completing swimming lessons, diving and sliding boards attract both boys and girls while mothers watch from the relative safety of picnic benches, waiting for the next request for food from the concession stand. (DGTH.)

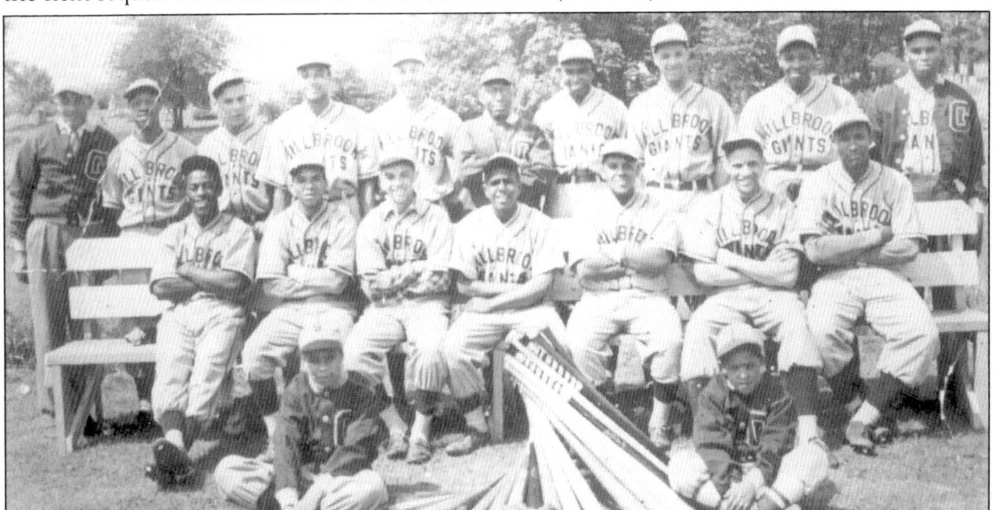

The Millbrook Giants. In the 1930s and 1940s, local semiprofessional teams organized under the National Baseball Congress. The Millbrook Giants practiced on an Elm Street lot and played Sunday games in the Tri County League from Connecticut and Massachusetts to upstate New York. Managed and sponsored by Ernest Duncan Sr., the team core represented friends and relatives like Preston, Monroe, and Austin Bennett. Duncan also recruited Poughkeepsie athletes Walter Patrice and Bob Magill, talented additions. WWII interrupted play, and the league closed in the 1950s. (MJB.)

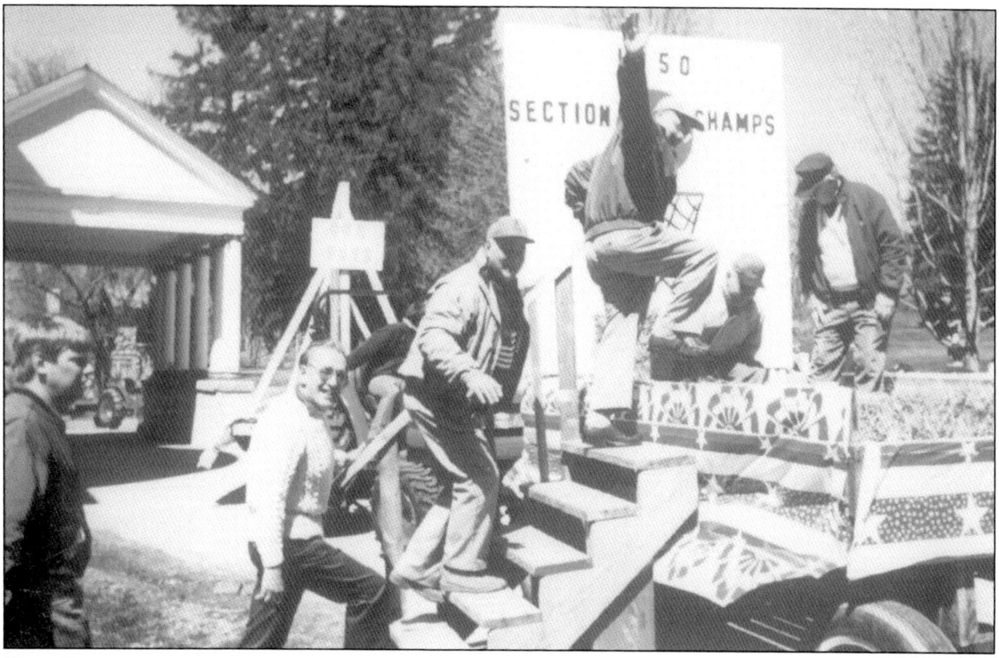

The Basketball Champions of 1950 in 1999. When Millbrook High School basketball players won a state championship in 1999, it was the signal for a community parade and party. Mayor Ciferri presented them with the key to the village and legislator Margaret Fettes brought commendations from the county. No one was happier for the kids, though, than Brian Hicks and the other members of the 1950 team, who had also brought home a championship in their time. Sports do indeed bring a community together. (JK.)

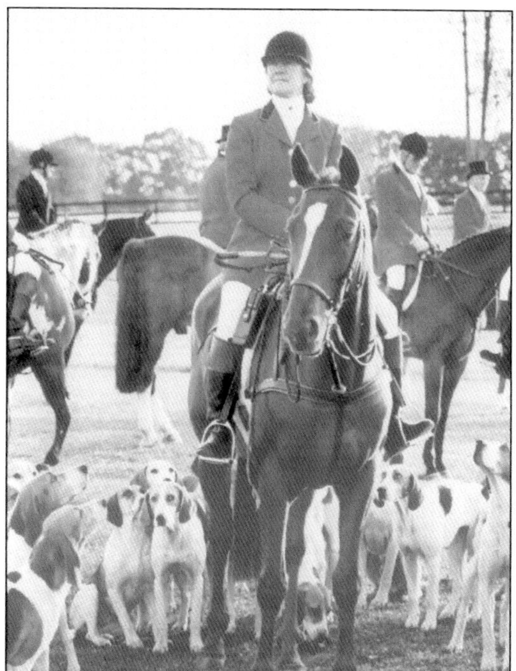

Betsy Park, Huntsman. Washington's vast unfenced farm estates suited the conventions of English fox hunting to perfection. In 1907, Charles C. Marshall and Middleton O'Malley Knott, Bennett Riding Master, introduced the sport here. Within two years, Millbrook Hunt was firmly established by Master Oakleigh Thorne. Over the years, both men and women have been selected for leadership. The Chadwells—Elias followed by his son, Earl—served as Huntsmen from 1928 to 1977. Since 1978, Betsy Park has held that post. Farnham Collins, Dick Verilli and Nancy Stahl are joint Masters. (MH/NS.)

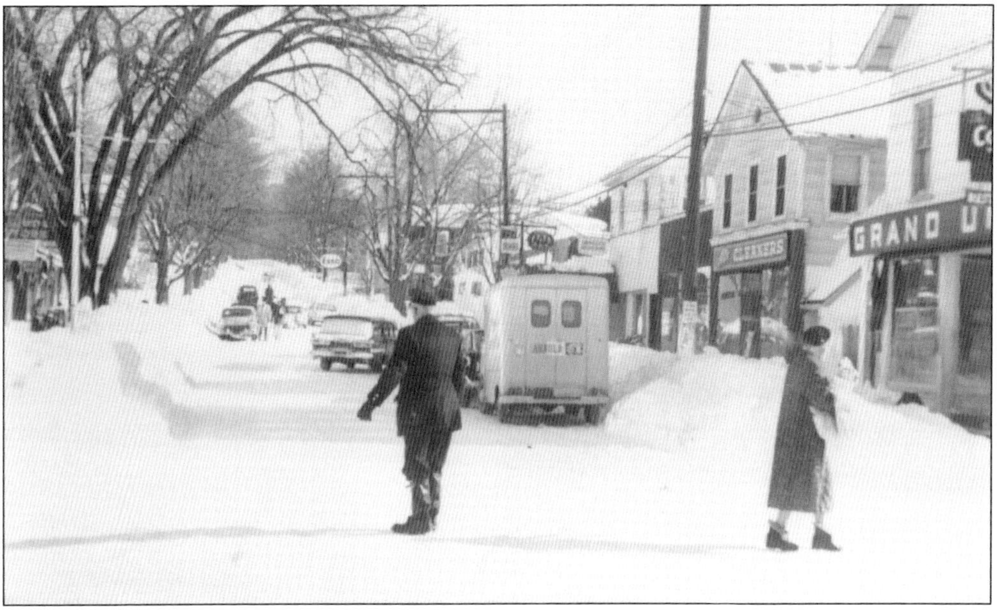

EARL CUNNINGHAM, VILLAGE POLICEMAN. Millbrook has had its own police force since 1897, when the trustees hired Charles Duncan at $1.50 per day to keep the peace seven days a week. Earl Cunningham followed in that tradition of duty first. His familiar face, directing traffic and helping ladies get across the street with groceries from the old Grand Union made him a respected member of the community. (JK.)

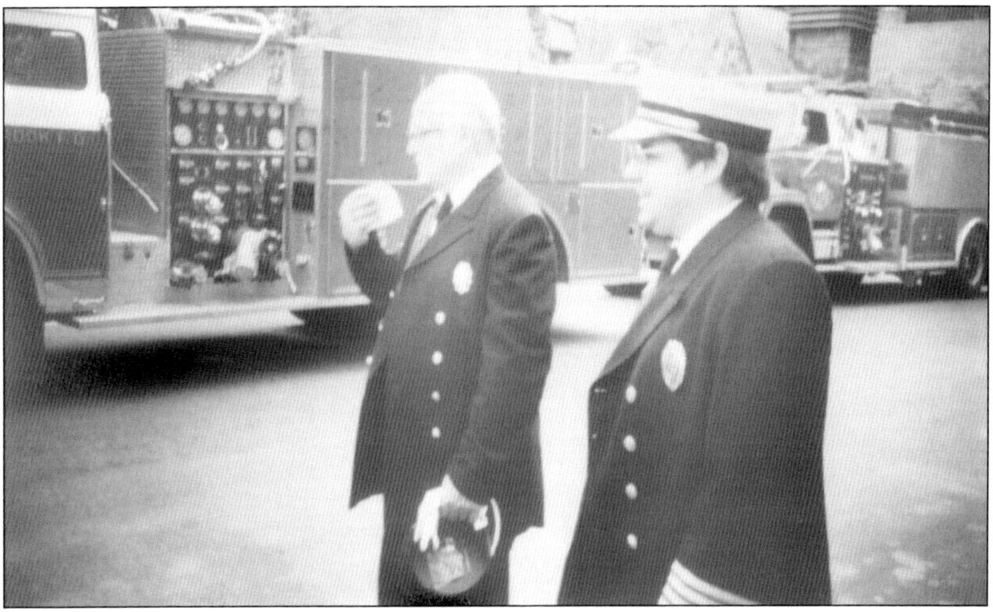

MILLBROOK FIREMEN. Before 1916, bucket brigades sufficed, but a major fire that year and a limited water source led to the development of not only a better equipped fire department, but also a community water system. In this 1960s photograph, volunteers Mickey Prisco and Mike Massarone proudly view the new fire truck. As in all community institutions these days, volunteers at the station on the green are prized, thanked by community support at parades and fundraising events. (JK.)

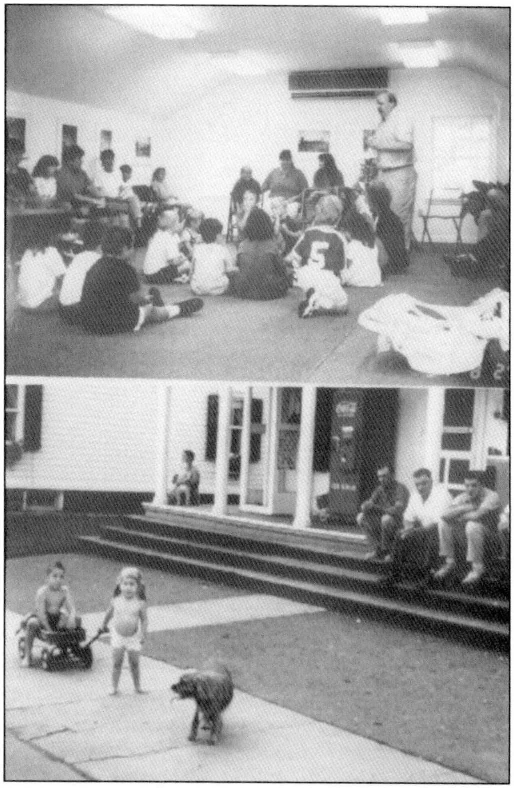

The Meyer and Kading Stores. Certain private enterprises become community institutions. In the 1950s, John Kading's Corner News Store housed family quarters upstairs and the business downstairs. Here one could pick up local papers, the *Times* and the latest local gossip from front porch chats with John. Kading's also nurtured Scott and Allison Meyer's dream bookstore, Merritt's, in its infancy. Merritt's newest quarters are a place where annual kindergarten socials coexist comfortably with book signings by world-renowned lights of the literary world. (JK/SM.)

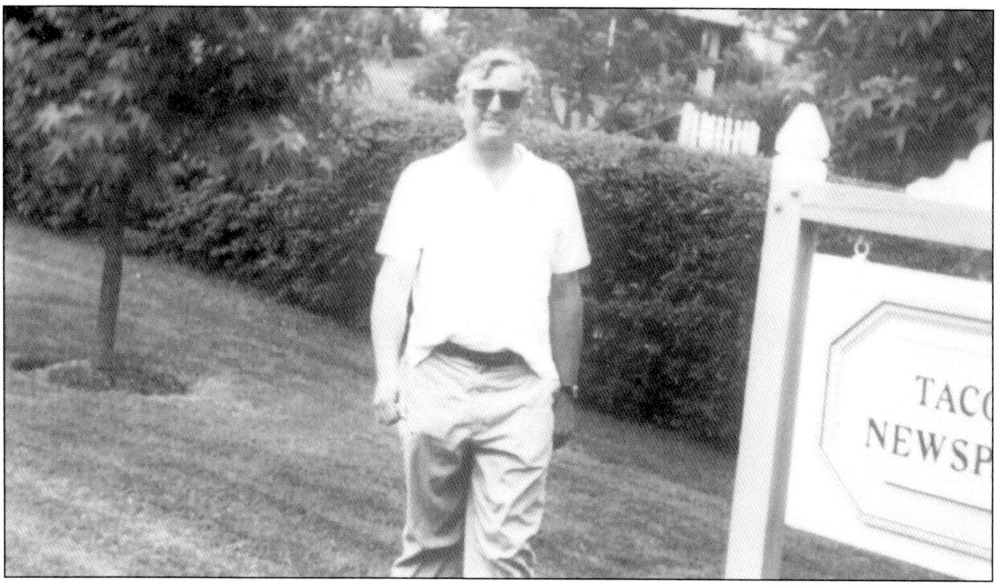

The Town Crier. Those who keep us informed about town issues, local institutions and our neighbors' successes or tribulations have an important role in community building. In this era of electronic communications, local papers are still the most complete source of small town news. The *Millbrook Roundtable* began in the 19th century. Hamilton and Helen Meserve bought the paper and consolidated several weeklies under the banner of the *Taconic Press* to become crier for several towns. (JK.)

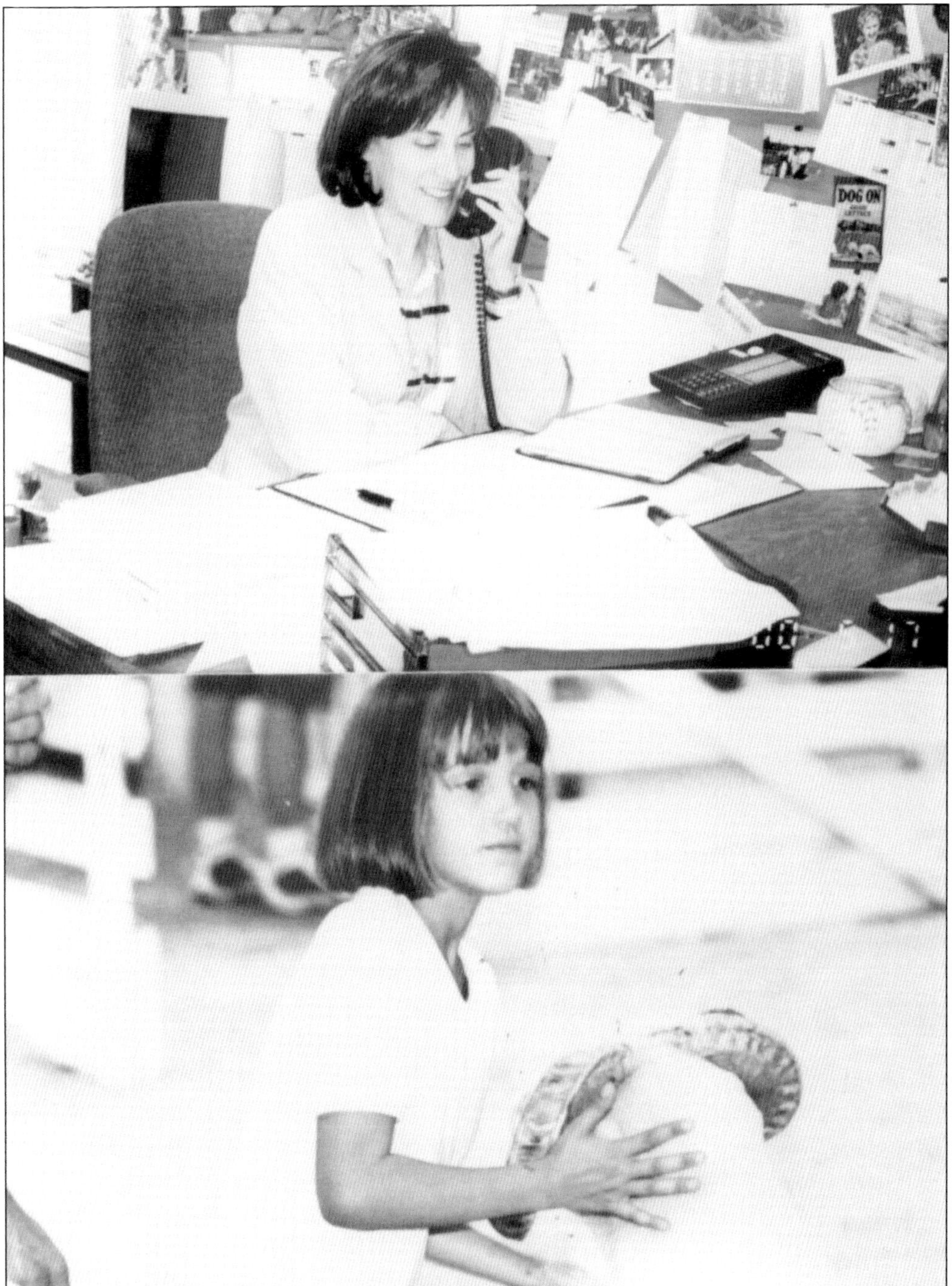

COOPERATIVE EXTENSION AND 4-H. Cornell Cooperative Extension, a rural presence for more than a century, helps farm families with everything from animal husbandry, crop pest control, and canning to community development. Recent changing agrarian patterns find agents like Judy Schneyer and Dave Teator focusing more on the last, reaching into the broader community. Members of 4-H, such as young Cynthia Kading, care little about all this, as long as their sheep or calf wins a ribbon at the fair. (CE/JK.)

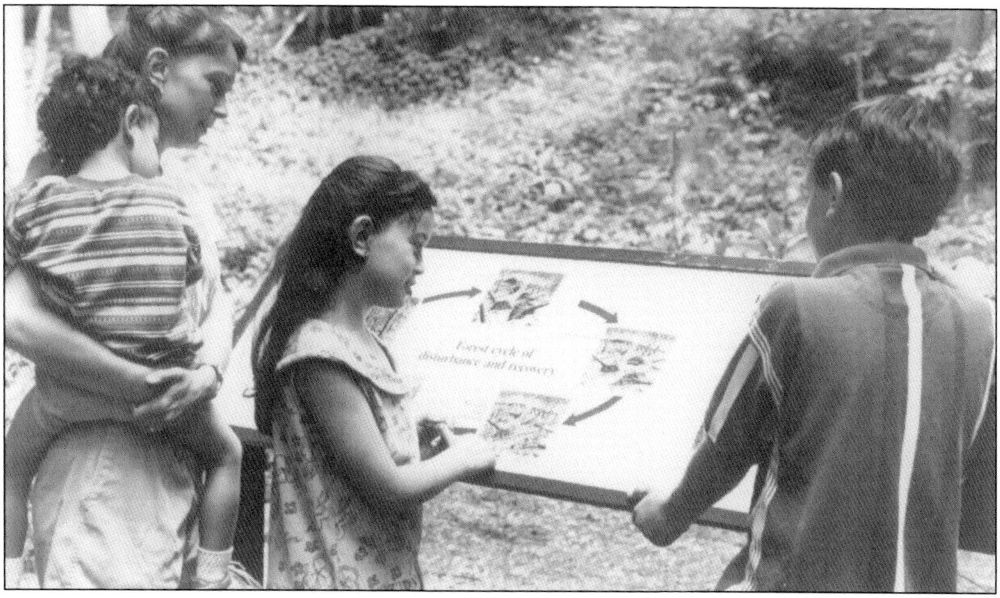

THE FUN IS IN LEARNING. The Institute of Ecosystem Studies makes learning a pleasure. The institute, an internationally recognized research and education facility, is located at the Mary Flagler Cary Arboretum on NYS Route 44A. Visitors enjoy its nature trails, tropical greenhouse, and display gardens, including the Fern Glen, where photographer Peter Klose captured both the beauty of the site and its educational mission. (IES/PK.)

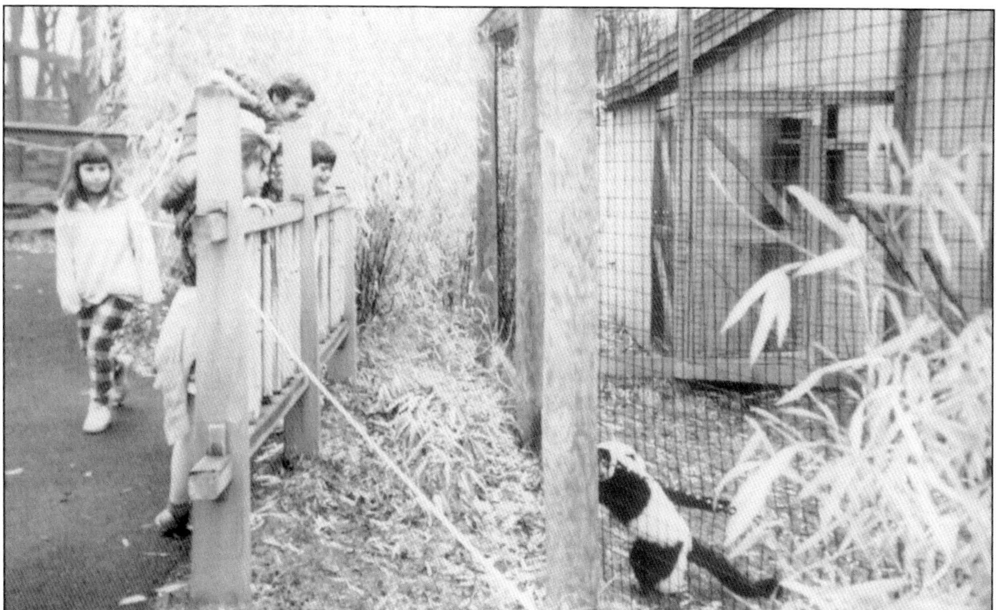

GOING TO THE ZOO. A child's first impression of Trevor Zoo on Millbrook School campus is usually pure delight at the nearness of exotic animals and birds. Otters cavort in the stream, emus peer disdainfully down, and lemurs return visitors' curious stares. This renowned zoo founded by Frank Trevor in 1936 includes seven endangered species among the 50 different species represented in its collection. Animals are cared for, in part, by Millbrook School students as part of the school's community service program. (JG.)

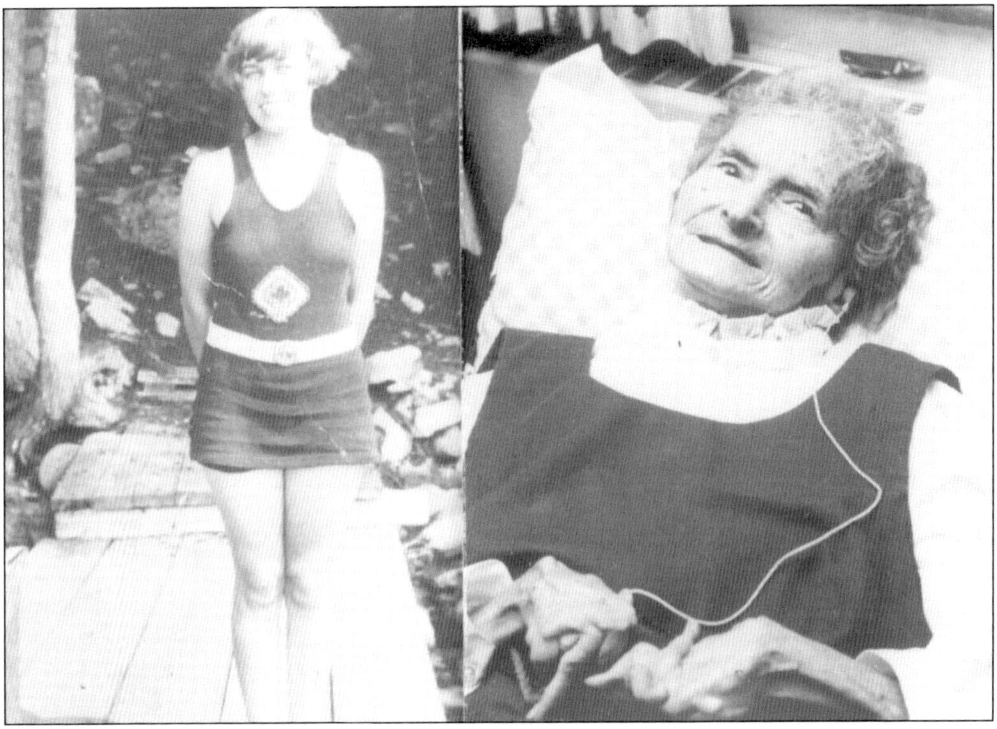

Louise Tompkins, Washington Historian, c. 1920 and 1980. Debilitating arthritis killed her dream of teaching physical education, but it could not destroy her spirit. With advocacy of Sen. Frederick Bontecou's family, she gained a place in the county infirmary, where she built a new life as town historian, organizing young history students through her support network. With fingers fused to hold a pencil, pages blown to the floor for a volunteer to collect, she wrote a weekly column that conveyed her courageous spirit and won a Presidential commendation. (MA/DGTH.)

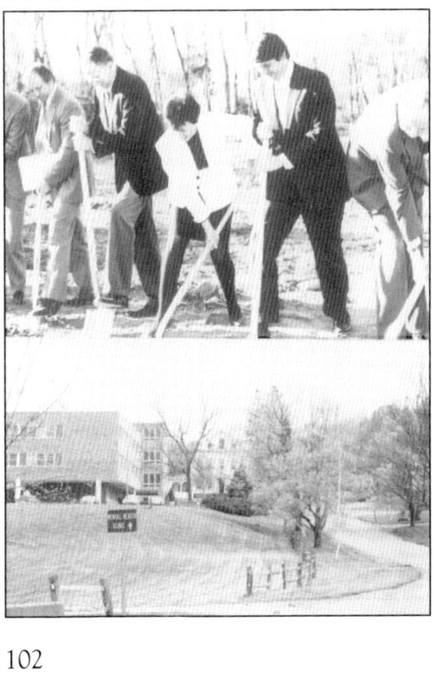

Officials Breaking Ground for Senior Housing. The 1980s saw rising interest in the concerns of seniors. Mayor Michael Murphy, whose great grandfather had overseen the Dietrich estate and Millbrook's first power plant, broke ground for a new senior housing complex on Alden Place. For Millbrook resident Congressman Hamilton Fish, County Executive Pattison, Senator Rolison, and Planning Commissioner Akeley this was a time of optimism. The 1990s, however, saw the closing of the County Infirmary, despite great local outcry. (MM.)

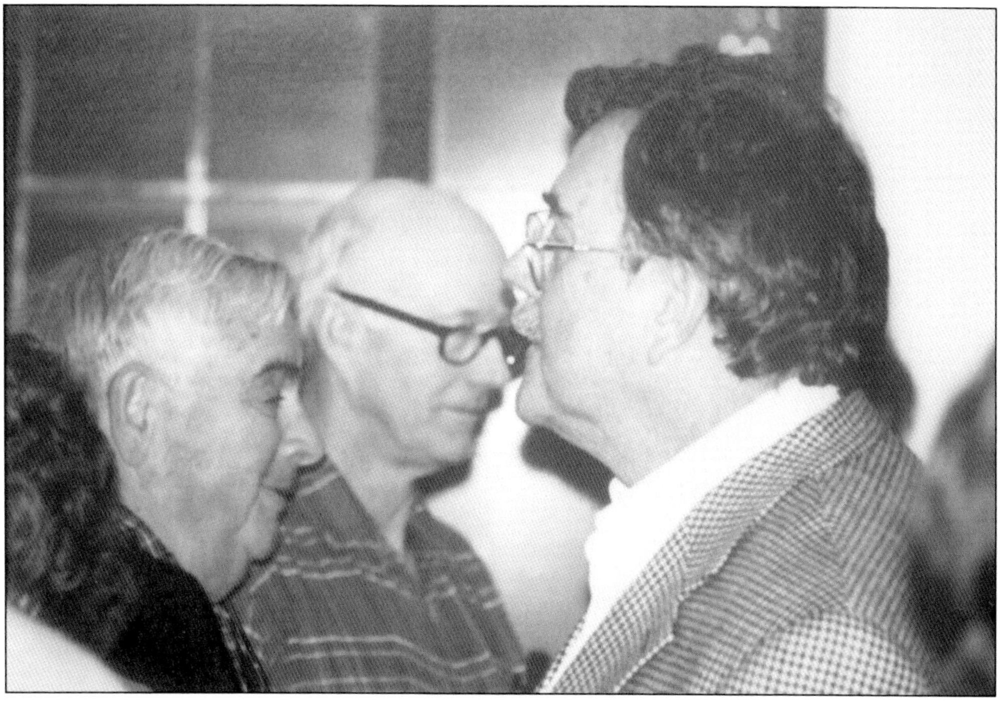

The Town Historian at a Historical Society Meeting, 1999. Washington has been fortunate in both its municipal historians and active historical society. With Louise Tompkins's passing, Bennett history professor Carmine Di Arpino served until his death. Here, art teacher and current town and village historian David Greenwood enjoys an informative exchange with Bert Velletri at a 1999 Washington Historical Society meeting addressing the history of the local Italian community. An attentive and informed membership, always prepared to set the record straight, contributes to a growing fund of local history materials. (SBSSB.)

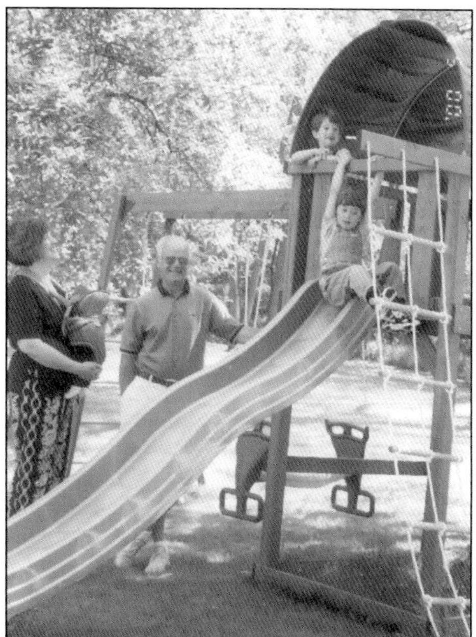

Millbrook's Newest Residents. As mother Karen Outwater and grandfather Ron Finn from Beekman look on, Daniel and Timothy perform on their backyard jungle gym on College Lane for their brand-new brother, Andrew, snoozing in his mother's arms. Teachers Jim and Karen Outwater recently moved to one of the few parts of Washington where suburban development appears—the former Four Corners–Oak Summit area along Route 82. Residents new and old, part of a growing rural community, must work together to sustain the environment that they all cherish. (JG.)

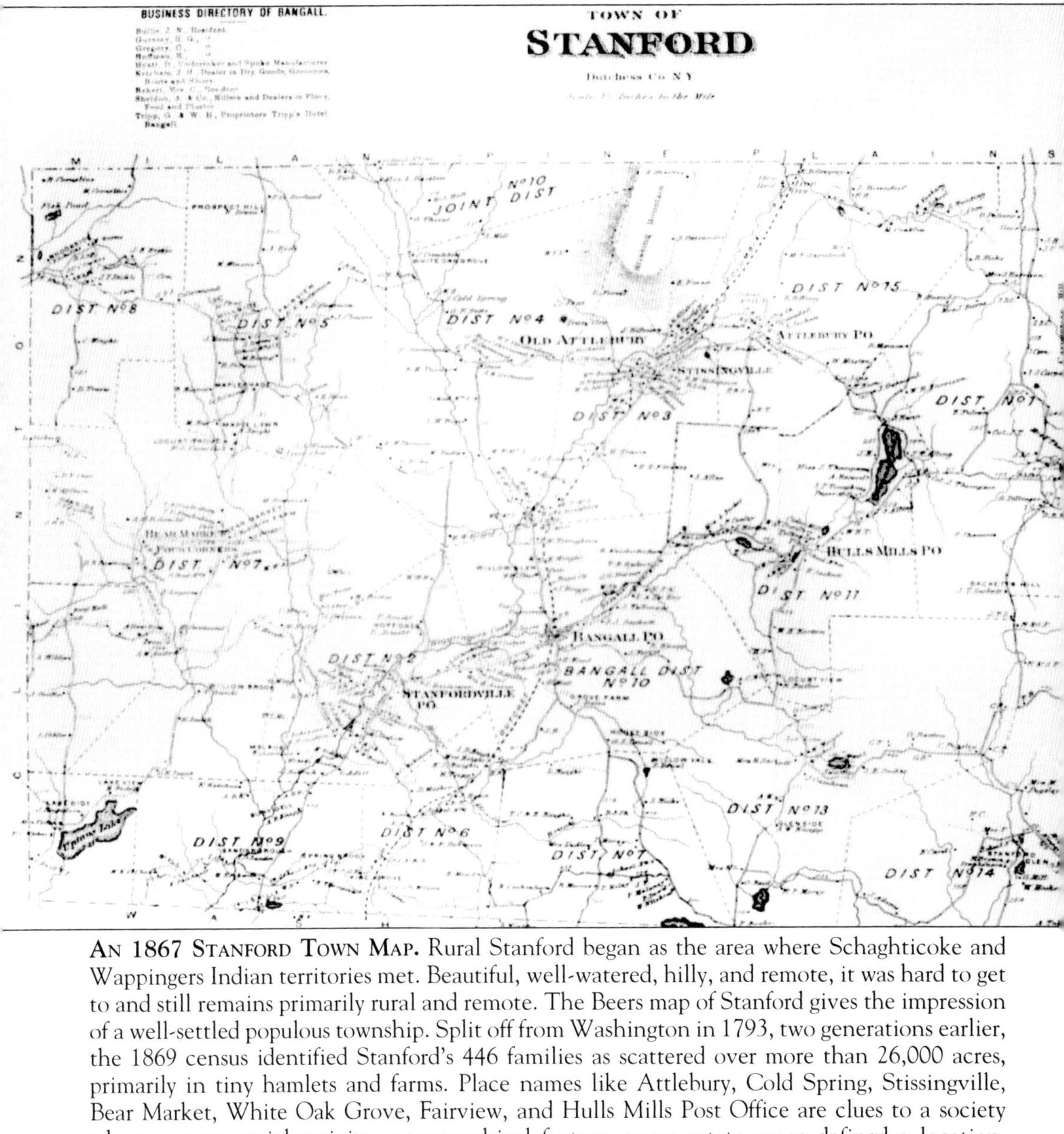

AN 1867 STANFORD TOWN MAP. Rural Stanford began as the area where Schaghticoke and Wappingers Indian territories met. Beautiful, well-watered, hilly, and remote, it was hard to get to and still remains primarily rural and remote. The Beers map of Stanford gives the impression of a well-settled populous township. Split off from Washington in 1793, two generations earlier, the 1869 census identified Stanford's 446 families as scattered over more than 26,000 acres, primarily in tiny hamlets and farms. Place names like Attlebury, Cold Spring, Stissingville, Bear Market, White Oak Grove, Fairview, and Hulls Mills Post Office are clues to a society where a commercial activity, a geographical feature, or an estate name defined a location. Following New York State requirements to make public schooling freely available meant building numerous one- or two-room schoolhouses within walking distance for a dispersed rural population. Bangall and Stanfordville, less than 2 miles apart, qualified for the title of the town center jointly in the mid-19th century, by virtue of the number of businesses and the mills gathered there. Today, although still remote and rural, it boasts a population that is double that of 1867 and is beginning to feel the push of suburban development. (DCHS.)

Six

Stanford

Stanford, the northernmost land in the Great Nine Partners Patent, was settled in the 18th century by relatives of original patent holders increased by New Englanders seeking space and personal freedom. A recent Stanford history states that since its formation as a town in 1793, carved from the northern portions of Washington, its population steadily grew smaller. The census average of about 1,500 residents reported over the centuries has doubled in recent years, as its rural charms become appreciated.

Local Stanford family names abound in Washington—Amenia, Pine Plains, and Clinton—the towns sharing its borders. It takes determination to locate residents amid a myriad of overlapping school district lines and postal and telephone codes. Except for direct town services and elections, townspeople relate daily to those other identifying features.

Horse and cattle breeding farms flourish today in a town that has sustained a primarily agricultural economy responsive to the changing market conditions of many successive eras. However, during the 19th century, hamlets along the Wappingers also supported a surprising variety of water-powered industries. Stanford, too, has been a tourist town welcoming 19th-century road and railroad workers and a continuing stream of vacationers seeking rural hospitality, lakeside cabins and "dude ranches."

The Taconic State Parkway exit east at Bulls Head Road leads to the municipal and commercial town center, Stanfordville, an unincorporated hamlet bordering Route 82. Just around the corner is the other major hamlet, Bangall. Other early settlements—such as the ones at Hunn's-Thompson's Lake, Vailsville, McIntyre and Uptons Lake—have either become neighborhood place names or, with later development, are redefining themselves as communities.

Weekend visits exploring Stanford's beautiful countryside have turned many a city-bred visitor into an enthusiastic permanent resident and booster.

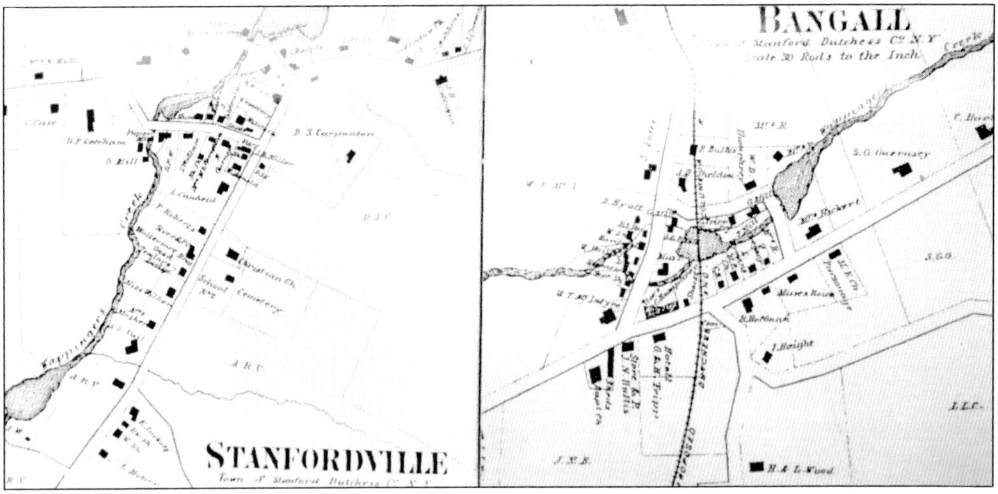

STANFORDVILLE AND BANGALL MAPS FROM 1867. These hamlets, within walking distance of each other, are on branches of Wappingers Creek, which provided power to the mills. Stanfordville, the governmental center of the town, stretches along an early north–south road connecting major stage routes between New England and the Hudson. Resulting travel led to the first businesses. Bangall hamlet, thought to be the earliest settled area in the town, continues to attract today's Sunday drivers to stores at the Y intersection where the Dutchess & Columbia Railroad station stood. (DCHS.)

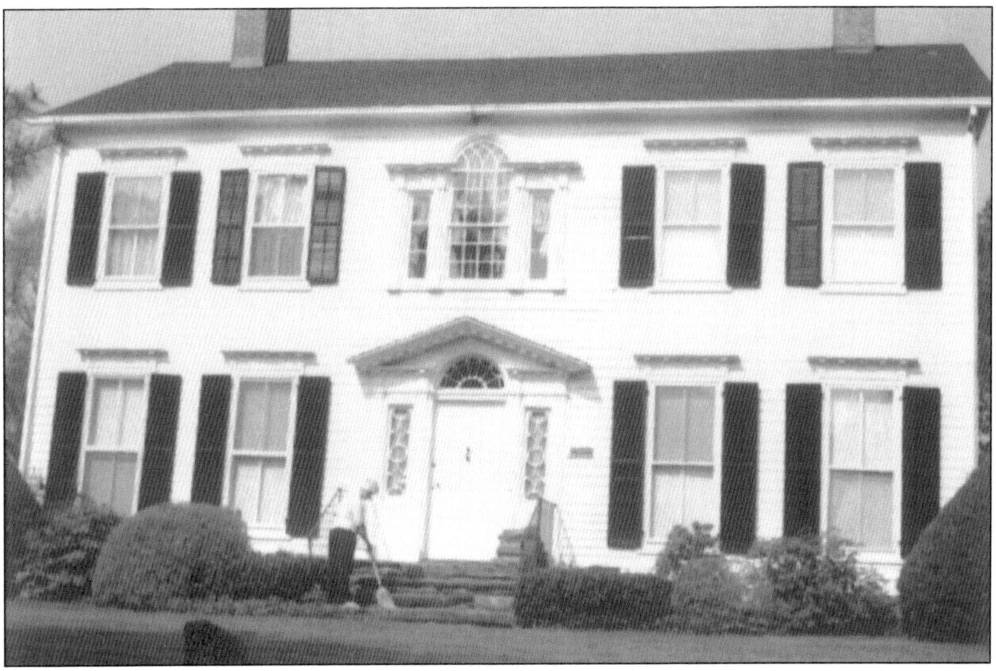

LANDMARK HOUSE, BANGALL. Col. Josiah Sutherland probably built the core of this Georgian house c. 1815 at the intersection of roads to Bangall-McIntyre and Hunn's Lake. After 1869, postmaster John Bullis's family lived here. In 1967, New York City businessman Bob Renshaw and his wife, Joy, discovered the house and hamlet and decided this was where they would raise their family. Two centuries of owners have watched Bangall slowly change from milling to railroading center to rural tourist attraction. (JBR.)

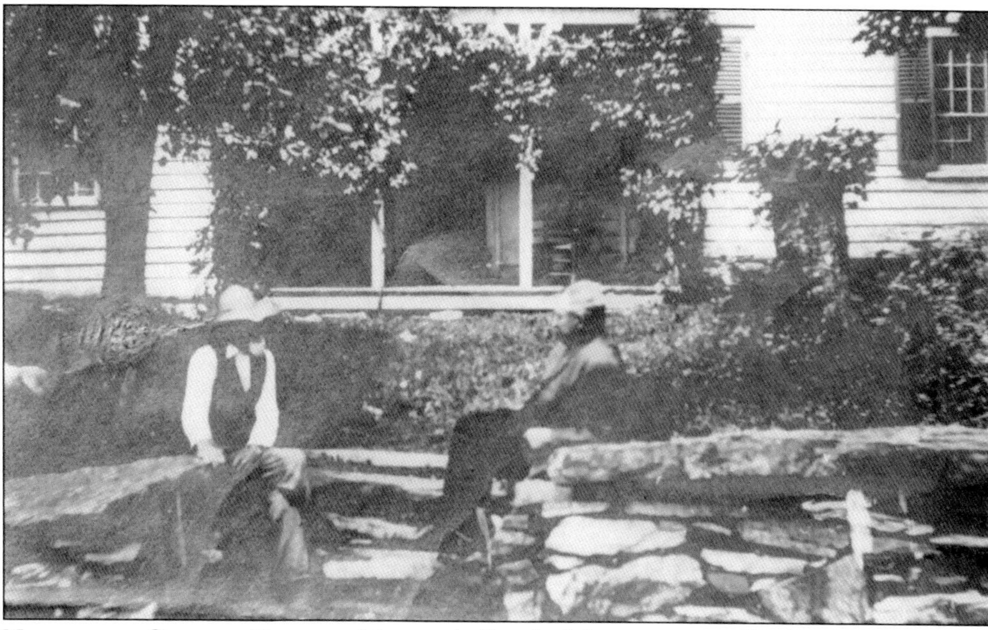

Nineteenth-Century Farmers. Most early Stanford farms were small subsistence farms of a few hundred acres. Weary farmers like these two faced an endless array of chores. The Butts farm near the locally renowned Cold Spring, one of several family compounds in Stanford, was typical. The Butts family came to Dutchess County from Rhode Island in the mid-18th century. Descendants spread throughout central Dutchess, from Butts Hollow on old maps of eastern Washington, west to the Hudson and beyond. (RRB.)

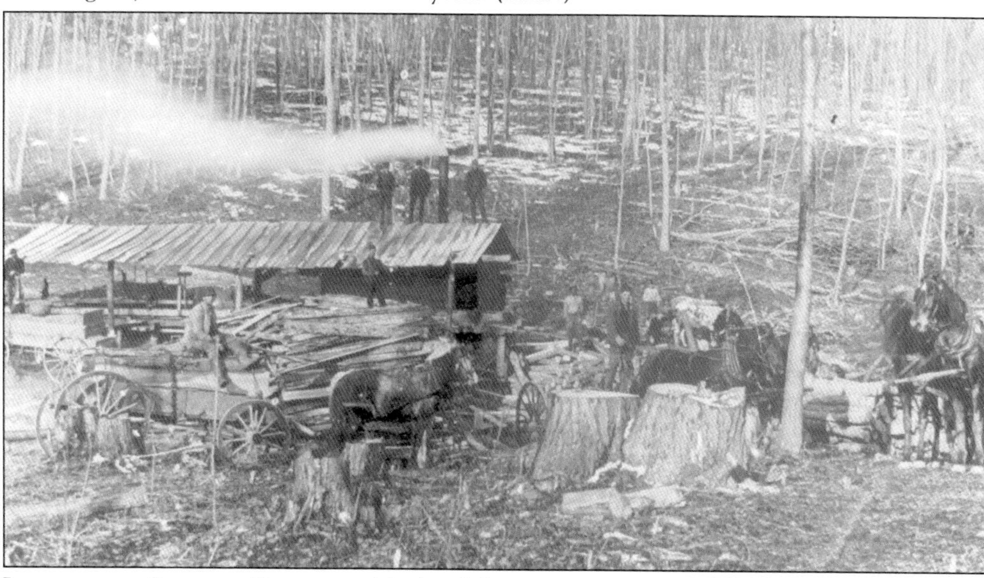

Logging on Leavitt Property. Much of the town was covered by forests. Farmland was reclaimed from tree-covered hills to provide pastureland and fields for cultivation. Gristmills and sawmills abounded near streams, and farmers welcomed both services. Businesses and mill owners themselves were also sawmill customers needing wood for building and for heating before other fuels became cheap. By the late 1800s, logging tasks were lightened, powered by steam engines. (SHS.)

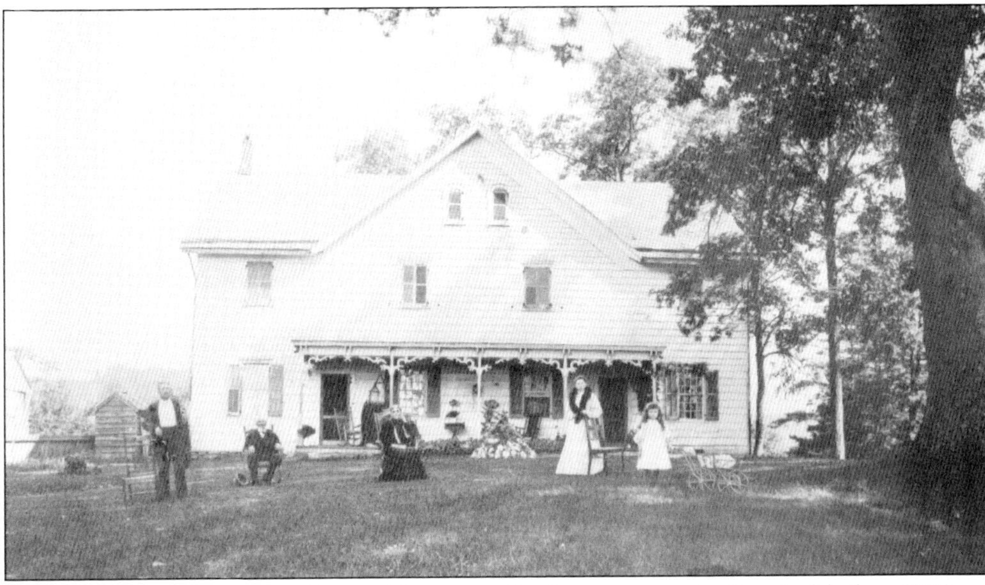

THE HIRAM VANDERWATER FARM. Clues to a Quaker presence in Stanford before 1800 are found in local histories, folklore, cemetery markers, and architectural history. The residents pose outside this farmhouse near Stanfordville in the late 1800s. The Victorian front gable, shutters, and decorative porch woodwork barely disguise the simple lines and double entries of a former classic meetinghouse. The present Robert Willis home was also once a meetinghouse. The Bull's Head–Oswego Meeting stands near the parkway. (DBTH.)

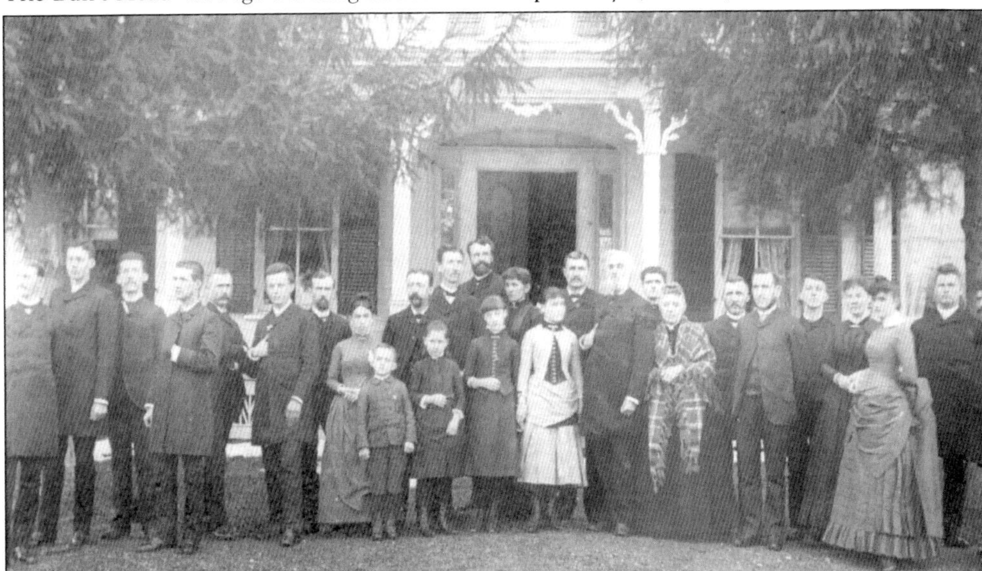

THE CHRISTIAN BIBLICAL INSTITUTE. Community religious life was energized by the coming in 1872 of the Christian Biblical Institute, a seminary training boys for the ministry. Bangall houses of worship were constructed early by Baptists who came *c.* 1755 and by Methodists sparked by the Great Awakening of the early 1800s. Stanfordville's First Christian Church congregation (now the United Church of Christ), organized *c.* 1837, began building in 1843. Sisters Hill Road was named for a Catholic retirement home for nuns built early in the 20th century. (SHS.)

The Dam at Bangall. Acts of nature are often seen as expressions of celestial wrath. At Stanfordville and Bangall, where the main branch of the Wappinger Creek meets several feeder streams, the annual rush of water frequently exceeds the stream beds. Floods are a regular occurrence. As long as houses of worship were spared, the loss of replaceable dams, bridges, walkways, and occasional dwelling and business damage seemed a small price to pay for the gift of cheap power that the water provided for more than two centuries. (SHS.)

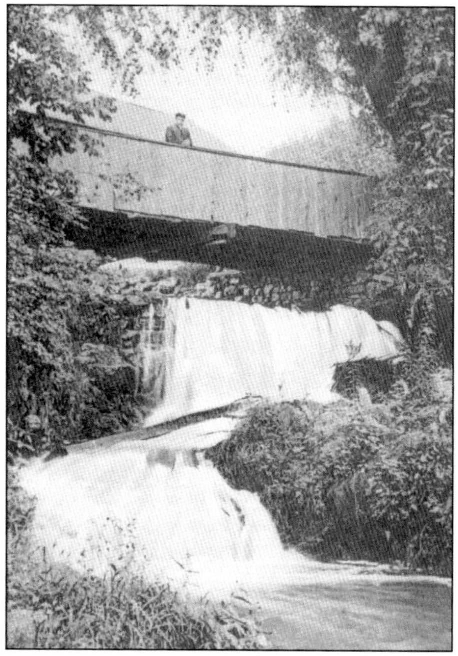

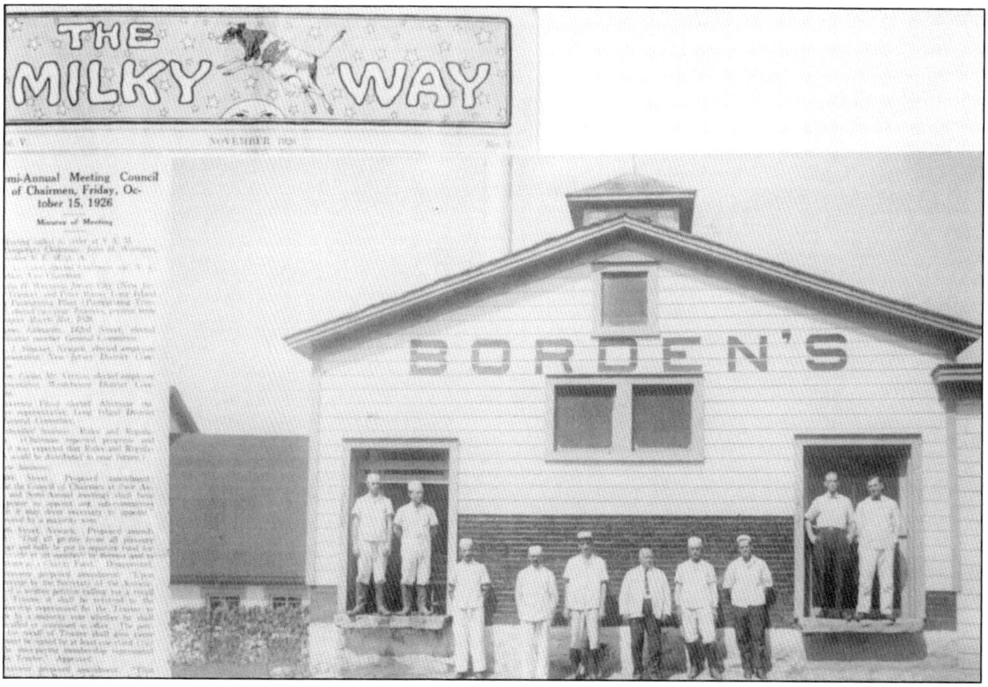

Stanford Industry. Stanford waterpower supported surprisingly diverse industries: sawmills; gristmills; cider mills; wrapping paper, cheese, shoe, and axle factories; and a wheelwright. The Borden plant, managed by Irving Bogle, was part of a string of northeast milk processing plants bringing fresh local dairy products to city markets along the rail network constructed mid-19th century. The Milky Way, more than a distant heavenly body, was a commercial concept and regular company newsletter keeping producers and workers in touch with the latest industry news. (JB/DBTH.)

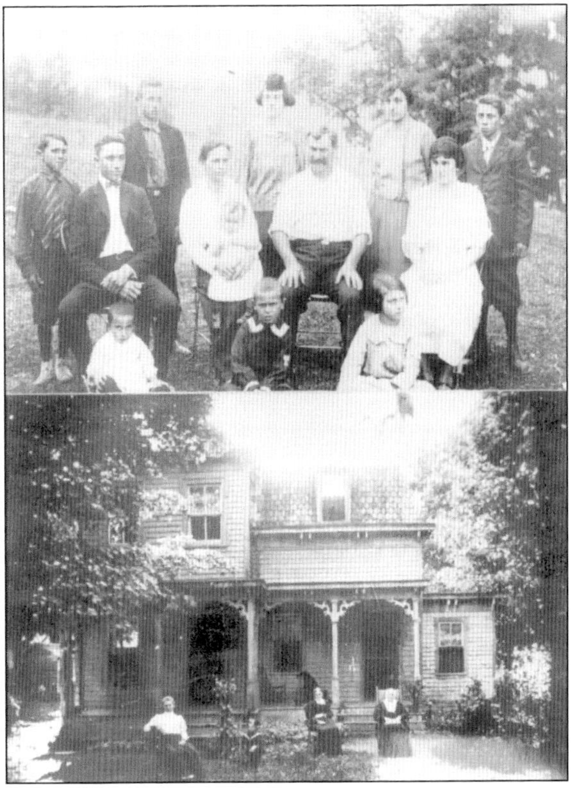

From Farmer to Businessman. John Battistoni Sr. and his wife came from Italy in the 1890s. Their married life here began on a farm, where they raised vegetables and a large family. John became a successful timber dealer. He opened a Bangall grocery store *c.* 1920 and moved the family to Stanfordville. Old Stanford residents, descendants of the Palatine Germans, New Englanders of English and Scottish descent, and African Americans who first settled here, became neighbors and customers. (JB)

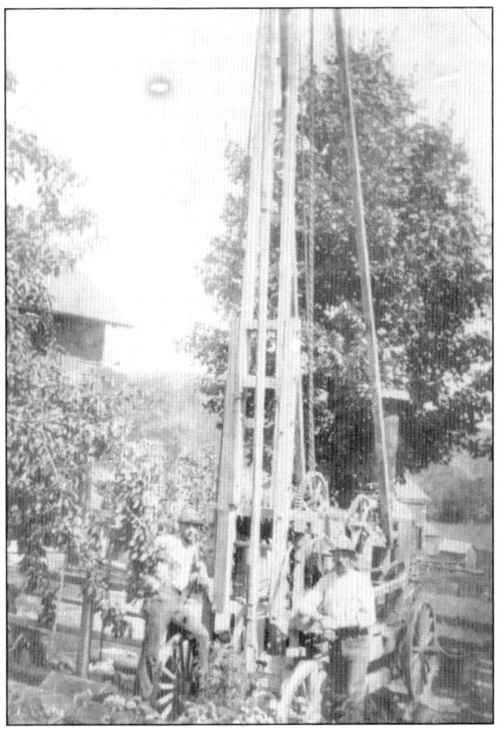

Well Drillers. Well drillers are essential to rural communities without water systems. Front yard wells and dippers signaled a choice site for a home. Early settlers looked for land with a stream or spring for an easily accessible water supply. Marshy areas yielding water when a shallow "point" was dug were good, too. Later residents depended upon a local well driller who knew the territory and had the equipment. Steam engines to run the drills eased labor. Stanford home owners still depend upon wells. (SHS.)

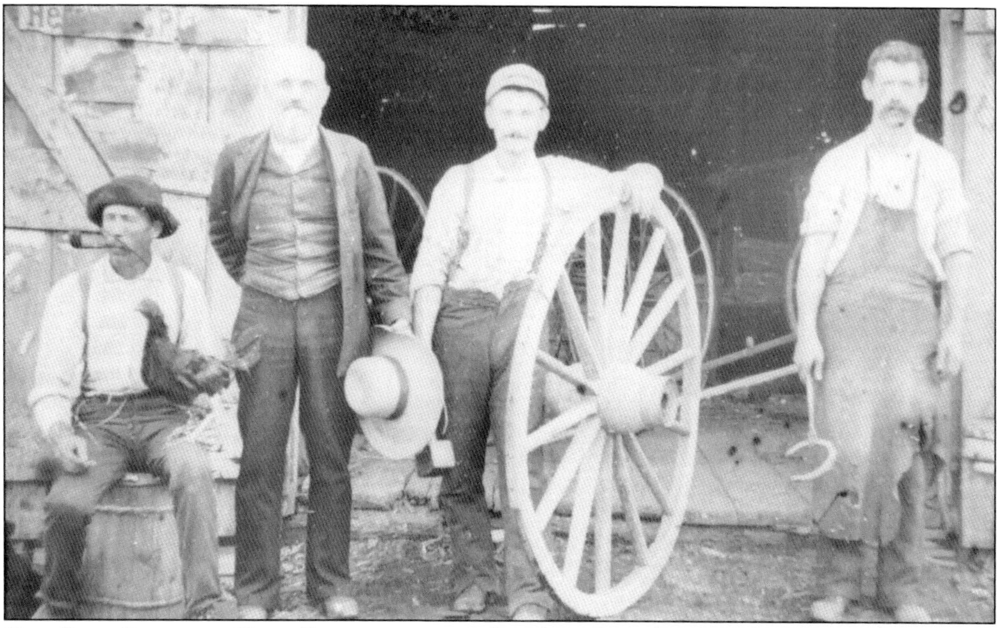

One-Stop Shopping. Bangall was never very big, but if you lived in the vicinity and needed something, it meant Bangall, Stanfordville, or a major trip to Poughkeepsie. This photograph may have been an advertisement. A visit to this blacksmith's shop could solve several major technical problems. He shod the horses, made or mended tools and farm equipment, and constructed wagon wheels. For those who liked their entertainment rough around the edges, there was cockfighting in the rear of the barn at Bangall. (SHS.)

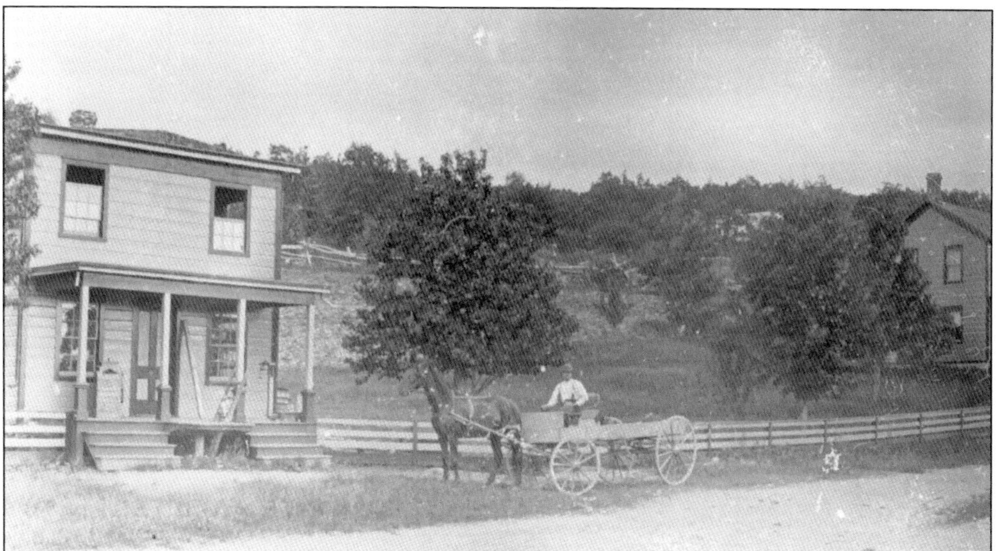

Getting Fed in Bangall. For more than a century, this spot has been a place where the thirsty or hungry could be satisfied. Opposite the proposed depot was Andrew Smith's ice-cream parlor. A few years later, it became Battistoni's grocery. When Prohibition ended, they opened a bar and restaurant famous for its soup made with Hunn's Lake turtles. Battistoni donated the green to the hamlet in 1946. Today, the Stage Stop Inn provides the food to hungry passers-by. (JB.)

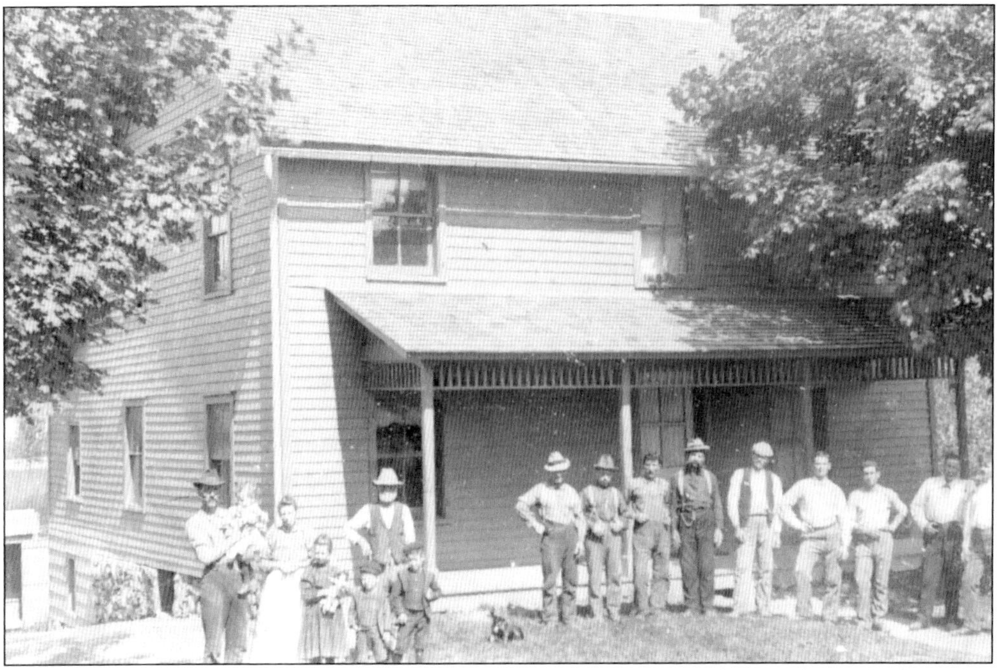

Railroad Workers' Accommodations, 1870s. When the railroads were being built in this part of Dutchess, the population swelled for several years with the men who built them. It was something of a boon to the farms in the area, converted into impromptu boardinghouses. Workers' sleeping accommodations in barns and attics may have been simple and crowded, but the workers were fed well with the bounty from the kitchen gardens, chicken coops, and dairy sheds of the farmers' wives. (SHS.)

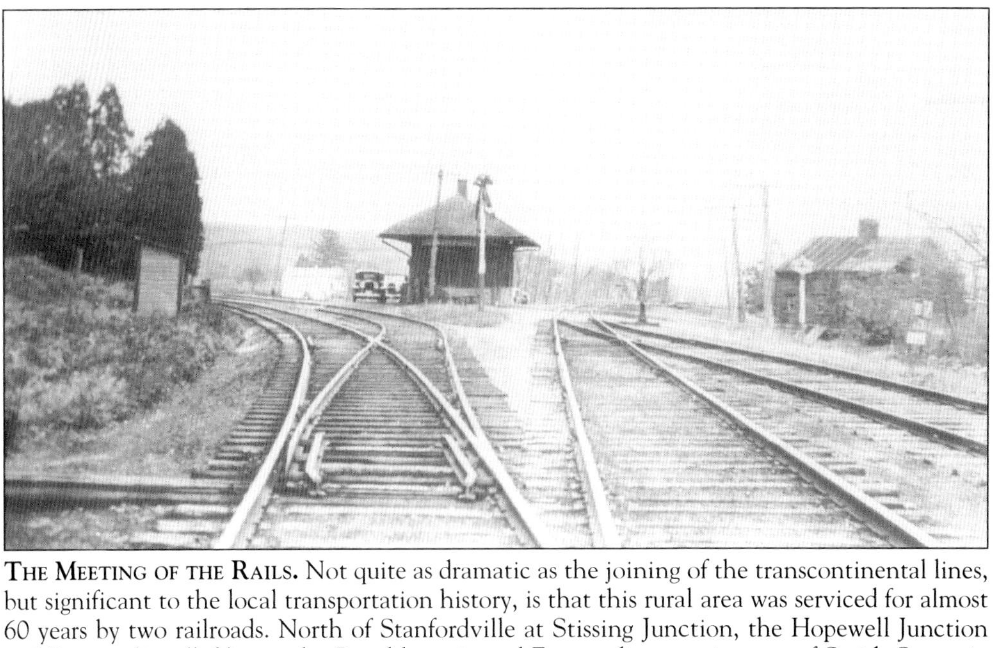

The Meeting of the Rails. Not quite as dramatic as the joining of the transcontinental lines, but significant to the local transportation history, is that this rural area was serviced for almost 60 years by two railroads. North of Stanfordville at Stissing Junction, the Hopewell Junction and Beacon line (left) met the Poughkeepsie and Eastern line coming out of Smith Street in Poughkeepsie through Pleasant Valley. You could get almost anywhere from here. (HC.)

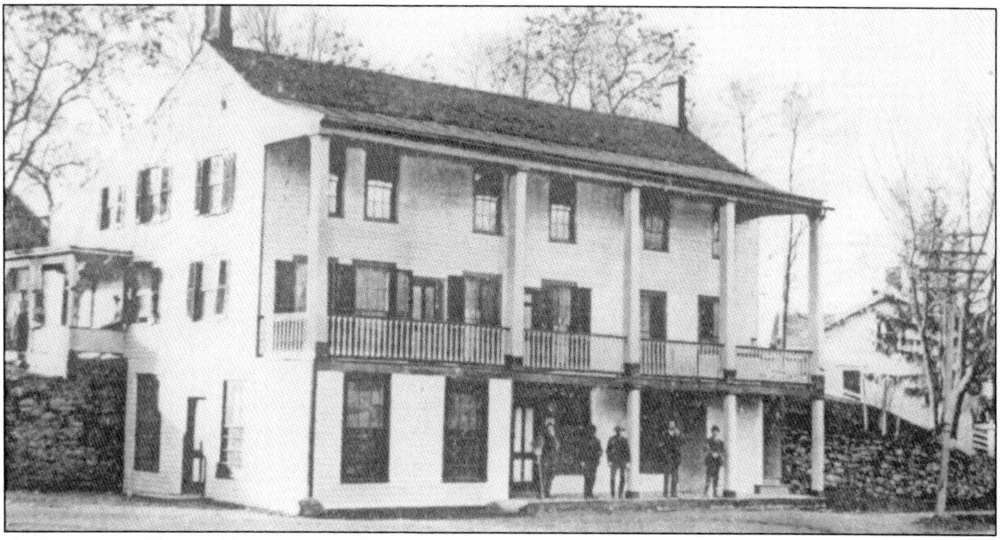

A Germond Hotel Postcard. The economic impact of the railroad felt in Millbrook spilled over by 1870 into Stanford hamlets and farms. Inexpensive countryside farm vacations had already begun to attract summer boarders from more urban communities in the valley. With better transportation, both longer and shorter visits from farther afield became possible. Mrs. Viola Germond's Bangall hotel was one of two hostelries only a short walk from the depot. Good food, country walks, and planned activities pleased guests whose postcards were Germond's best advertisements. (SHS.)

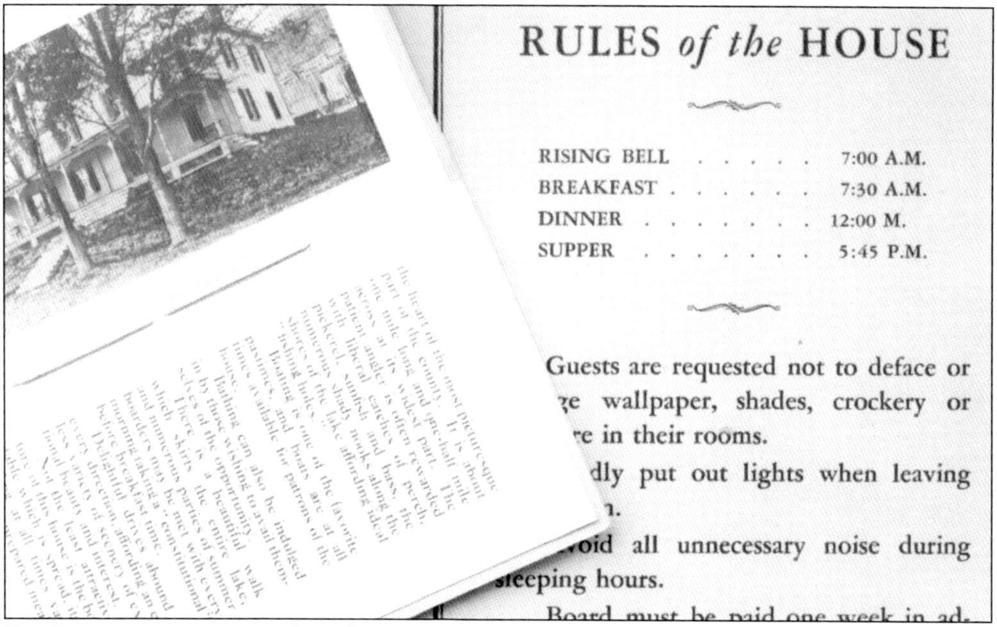

The Rules of the House. The Dillinger guesthouse overlooks beautiful Hunn's Lake. Here, visitors relaxed during restful but orderly vacations that centered around Mrs. Dillinger's home-style meals, which were taken with the family at the same table. Between the rising bell and lights-out, they were offered opportunities to fish, hike, swim, or chat with other guests while rocking on the front porch. Hunn's Lake had a dance hall for those so inclined, but dancers had better tiptoe if they came in late. Furthermore, it was necessary to pay a week in advance. (SHS.)

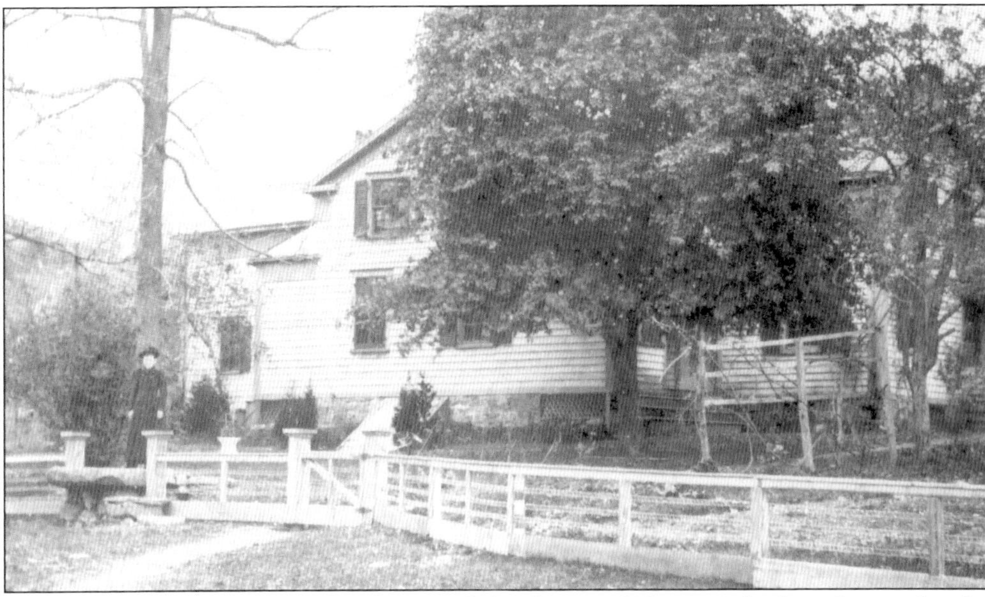

Farms Leave Hunn's Lake. Some mourned the change of Hunn's Lake from farming hamlet to vacation venue, but others saw opportunity. The name of Thompson's Pond was changed to Hunn's Lake. The hamlet supported paper manufacturing as well as subsistence farming before the lake began to attract tourists. The 20th-century dance hall and Prohibition-era roadhouse gave way to private camps. Today, suburban residences and weekend homes sprout near Roseland Resort, a year-round dude ranch attracting families. (SHS.)

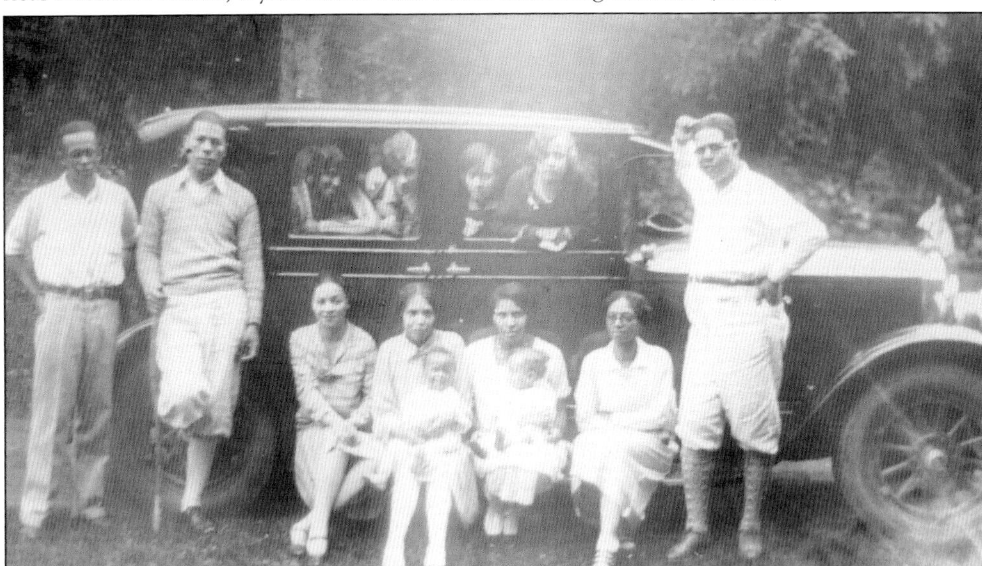

The Taylors, Johnsons, and Guests. The farm once owned by Quaker Mary Arnold, thought to be part of the Underground Railroad, is at the intersection of Bulls Head (County Road 19) and Gristmill Roads. Members of the Taylor-Johnson family became its owners in the early 1900s, with several generations sharing the farmhouse. Seated on their mothers' laps by a visitor's car are tiny cousins Dorothy and Marion Johnson. Knickers were the latest fashion for country jaunts in the 1920s. (MJB.)

Summer Residents. The Butts's family devotion to Stanford brings them back from all over the country. Their Cold Spring farm, in and out and back in the family over almost 200 years, is still home base. The alternative was Upton Lake, where this Poughkeepsie contingent spent its summers. Mother Harriet came out with the children, Marion and Franklin, when school closed. Their carefree days were spent swimming and exploring the surrounding territory. Mother kept house and entertained frequent guests, catching up on the news by mail. (RRB.)

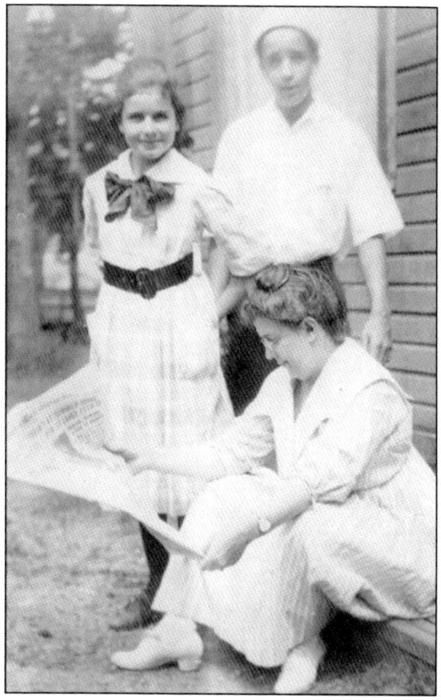

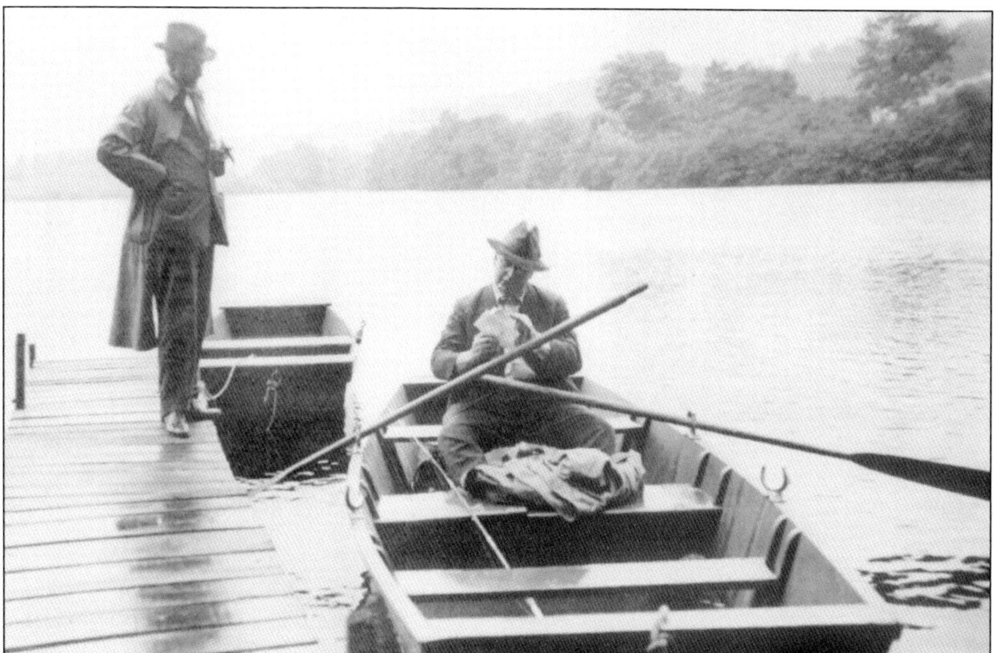

Weekend Fathers. Ralph F. Butts, still in his working clothes, must have been itching to get at his fishing, but Jake Strong appears to need mail checked first. Some families with lakeside camps were separated all week long. The car or rail spur connecting Upton Lake and its icehouses with the world brought breadwinners and wives together. Weekends meant picnics, fishing, swimming, or blowing cigar smoke into the quiet country air. For excitement there was an amusement park with rides, a dance hall, and food vendors. (RRB.)

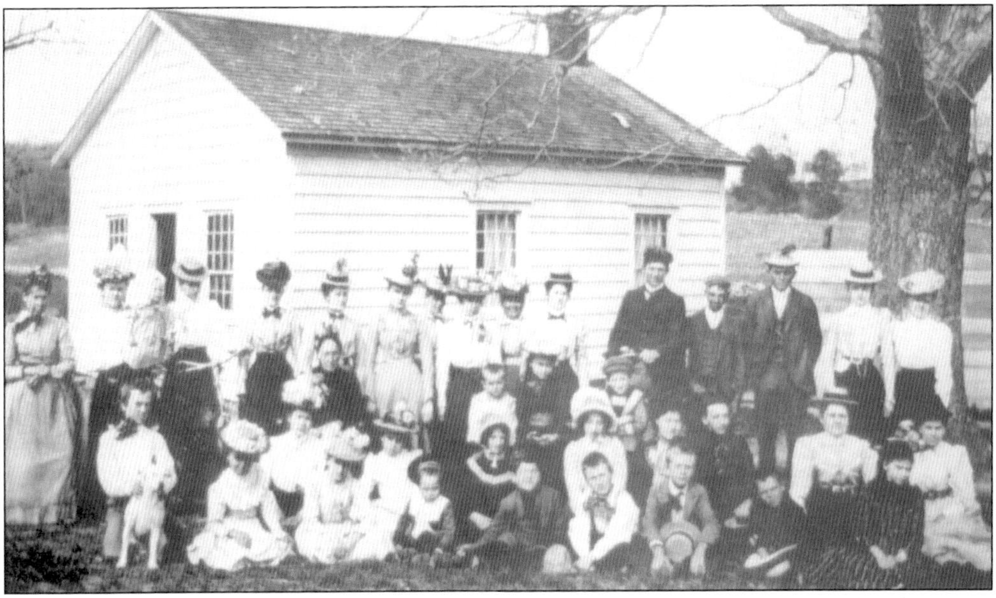

A Knight Road Schoolhouse Picnic, c. 1900. The children and families of School District No. 9, one of 14 local districts, ended the year with a picnic at the schoolhouse. Dorothy Burdick's father and mother, Mr. and Mrs. Frank Barton, attended. Neighborhood schools, where the basics were taught even to adults, ended a generation later. When this school off Route 82 on the Washington line was closed, the property was purchased by the Whitlocks and the building was removed and rebuilt elsewhere. The grounds were given to the town as parkland. (DBTH.)

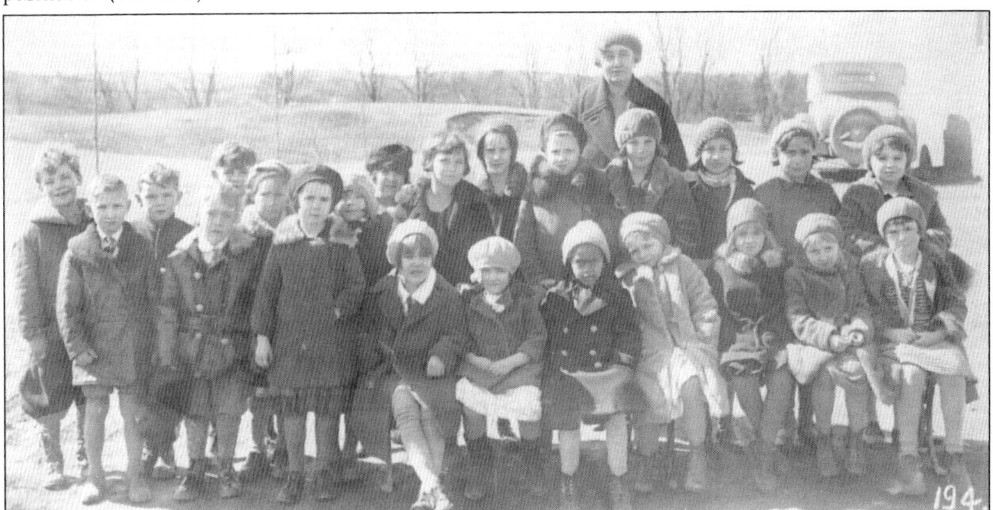

Stanford Union Free School First and Second Graders, 1931. Among those entering the Stanfordville Union Free School built six years earlier were schoolmates Marion Johnson, Dorothy Barton, and Mary Lou Benham. They were spared the hardships of one-room schoolhouse scholars who carted drinking water, fed the stove, and battled snowbanks on foot to complete eight grades. Separate rooms kept youngsters of the same age together through tenth grade, after which they were transported to Pine Plains or Millbrook to complete high school. (MJB.)

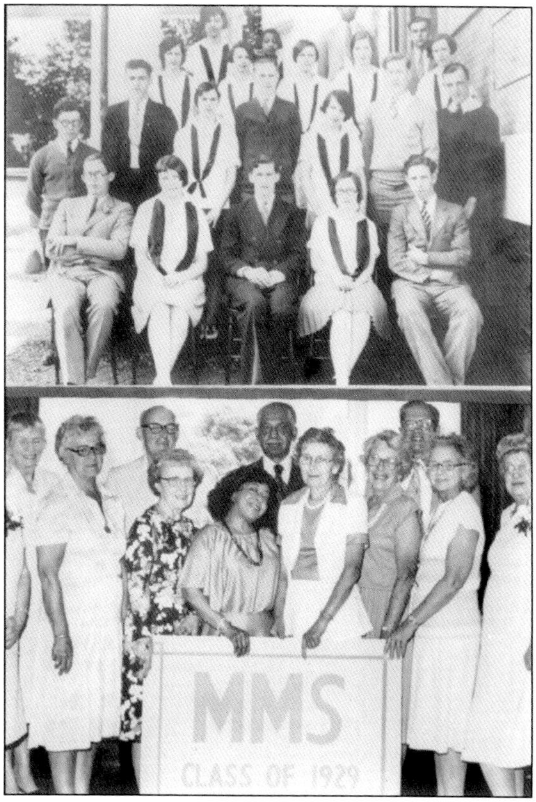

MILLBROOK'S STANFORD GRADS. Some members of the Millbrook Memorial School class of 1929 were from Stanford. At their 50th reunion, they relived their experiences. Once, eighth-grade "testimonials" from neighborhood districts ended formal education. Later, tenth-grade Union Free School certificates provided evidence of education. By the 1920s, school boards paid transportation and tuition fees for Stanford high school juniors and seniors to go to Millbrook, Poughkeepsie, or Pine Plains. These grads had done it all in one-room, Union Free, and transfer district schools. (DBTH.)

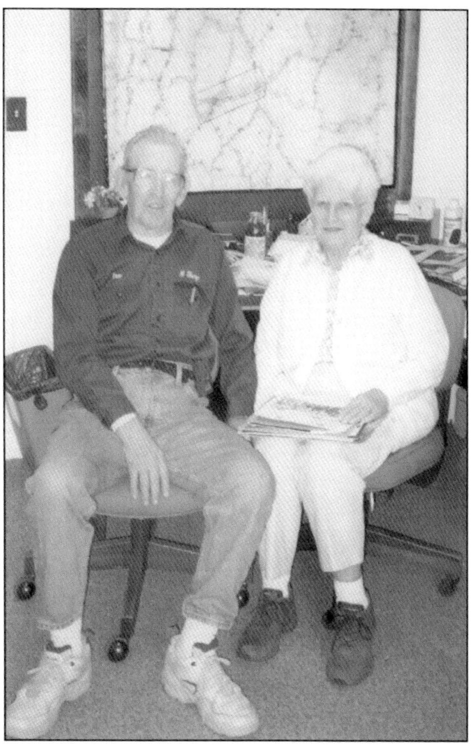

A HOME AWAY FROM HOME. Dorothy and Irving Burdick find a moment's rest in the Stanford Town Hall on school district voting day in 2000. They are comfortable in the building where they went to school and where they have spent many hours in community service. The former schoolhouse, transferred to Pine Plains during the 1950 centralization, was still in good shape when residents agreed in 1972 to buy it back as the town hall for $55,000 from the new district. Dorothy's historian's office once belonged to Irving during his seven years as town supervisor. (JG.)

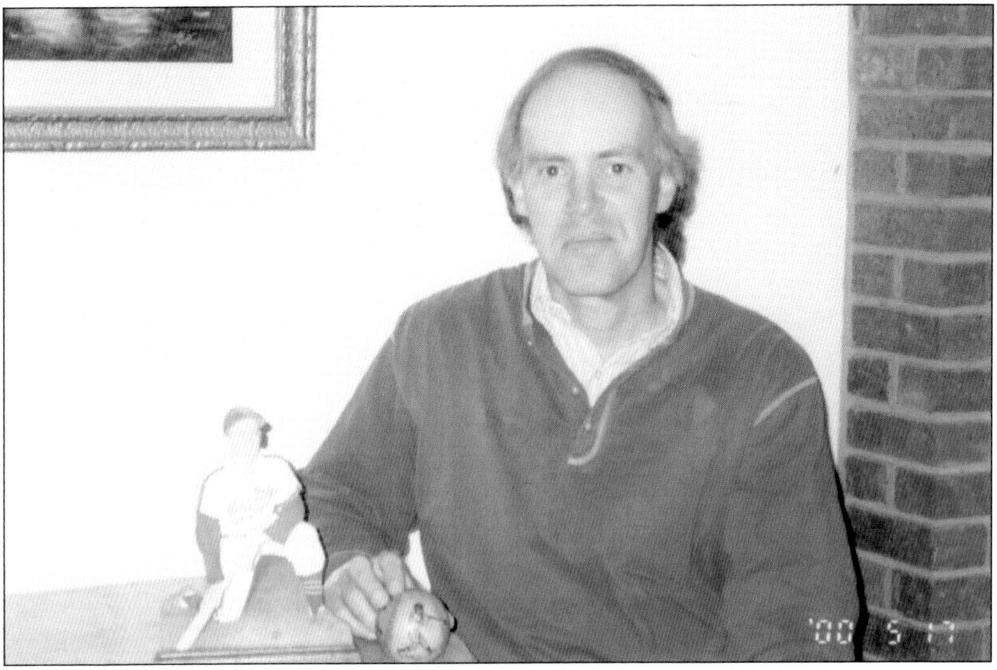

Austin Knickerbocker, a Hometown Hero. Stanford's history is filled with generations of community-minded Knickerbockers, but baseball fans know Austin best. Under Fritz Jordan's guidance, his high school athletic record leading to college ball could have meant major league stardom, but WWII intruded. Entering the minors after the war at age 27 limited him to only one year in the majors with the Philadelphia A's. Son John holds part of mother Helen's treasured memorabilia, a statuette and signed ball testifying to Austin's hitting skills. (JK.)

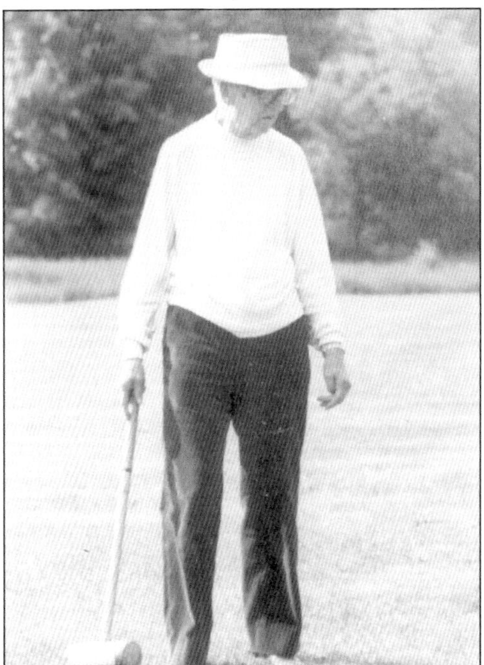

Alfred Butts, Working at Play. Alfred Butts took on innumerable challenges. He was an architect, stamp collector, inventor, artist whose work is owned by the Metropolitan Museum of Art in New York City, and monograph writer on games. In 1939, he invented a game called Criss-Cross Words—what became Scrabble, the popular word game, in 1948. He used his Scrabble earnings in 1953 to reclaim Butts's Homestead near Stanford's Cold Spring. He and wife, Nina, made their home, now owned by nephew Robert, a venue for frequent family reunions where conversation, word games, and croquet competed for attention. (RRB.)

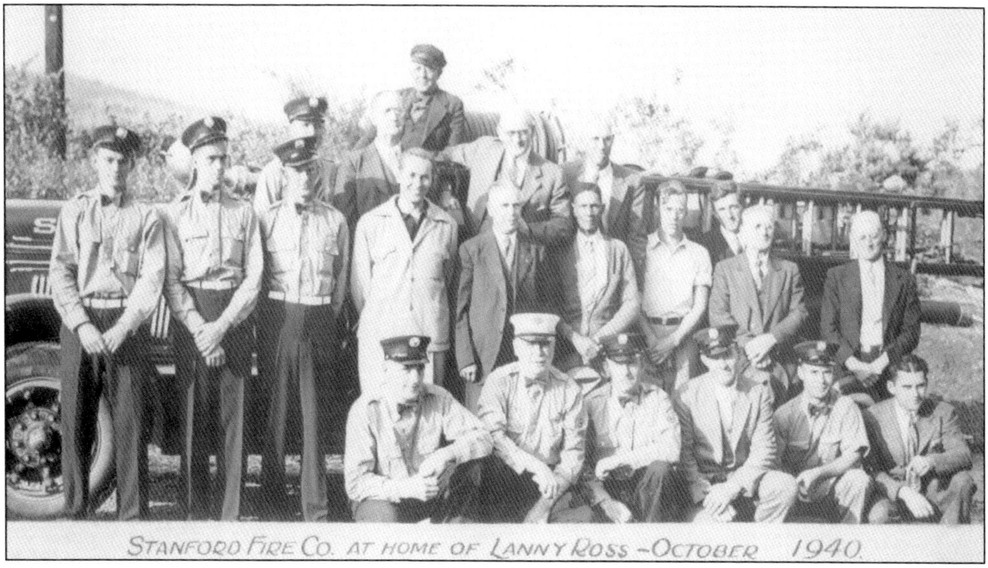

LANNY ROSS, CENTER, SINGING FIREMAN. America's favorite balladeer and radio star of the 1930s and 1940s was Lanny Ross. Like other celebrity residents, he welcomed the friendship of neighbors who respected personal privacy. A Christmas card sent to Jay Knickerbocker from New Guinea during WWII and this photograph in the Stanford Fire Company are reminders of his friendship. He generously brought his whole show here for a fire company benefit and entertained fellow volunteers at Melody Farm, his dairy farm on the Bangall-Amenia Road. (SFC.)

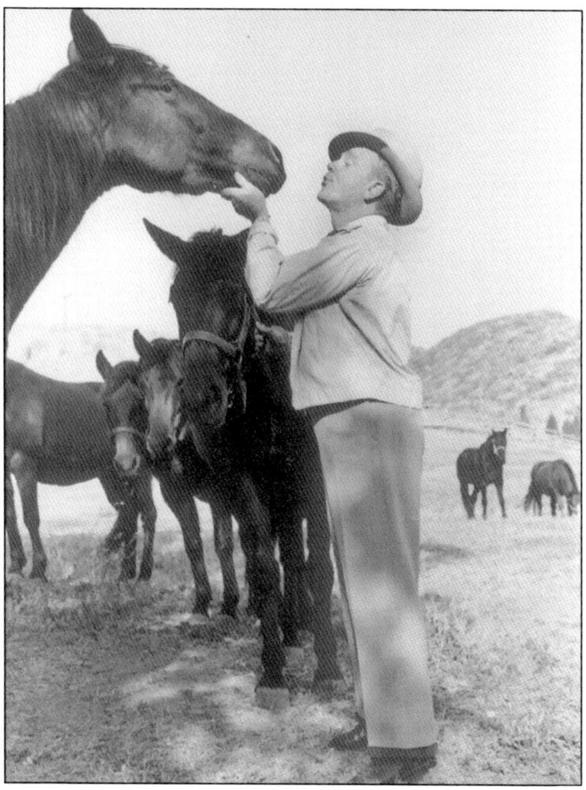

STANFORD'S YANKEE DOODLE DANDY. Jimmy Cagney loved Stanford, and Stanford loved him back. In 1955, the former Ross dairy farm became Cagney's horse farm and the place where he turned his talents to painting lively, colorful oils. His family's modest stone ranch house overlooked the pond and fields where horses scampered and grazed. He was a familiar and free spirit in the community, waiting patiently for a haircut at Al Perry's shop or, on a whim, purchasing the Bangall post office outhouse for his pasture art studio. (KS.)

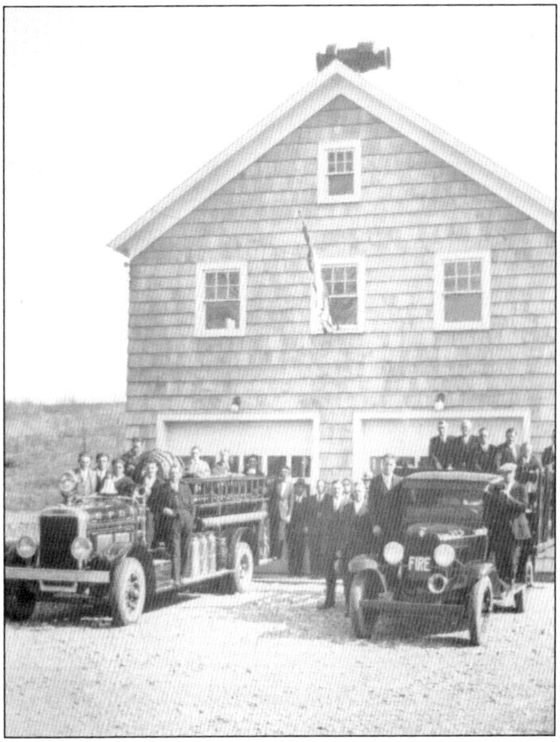

STANFORD GETS A FIRE COMPANY. Rural Stanford had no fire department for two centuries. Local folks put fires out themselves, called for help, or stood around watching them burn. Fires destroying Harrison's and Van de Water's stores forced the community, under Grange leadership, to organize a much appreciated volunteer company. By 1931, they were fully equipped and trained. Appreciation of firefighters is expressed in many ways besides dinners and parades. The firehouse was draped in George Beckwith's memory. Irv Burdick's service merited a plaque on the ambulance. (SFC.)

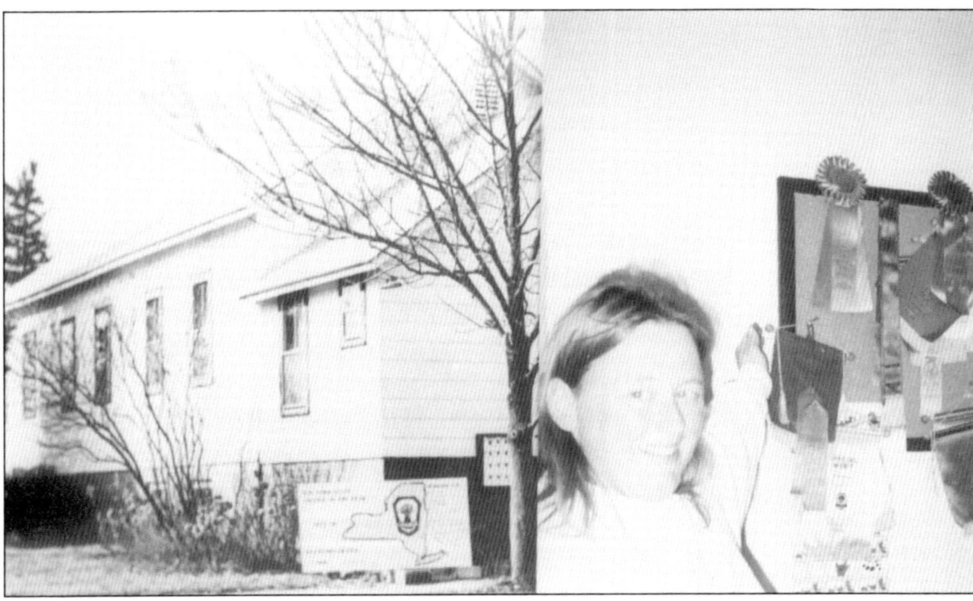

STANFORD GRANGE NO. 808. One of Stanford's most influential institutions, now led by Cathy Stark, is the Grange. With the national agrarian movement following the Civil War, rural Granges sprung up nationwide to help farmers. After an abortive start earlier, Stanford Grange No. 808 was chartered in 1896. For two years, 1977 and 1978, it was New York's top Community Service Grange. Its current 80 members mix farm, civic, and community interests in a building available to all town groups; it was constructed in 1944 on the foundations of the former Christian Biblical Institute. (SG/CS.)

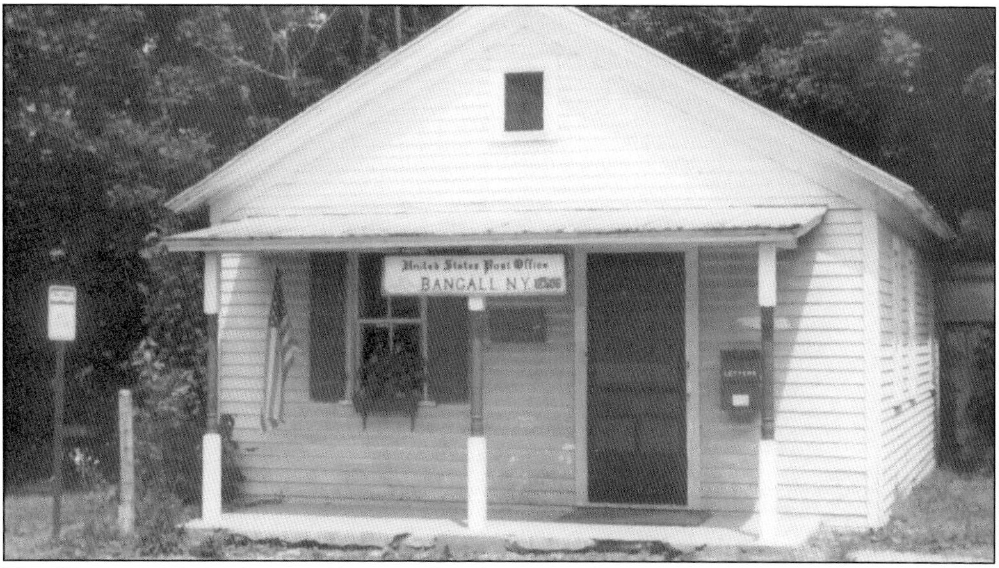

The Bangall Post Office. This tiny hamlet post office has been a community gathering place since its 1915 construction, 12 years after National Grange advocacy won farmers Rural Free Delivery. With RFD, ten hamlet post offices in private homes around the town were eliminated. This one remains from the days when postmasters owned the buildings and the postal service was handled by contract and appointment. Harrie Knickerbocker, postmaster in 1915, owned the building, but the ground under it belonged to the Churtons. Dolores Straley is postmaster currently. (DS.)

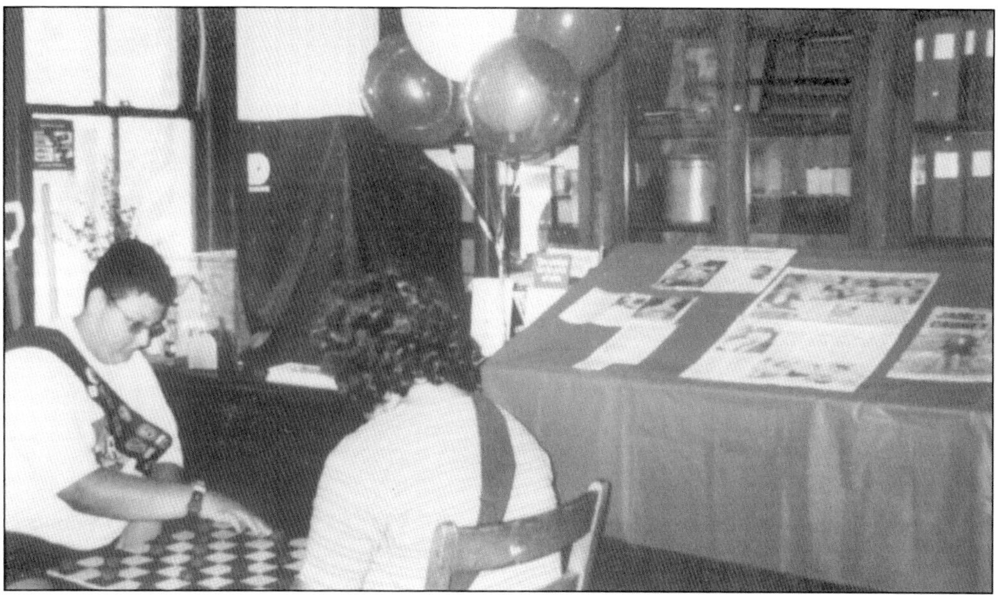

A Historic Game of Checkers. A checker board at the post office, owned by the Stanford Historical Society since 1973, gets a frequent workout from these young patrons, Orton family members and also members of the society. The organization got its start in 1969 from local historians like Stanley Willig, Newton Deuel, and Elinor Beckwith, who were also inveterate collectors. The collections of the society, on display in the post office, along with the checkers, encourage lingering and conversation. (DS.)

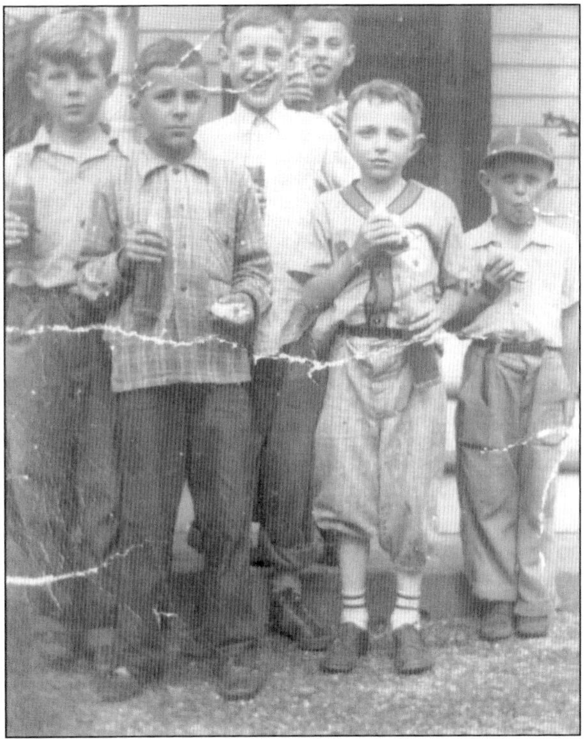

PLAY BALL ANYONE? In the 1930s and 1940s, before town recreation programs and Little Leagues, children designed their own diversions. Boys pick-up games of the past may not have featured elaborate uniforms or even stuck very closely to the rules of the game, but they generated as much enthusiasm as those of today. Everyone got a chance to pitch, hit, and run, even the weaker players. Moreover, the mothers of Battistoni, Place, Post, and Spohr children did not have to chauffeur them anywhere. (JB.)

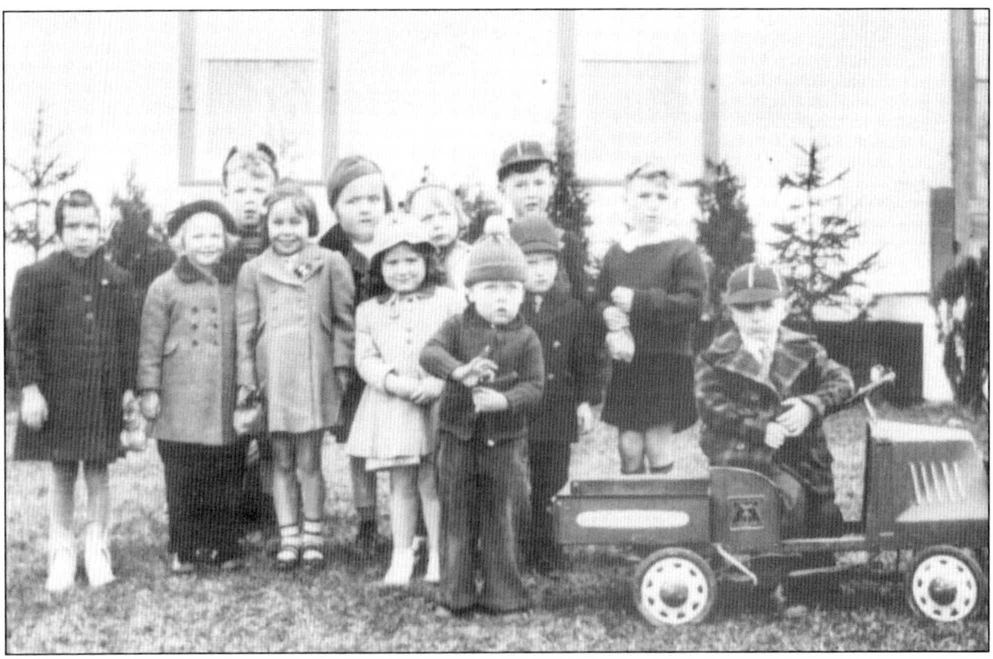

HAPPY FIFTH BIRTHDAY TO JOHN. Children's birthday parties and small towns go together, but they can be hard on both guests and hosts. No one knows what to wear or what to bring for a gift. Birthdays are especially trying for the guest of honor. John Battistoni III's sober expression may have been because girls were invited. Maybe he got the wrong model truck. It might have been that second helping of ice cream. More likely, he was tired and it was nap time. (JB.)

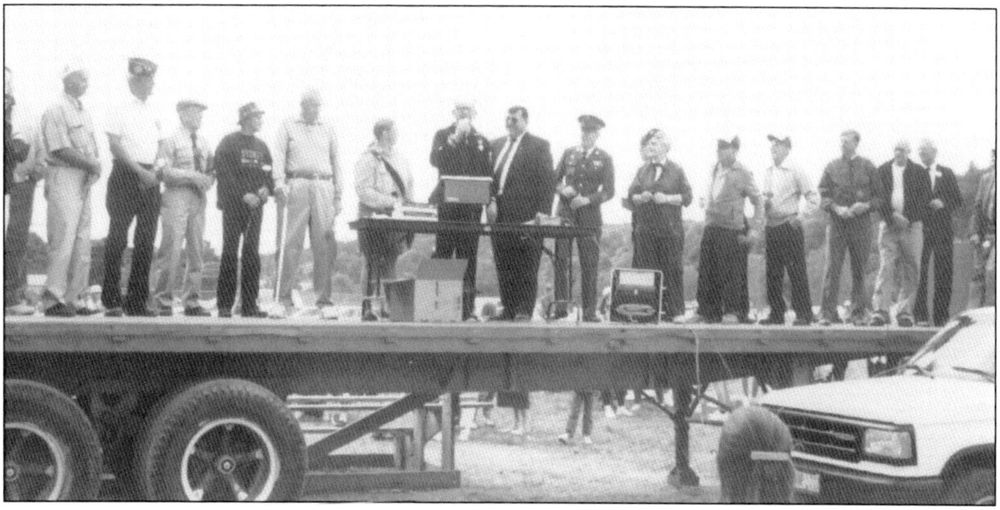

COMMUNITY DAY 1995. Community Day every September celebrates rural town life. Parades, organizational booths, games, and food draw far-flung neighbors to Stanfordville for a day of fun. The Grange uses this occasion to make its annual National Community Service Award to local organizations or individuals. In 1995, those who served in WWII were honored. Cathy Stark, Grange master for almost two decades, shared the platform with Cooperative Extension's Dave Teator. Moose Karn, Donald Spiers, Jack Eagan, Dorothy Burkowske and Irv Burdick were among the veterans contingent. (SG/CS.s)

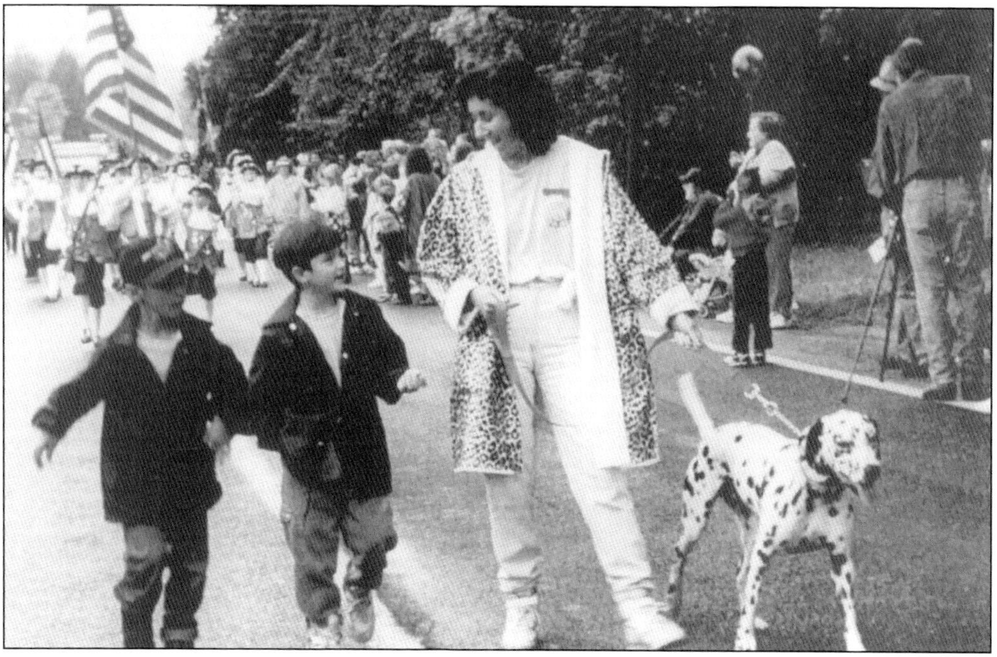

HAPPY BIRTHDAY, STANFORD. The celebration in 1993 topped them all. A town does not get to be 200 more than once. The public program included speeches from town and county officials, proclamations and public acknowledgments of the importance of history and historians. The parade was bigger and better; all, including the family pets, were invited to participate. The action was caught on video, enlivened by the music of both local and out-of-town bands. (DBTH.)

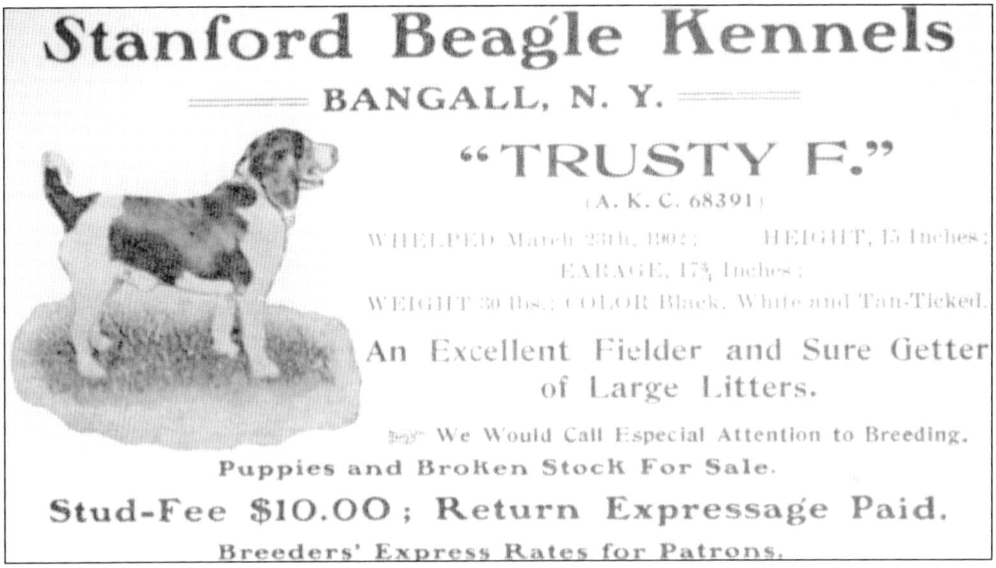

EXCELLENCE IS IN THE BREEDING. Whether it is cattle, horses, or dogs, Stanford animals have a reputation for excellence. A letter written in 1915 to Stanford Kennels from a customer in North Carolina began, "I like the build of your Beagles" and continued, describing in detail what the dog ordered should look like. High standards and attention to demanding customers' wishes keep today's breeders, trainers, and horse farm operators like Jesse and Gayle Bontecou in business. (SHS.)

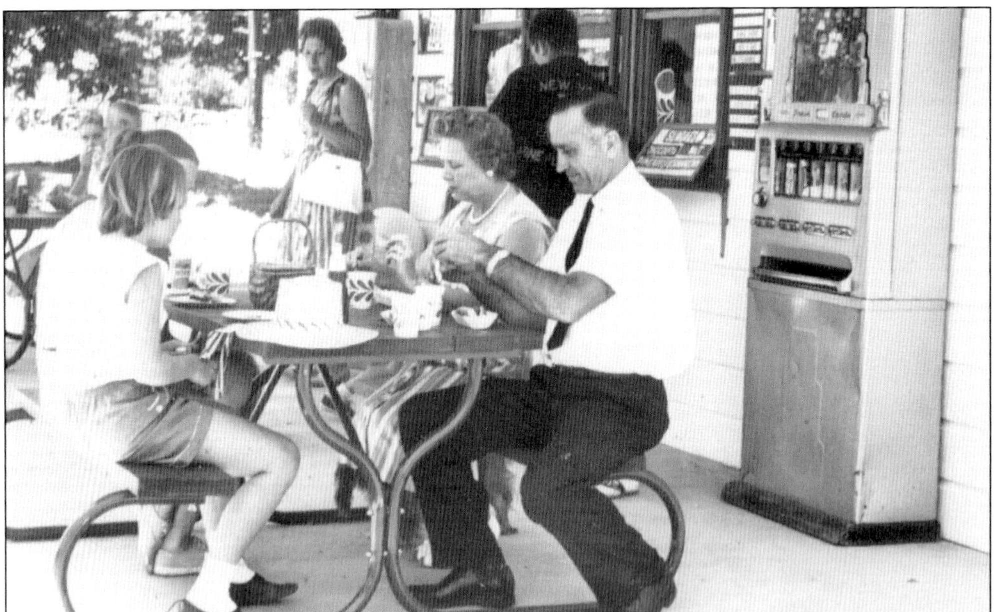

WOOFING IT DOWN AT "HOME PLATE." John Battistoni Jr. and his wife, Kathleen, check out the food concession of the town recreation park, opened in the 1950s. John Battistoni Jr. began the family tradition of serving in government. The years following WWII brought serious issues to even small rural towns, requiring full-time commitment from part-time public servants. John's experience in family business and as road commissioner served him well as supervisor of a town beginning to face development pressures and demands for increased services. (JB.)

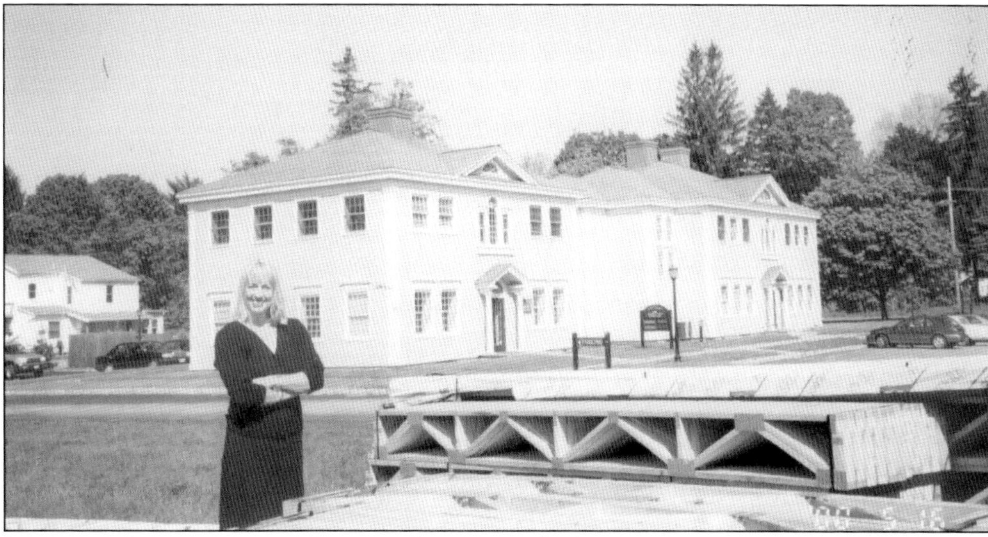

STANFORD GETS CENTERED. For years, linear growth along Route 82 defied attempts to define a town center. The question for the moment has been settled. It is Stanfordville, in the same vicinity selected a century ago by the Christian Biblical Institute. Village Centre, the attractive complex owned by Deirdre and Kevin Cunningham, is across the street from the Grange hall, where the main building of the institute stood. (JG.)

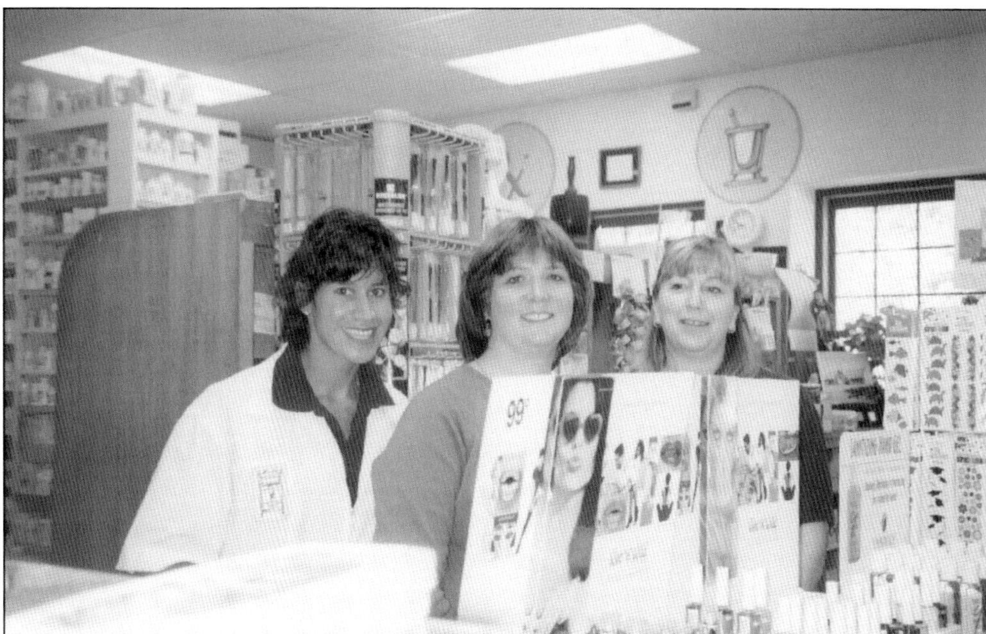

PHARMACISTS ON DUTY. Owner-run family businesses in this day of franchises and pharmaceutical chains are a rarity, needing community support. The constant flow of cars at Sean McCarthy's pharmacy in Village Centre is evidence of Stanford's approval. He returns the favor by volunteering as chief of the fire company while wife Eileen, Darlene Hicks, and pharmacist Ruthy Otero serve customers here. Sean is expanding next-door, helping to anchor the new center. (JG.)

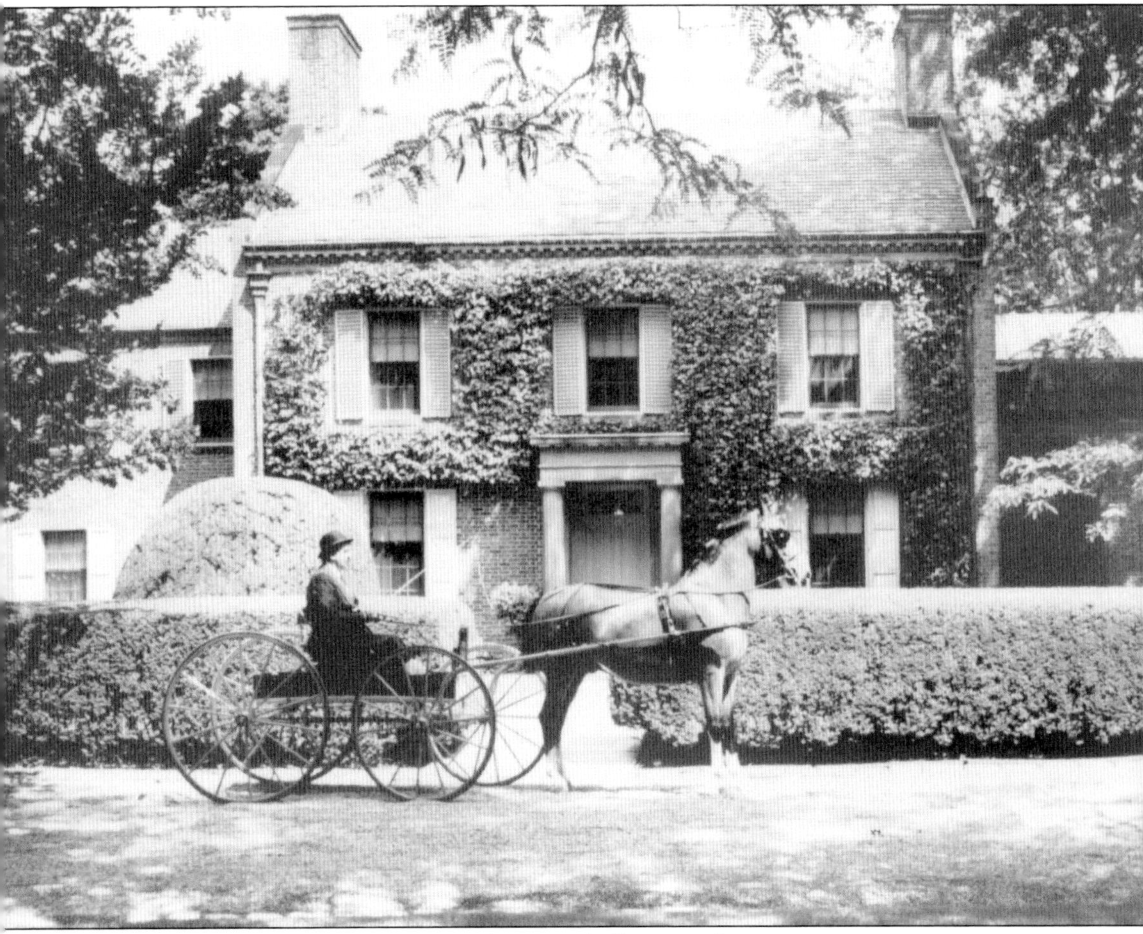

WETHERSFIELD. From 1937 to 1989, Chauncey Stillman—who was an investor, art connoisseur, philanthropist and conservationist—created this magnificent hilltop estate with its carriage house collection, formal gardens and incomparable views, integrating art, architecture and the environment into a personal artistic vision. Stillman provided for its protection and for public appreciation of his antiques and art collections through the creation of the Homeland Foundation, which supports the museum and estate grounds. Through his beneficence and a professional staff, Stanford now boasts a renowned museum welcoming visitors each summer and fall. (HF/JS.)

ACKNOWLEDGMENTS

This book could not have been written without the help of many individuals and organizations. The initials after each caption acknowledge the lender. A special word of thanks is due to the town historians: Vincent Vail, Joann Mirocco, Emily Johnson, David Greenwood, and Dorothy Burdick, and to Dutchess County Historical Society (DCHS), Dutchess County Landmarks, the Beekman Historical Society, Union Vale Historical Society (UVHS), LaGrange Historical Society (LHS),Washington Historical Society, and the Stanford Historical Society (SHS).

We are also indebted to Roger Akeley, Richard Birch, and Dennis Amone of the Dutchess County Department of Planning and Economic Development (DCDPEC) for their help in producing the map of the area and to Heyward Cohen (HC) for the material pertaining to trains.

Taconic State Parkway—Franklin D. Roosevelt Library (FDRL): Lynn Bassanese, Mark Renovitch, Raymond Teichman, Alycia Vivona; New York State Department of Parks, Recreation, and Historic Preservation: Kathleen La Frank; Taconic Region (TR): Melodye Moore; New York State Department of Transportation: Philips C. Crocker, Joseph Foglietta, Michael George, Colleen McKenna, Richard Shaw; Washington Town Historian David Greenwood (DGTH); and Ruth and Robert Hogan (RRH).

Beekman—Town Historian: Vincent Vail (VVTH); Town Clerk: Virginia Ward; the Beekman Library Association: Lee Eaton (BL); the Mount Zion Baptist Church: Beatrice L. Johnson; Debbie Boden; Tonya Slocum Capalbo (TC); Dalton Farm (DF); Eleanor DeForest; Robert Ferris (RF); Marian Hait; Blanche Hait; Ruth and Robert Hogan (RRH); Stan Horton; Gay Kendall; Wilbur Knapp; Hilde and Rudolph Littauer; Amy Hoag Lynch (AHL); Gael and Sheridan Morey (GM); Margaret Ostrander; Jerry Ramage; Duane and Jane Barber Smith; and John White.

Union Vale—Town Historian: Joann Miracco (JMTH); Town Clerk: Mary Lou DeForest (MLdeF); Town Supervisor: Lisette Hitsman (LH); Union Vale Fire Department (UVFD); James and Marian Coffin Andrews (JA); Marian V. Briggs (MB); Joyce Belterman; Jim Coffin (JC); Judith Coombs; Margaret G. Fettes (MF); Andrea Fountain (AF); Jane Geisler; Ruth and Robert Hogan (RRH); Deborah and Peter Krulewitch (DPK); Amy Hoag Lynch (AHL); RayVail; and Rev. Jim Wickstead.

LaGrange—Town Historian: Emily Johnson (EJTH); Town Supervisor: George Wade (GW); LaGrange Fire District: Jeffrey C. Kaiser, Andy McGarry, Shawn Murray, and Sonny Phelps; Paul and Jo Case (PJC); Rosemary Christ (RC); Tess Fowler; Marguerite B. Hubbard (MBH); Fran Jacob (FJ); Barbara Lumb (BL); Betty A. Lundewall (BAL); Louise McDermott (LMcD);

Dom O. Napoleon (DON); Sonny Phelps; Vivian Quinn (VQ); Claire N. Sleight (CNS); Mark D. Titus (MDT); Nancy Wade (NW); and Doris Washburn (DW).

Washington and Millbrook—Town and Village Historian: David Greenwood (DGTH); Town Clerk: Mary Alex (MA); Cornell Cooperative Extension (CE); Institute of Ecosystem Studies: Jill Cadwallader (IES/PK); Millbrook Hunt: Farnham Collins, Nancy Stahl (MH/NS); Millbrook Library: Muriel Verdibello and Nancy Rogers (ML/NR); Millbrook Preparatory School: Jill Kane (MS); St. Peter's Church; the Stanley Benham and Sidney Smith Benham Collection (SB/SSB); Virginia Benham Augerson; Sandra Beach (SB); Marion Johnson Bennett (MJB); John Blauhut; Marian V. Briggs (MB); Margaret G.Fettes (MF); David and Nancy Greenwood (DNG); John Kading (JK); Eugene Klein; Peter Klose; Stephanie Mauri; Scott Meyer (SM); Michael Murphy (MM); Karen Outwater; Walter Patrice; Vincent Vail (VV); and Vincent G. Westman (VGW).

Stanford—Town Historian: Dorothy Burdick (DBTH); Town Clerk: Marge Willis; Homeland Foundation Inc.: Jeanne Stalker (HF/JS); Stanford Fire Company (SFC): Al Bowen; Stanford Grange No. 808 (SG/CS); John Battistoni III (JB); Barbara Battistoni; Marion Johnson Bennett (MJB), Irving Burdick; Robert R. Butts (RRB); Evelyn Stevenson Butts (EB); David and Nancy Greenwood (DNG); Kevin and Deirdre Cunningham; Darlene Hicks; A. John Knickerbocker (AJK); Stephanie Mauri; Sean and Eileen McCarthy; Joy and Bob Renshaw (JBR); Karen Staats (KS); Bea Sheffield; Cathy Stark (CS); Delores Straley; and Marge Zimmerman

Reading List

The town historian and the historical society of each community have produced very useful historical materials. Contact the society, the town historian, or the Dutchess County Historical Society and arrange an appointment.

Caro, Robert A. *The Power Broker: Robert Moses and the Fall of New York*. New York: Vintage Books, 1975.

Dutchess County Historical Society, ed. Yearbooks 1914–1995. An index of articles is available at the society's headquarters at the Clinton House, 549 Main Street, Poughkeepsie, NY 12601.

Dutchess County Planning Board prep. *Landmarks of Dutchess County 1683–1867: Architecture Worth Saving In New York State*. New York: NYSCA, 1969.

Hasbrouck, Frank. ed. *The History of Dutchess County, New York*. Poughkeepsie, N.Y.: S.A. Matthieu, 1909.

Jeanneney, John and Mary L. *Dutchess County: A Pictorial History*. Norfolk, Virginia Beach: the Donning Company, 1983.

Poucher, J. Wilson M.D. and Helen Wilkinson Reynolds. *Old Gravestones of Dutchess County, New York*. Poughkeepsie: DCHS, 1998.

Reynolds, Helen Wilkinson Reynolds. *Dutchess County Doorways and Other Examples of Period-Work in Wood 1730–1830*. New York: William Farquhar Payson, 1931.

Reynolds, Helen Wilkinson. *Dutch Houses in the Hudson Valley Before 1776*. New York: Payson & Clarke Ltd., 1929.

Smith, James H. assisted by Hume H. Cale and Wm. R. Roscoe. *History of Duchess County, New York*. Syracuse, NY: D. Mason & Co., 1882.

Smith, Philip H. *General History of Duchess County from 1609–1876*. Pawling, NY: Published by the author, 1877.

Transformations of an American County Dutchess County, NY 1683–1983. Poughkeepsie, NY: Dutchess County Historical Society on behalf of the Dutchess County Tercentenary Advisory Committee, 1986.